D1475011

PRACTICAL MANAGEMENT SERIES

The Ethics Edge

Edited by
Evan M. Berman
Jonathan P. West
Stephen J. Bonczek

International
City/County
ICMA
Management
Association

PRACTICAL MANAGEMENT SERIES
Barbara H. Moore, Editor

The Ethics Edge
Accountability for Performance
Balanced Growth
Capital Projects
Current Issues in Leisure Services
Fire Services Today
Local Economic Development
Long-Term Financial Planning
Managing for Tomorrow
Pay and Benefits
Performance Evaluation
Personnel Practices for the '90s
Police Practice in the '90s
Practical Financial Management
Quality Management Today
Resolving Conflict
Shaping the Local Economy
Strategic Planning for Local Government

The Practical Management Series is devoted to the presentation of information and ideas from diverse sources. The views expressed in this book are those of the contributors and are not necessarily those of the International City/County Management Association.

Library of Congress Cataloging-in-Publication Data

The ethics edge / edited by Evan M. Berman, Jonathan P.
   West, Stephen J. Bonczek.
      p.   cm.—(Practical management series)
      Includes bibliographical references.
      ISBN 0-87326-161-5
      1. Political ethics. 2. Business ethics. 3. Professional
   ethics. 4. Social values. I. Berman, Evan M. II. West,
   Jonathan P. (Jonathan Page), 1941– . III. Bonczek,
   Stephen J. IV. Series.
   JA79.E8236 1998
   172—dc21   98-12422
                                                              CIP

Printed in the United States of America
2004 2003 2002 2001 1999 1998
7 6 5 4 3 2 1

 The Ethics Edge

The International City/County Management Association is the professional and educational organization for chief appointed management executives in local government. The purposes of ICMA are to enhance the quality of local government and to nurture and assist professional local government administrators in the United States and other countries. In furtherance of its mission, ICMA develops and disseminates new approaches to management through training programs, information services, and publications.

Managers, carrying a wide range of titles, serve cities, towns, counties, and councils of governments in all parts of the United States and Canada. These managers serve at the direction of elected councils and governing boards. ICMA serves these managers and local governments through many programs that aim at improving the manager's professional competence and strengthening the quality of all local governments.

ICMA was founded in 1914; adopted its City Management Code of Ethics in 1924; and established its Institute for Training in Municipal Administration in 1934. The institute, in turn, provided the basis for the Municipal Management Series, generally termed the "ICMA Green Books."

ICMA's interests and activities include public management education; standards of ethics for members; the *Municipal Year Book* and other data services; urban research; and newsletters, a monthly magazine, *Public Management,* and other publications. ICMA's efforts for the improvement of local government management—as represented by this book—are offered for all local governments and educational institutions.

Foreword

The importance of ethics in government cannot be overstated. In a time when many citizens have a fundamental distrust of government employees and institutions, when instances of wrongdoing in government attract sensational media coverage, and when concerns about fairness and equity assume major proportions, government managers must rise to the challenge of fostering ethics in their organizations.

ICMA has been in the ethics business for decades, and the ICMA Code of Ethics is a source of guidance—and pride—for professional local government managers. ICMA adopted its code of ethics in 1924 and has revised it over time in response to changing needs and views. Subscription to the code is a condition of membership, and the association maintains an active and effective enforcement program.

The present book, *The Ethics Edge*, represents a continuation of ICMA's efforts to educate and assist managers in this important area. It replaces an earlier volume, *Ethical Insight, Ethical Action*, with updated selections for today's management environment. ICMA also provides ethics training and advice for members.

ICMA is grateful to Evan M. Berman, Jonathan P. West, and Stephen J. Bonczek for editing this volume; to Donald C. Menzel, James S. Bowman, and Elizabeth K. Kellar for their original contributions; and to the publishers and authors who granted ICMA permission to reprint materials for inclusion.

ICMA staff who contributed to this project were Barbara Moore, editor of the Practical Management Series; Jane Gold, who edited the original selections and coordinated production; Dawn Leland, director of publications production; and Julie Butler, editorial assistant.

Like other books in the Practical Management Series, *The Ethics Edge* is intended to provide the best of current thinking on important management topics.

William H. Hansell
Executive Director
International City/County
Management Association

About the Editors and Authors

Evan M. Berman is a faculty member in the Department of Public Administration at the University of Central Florida. He has previously taught at the University of Miami; Dr. Berman also served as a policy analyst for the National Science Foundation and as a consultant to the U.S. Congress. He is active in the American Society for Public Administration and is the 1998–1999 Chair of the Section of Personnel and Labor Relations. Dr. Berman has published widely on the topics of ethics and productivity improvement in local government, and frequently assists local governments in conducting their citizen surveys and community-based planning activities. His latest book is *Productivity in Public and Nonprofit Organizations* (Sage, 1998).

Jonathan P. West is professor and chair of political science at the University of Miami and director of the graduate program in public administration. Previously he taught at the University of Arizona and at the University of Houston; Dr. West also served as a management analyst in the office of the U.S. surgeon general. For the past ten years, he has taught a graduate course on ethics in the public sector. Dr. West has published widely on the topics of ethics and productivity. His latest book is *Quality Management Today* (ICMA, 1995). He is coauthor of chapters in three editions of the ICMA *Municipal Year Book*, including a 1993 article on ethics in local government. He is the managing editor of *Public Integrity*, a journal cosponsored by the Council of State Governments, the American Society of Public Administration, and the International City/County Management Association.

Stephen J. Bonczek is managing director in Reading, Pennsylvania, and has a master's degree in public administration from Wayne State University. He has extensive executive management experience in local government, including city manager in East Pointe and Southgate, Michigan; and Largo and Cocoa, Florida, where he also served on the Florida City/County Management Association Ethics Committee. Mr. Bonczek has written numerous articles on ethics *for Public Personnel Management, Public Management*, and other publications. He has made presentations for public professional organizations and has been an adjunct instructor in public administration and ethics for Wayne State University, St. Petersburg Junior College, Barry University, and the University of Central Florida.

Following are the affiliations of the contributors at the time of writing:

James S. Bowman, professor, Department of Public Administration, Florida State University.

Patricia L. Brousseau, executive vice president, Institute for Global Ethics.

Gary B. Brumback, senior policy analyst, U.S. Department of Health and Human Services.

Anita Cava, associate professor, Department of Business Law, University of Miami.

Stephen L. Carter, professor, School of Law, Yale University.

Steven Cohen, associate dean, School of International and Public Affairs and director, Graduate Program in Public Policy and Administration, Columbia University.

Stephen Covey, founder and chair of the board, Covey Leadership Institute.

William Eimicke, director, School of International and Public Affairs Management Training Center and Program in Politics and Public Policy, Columbia University.

Mark W. Huddleston, professor, Department of Political Science and International Affairs, University of Delaware.

Richard W. Hug, associate professor, Division of Public and Environmental Affairs and Political Science, Indiana University Northwest.

Michael Josephson, author and founder, Josephson Institute of Ethics.

Elizabeth K. Kellar, deputy director, International City/County Management Association.

Rushworth M. Kidder, founder, Institute for Global Ethics.

Peter Kobrak, professor, Department of Political Science, Western Michigan University.

Carol Lewis, professor, Department of Political Science, University of Connecticut.

Donald C. Menzel, professor, Division of Public Administration, Northern Illinois University.

Lloyd A. Rowe, professor emeritus, Division of Public and Environmental Affairs and Political Science, Indiana University Northwest.

Joseph C. Sands, doctoral student, Department of Political Science, Princeton University.

James Svara, professor, Department of Political Science and Public Administration, North Carolina State University.

Dennis F. Thompson, professor, Harvard University.

Montgomery Van Wart, associate professor, Department of Political Science, Iowa State University.

Contents

Part 3
The Ethical Frontiers

Introduction

Evan M. Berman, Jonathan P. West, and Stephen J. Bonczek

This book, *The Ethics Edge,* brings together articles that provide new insights on values in government and the public administration profession. It highlights state-of-the-art ethics management practices and emerging ethical issues.

Clearly, ethics shape and define the nature of public professions. Managers and employees who are informed by ethics have an added "edge" because they are more likely to know the right thing to do, to undertake these actions, to justify actions on the basis of professional and moral criteria, and to protect themselves against being blindsided by allegations of ethical impropriety. These competencies are critical in today's managment environment; they occur because ethics mold the aspirations and roles that managers fulfill in their organizations and jurisdictions, and help define core values and beliefs that direct managerial action. By contrast, managers who act without regard to core values and professional ethics are taking ethical risks that may jeopardize the public interest, their careers, and the reputations of their jurisdictions.

The past decade has witnessed a resurgent interest in ethics. Such interest follows the "decade of greed" of the 1980s, which left government with a public trust deficit and a profession besieged by advocates of ideologies that favor scaling back the role and size of government. The causes of these conditions and attacks are varied and include, among other things, public backlash to perceived growth of government, problems in the private sector, and unscrupulous actions by a few high-profile public officials. As a result of these developments, new efforts were under way by the late 1980s in many jurisdictions and among professional organizations to rebuild public trust and respond to vitriolic attacks on the character and competence of public managers. Ethical responses often followed two separate, parallel tracks—one legal, the other behavioral. Laws were adopted to minimize wrongdoing, and training efforts were undertaken to help employees and managers do the right thing. Ethics activities during the past decade can be understood as the further development of these two orientations.

Two-track responses

The legal response to ethical concerns has been the passage of laws and policies prohibiting unethical activities, such as sexual harassment, discrimination, and invasion of privacy, as well as mandating ethical behaviors regarding conflict of interest, financial disclosure, and postservice employment with contractors. Governments at the subnational level have adopted many of these laws and policies. But while these laws have a deterrent effect on those who might engage in wrongdoing, this track also has some limitations. For instance, legal standards do not exist for all ethical areas of professional activity, and ethics laws are seldom sufficient to deal with a growing number of gray areas, such as the extent to which city managers can be involved in negotiating contracts with organizations that also employ their spouses. Another limitation is the unintended effect of vigorous prosecution: it sharply increases public awareness of ethical wrongdoing that, in turn, may decrease trust!

For these reasons, a second behavioral track has been implemented. Training and information are used to help managers and employees recognize and deal with unethical situations, and they provide guidance for dealing with such situations through consultative strategies and other efforts. These tools also aim to reduce instances of ethical wrongdoing by changing attitudes and increasing employees' awareness of ethics. Initially, many strategies center on developing codes of ethics that set forth the ethical values to guide organizations. Although codes have little impact when they merely "hang on the wall" or "collect dust on the shelf," they are effective when they help individuals and groups think through their values and aspirations. However, training efforts have become more specific, using a broader range of scenarios and strategies for ethical responsibility. ICMA contributed to these efforts by publishing *Ethical Insight, Ethical Action* (1988), a then state-of-the-art compilation of articles; *The Ethics Factor* (1988), a training package providing cases and exercises for local managers and employees in developing codes; and *Ethos* (1994), a multimedia CD-ROM that contains forty-two cases of ethical decision making. In addition, ICMA staff is available to assist its members by answering ethics questions that arise.

The dual legal and behavioral developments during the last decade now call for a new volume on ethics. Following these advances, *The Ethics Edge* examines lessons and insights that have been learned. For example, it discusses effective approaches in ethics management and the many challenges that public officials must confront; many of the same issues confront managers in the private and nonprofit sectors. It also discusses emerging issues in ethics that result from shifting frontiers in government: what are the ethics of managing information technology, building communities, maintaining dual-career families, and rebuilding public trust? In addition, this book presents recent articles that deal with fundamental ethical virtues such as integrity and honesty. These discussions examine ethics in new ways that have practical use for managers.

Enduring concerns

Enduring values are fundamental to the study of ethics, and their examination ensures continuity with the past. Clearly, the concept of professional ethics is not new. The ancient Greeks (Socrates, Aristotle) had much to say about moral imperatives and civic and political responsibilities. The philosophic writings of Immanuel Kant (the categorical imperative), Herbert Spencer (social Darwinism), Jeremy Bentham (utilitarianism), and others continue to provide insight and valuable guidance to today's public managers. American writings and political developments in the early 1900s also emphasized wholeness of character and professional responsibilities, albeit in the context of industrial society. Professional associations, including ICMA, adopted codes of ethics, declarations of ideals, and so forth. The content of these codes has not greatly changed over the years, even though contexts have greatly changed and professional organizations have routinely revisited their codes. The codes emphasize professionalism, personal honesty and integrity, support for employees and others, and respect for democratic processes. These are enduring values, many of which are also mentioned in the codes of corporate and nonprofit organizations.

The current upswing in ethical awareness implies that at some point these values must have been partially lost, deemphasized, or called into question. There is consensus that this is what occurred from the mid-1960s through the late 1980s. Mired in domestic strife, economic restructuring, and the development of international interdependencies, a new generation rejected traditional values in search of new paradigms. Today, as this generation has come to assume positions of power and influence in government, with Generation X at its heels, managers are finding worth in these traditional, time-tested values. The buzzwords of today—responsiveness, inclusion, openness, integrity, empowerment—are ethical values and orientations. Indeed, the role of ethics as a personal, team, and organizational orientation is increasingly acknowledged.

For some managers, functioning in an era of blurred moral distinctions and ethical ambiguity leaves them with a fuzzy moral compass, and efforts to determine the right thing to do can be confusing. For such managers, this book provides grist for the mill of ethical reflection on core values that can empower both managers and employees to increase responsiveness to organizational and social issues. For example, productivity improvement efforts must be driven by values of responsiveness (improvement for whom?) and openness (e.g., consultation with stakeholders about options and consequences) if they are to be effective, and managers must follow up their intentions with actions (i.e., exhibit integrity). Productivity improvement must be more than a set of technical procedures if it is to have a lasting impact. The articles presented in *The Ethics Edge* encourage managers to evaluate their ethical beliefs and analyze the ethical implications of their decisions. Understanding and acting on clearly articulated values is a powerful way for managers and employees to help foster more ethically sensitive organizations.

Selection of materials

This volume was designed to offer the best and most current literature on ethics in government. All the selections were published since 1990; fourteen out of twenty were published in 1995 or thereafter. Five selections were commissioned to fill significant gaps in the available literature. To obtain the best material available, it was occasionally necessary to select an article with more of a business than a public administration slant; however, by and large the emphasis is on local government applications.

For readers who search this book for specific information, the accompanying grid lists some important content categories and keys them to the corresponding chapters.

Contents

The articles in this volume are grouped under three general headings: "Foundations," "Implementation," and "The Ethical Frontiers." The first part discusses virtues, values, principles, dilemmas, and paradoxes and provides important background for those who are new to the subject of ethics in government. The second part encourages readers to move from considering important ideas to the world of action, where concepts and principles are put into practice. The third part explores specific cutting-edge issues at the frontier of ethics in the public sector.

	Virtues	Values	Principles	Codes	Training	Cases	Audits/Assessment Tools	Leadership	Stakeholders	Moral Reasoning	Communication/Dialogue	Consequences	Accountability	Public Opinion	Resistance	Justifications	Dilemmas	Law
The Six Pillars of Character	x	x	x															
The Insufficiency of Honesty	x	x																
Moral Compassing	x	x					x											
Ethical Dilemmas: Right vs. Right		x		x	x					x							x	
Paradoxes of Government Ethics												x	x	x				
Institutionalizing Ethics in Government					x	x		x	x	x			x		x	x		x
Creating an Ethical Work Environment						x		x										
The First Step in the Reinvention Process		x					x							x				
Achieving the Ethical Workplace		x						x	x						x	x		
Ethical Decision-Making in Business and Government			x	x		x				x							x	x
Strategies and Tactics for Managerial Decision Making						x					x	x					x	x
City Manager Perceptions ...			x	x														
Enforcing Administrative Ethics			x	x				x										x
The Professional Edge							x			x			x					
Is Public Entrepreneurship Ethical?						x		x				x						
Privatization and Cozy Politics						x		x	x			x						
Ethics Management in the Cyber-Workplace							x	x		x		x	x					x
Public Cynicism: Manifestations and Responses										x	x	x	x	x				
The Ethics of Community Building		x				x			x		x	x						
Current Ethics Issues ...			x		x	x											x	
Total	3	7	5	4	3	8	4	7	4	6	3	7	5	3	2	2	4	5

Readers may approach the material in this book either selectively or sequentially. Those who read selectively will identify and peruse the articles that appeal to their interests, viewing each article independently of the others. Those who prefer to read sequentially will read the articles that set the foundation before proceeding to those that deal with specific implementation and will conclude with the critical ethical issues facing government.

Part 1, "Foundations," begins with Michael Josephson's "The Six Pillars of Character." This article defines and clarifies the meaning of trustworthiness, respect, responsibility, fairness, caring, and citizenship—pillars that guide and improve the quality of ethical decisions. Josephson stresses the interdependence of these core values and principles and shows how each relates to the others. Stephen Carter's article, "The Insufficiency of Honesty," examines the differences between honesty and integrity—two elements of "trustworthiness" in Josephson's "six pillars"—reviewing the three steps to integrity and providing examples to illustrate the meaning of integrity in practice. In "Moral Compassing," Stephen Covey discusses principles as providing a moral compass. He distinguishes between principles and values and between management by maps (values) and leadership by compass (principles), offering practical examples of leadership by principles. Sidebars by the Council for Excellence in Government and by Rushworth Kidder that accompany these two articles provide further examples of statements of core values and guiding principles for public servants and of their potential utility in formulating a global code of ethics, respectively.

The fourth article in Part 1 builds on concepts contained in the first three articles by outlining a practical model for ethical decision making based on shared "core values." Patricia Brousseau presents dilemmas that involve "right vs. right" choices; she then applies three decision rules useful in resolving these dilemmas. The three decision rules are ends-based, rule-based, and care-based. The sidebar by James Svara describing the ethical triangle suggests three different approaches to administrative ethics—virtue and intuition (integrity), principle-based (justice/fairness), and consequences (utilitarianism). Part 1 concludes with an article titled "Paradoxes of Government Ethics," in which Dennis Thompson discusses three important misconceptions or "paradoxes" of government ethics that make education in democracy difficult: (1) the priority of government ethics, (2) the difference between government and personal ethics, and (3) the importance of appearance.

Part 2, "Implementation," describes some important operational concerns in implementing ethical principles in various organizational settings. Gary Brumback's "Institutionalizing Ethics in Government" introduces this section with an overview that identifies the causes and types of unethical behavior. He outlines the elements of a government ethics program and discusses selected elements, offering several specific examples. Brumback provides the backdrop for Stephen Bonczek's article, "Creating an Ethical Work Environment," which discusses more specific and practical strategies, such as ethical climate surveys and ethics training, for enhancing ethics awareness in local government. The crucial role of assessment has been highlighted by the "reinventing government" efforts under way in federal, state, and local governments. Montgomery Van Wart's article, "The First Step in the Reinvention Process: Assessment," describes and assesses the utility of seven assessment methods: (1) ethics assessments; (2) mission, values, and planning and vision statement assessments; (3) customer and citizen assessments; (4) employee assessments; (5) performance assessments; (6) benchmarking; and (7) quality assessments.

Next is "Achieving the Ethical Workplace," coauthored by Stephen Bonczek and Donald Menzel. These authors consider and discuss eight false assumptions that undermine efforts to enhance ethical awareness in public organizations, and they spell out the challenges involved in achieving and maintaining an ethical workplace. Following that, in "Ethical Decision-Making in Business and Government," Anita Cava, Jonathan West, and Evan Berman analyze both formal and informal strategies for achieving an ethical workplace. They include case analyses using codes of conduct and statutory guidelines (formal) as well as ethical principles (informal). In "Strategies and Tactics for Managerial Decision Making," Carol Lewis introduces additional guidelines for ethical analysis and then applies several elements in a decision-making checklist to the specifics of a perplexing local government case. Her chapter provides concrete guidance to public managers about the process of moral reasoning and the ways to determine ethical responsibilities. Lloyd Rowe and Richard Hug's article, "City Manager Perceptions of the ICMA Code of Ethics," examines perceptions of (1) the influence of the ICMA code as a source of ethical guidance compared with other potential sources, (2) its influence in several categories of managerial responsibilities, (3) the importance of the individual tenets of the code, and (4) the code's overall impact. Survey results reported by these authors indicate that ICMA members recognize the importance and value of their professional code. However, it is one thing to formulate a code and another to enforce it. In the last article in Part 2, "Enforcing Administrative Ethics," Mark Huddleston and Joseph Sands discuss three methods of ethics enforcement: (1) codes of ethics including laws, professional rules, and whistle-blower statutes; (2) "ethics police" with responsibility for enforcing standards; and (3) cultural strategies designed to create organizational climates conducive to ethical behavior.

Part 3 deals with newly emerging ethical issues. In the first article, "The Professional Edge," James Bowman observes that professionalism in the public service requires both technical competence and personal integrity. The central importance of ethics within the profession was lost for a period but has since regained salience. Bowman challenges public administration professionals to help ethics flourish in the future and suggests some ways to make that happen. Steven Cohen and William Eimicke, coauthors of the second article, explore the question, "Is Public Entrepreneurship Ethical?" They examine three entrepreneurial projects—the Orange County bankruptcy; a Visalia, California, hotel project; and an Indianapolis wastewater treatment plant—to identify a list of do's and don'ts for ethical public entrepreneurs. Entrepreneurial government has many features, one of which involves competition among service providers via such means as privatization. Peter Kobrak's article, "Privatization and Cozy Politics," addresses this issue. He reviews the literature and selected case studies to highlight the "cozy politics" that often accompany contracting for goods and services. Kobrak examines the consequences of the politicization of contracting out and offers recommendations regarding how to avoid the pitfalls of cozy political arrangements when developing public-private partnerships.

The fourth article in Part 3 addresses another contemporary issue with ethical implications. In "Ethics Management in the Cyber-Workplace," Donald Menzel explores ethical and managerial issues posed by the Internet, examines the pros and cons of Internet access for group life in public organizations, and explores the ethical challenges facing managers committed to promoting ethical values. Despite efforts to "reinvent" government and apply the latest management theories and technologies, citizens remain skeptical and cynical in assessing the performance of government. Evan Berman's article, "Public Cynicism: Manifestations and Responses," presents a theory of citizen cynicism concerning government, examines the extent of cynicism, and considers the ways that public officials can reduce the level of cynicism. Evan Berman and Stephen Bonczek then build on some of the foundation articles in their discussion of "The Ethics of Community Building." They address the importance of the ethical framework of community building, linking it to values, codes, trust, and cynicism in a multicultural environment. In the final article in Part 3, "Current Ethics Issues for Local Government

Managers," Elizabeth Kellar examines the current and emerging issues confronting local government administrators, including political activity, firing/severance, dual-career families and conflicts of interest, and threats to managerial objectivity.

Conclusion

This book of readings provides an orientation to ethics in government. It summarizes the key concepts and strategies that individuals and organizations use to deal with ethical dilemmas. It also highlights contemporary challenges and issues that face today's manager as he or she seeks to build and maintain an ethical climate in a public sector setting. The salience of ethical issues at all levels of government has risen in recent years. While ethics in government is not a new topic, the types of ethical challenges confronting managers as we enter the next millennium are different. Public sector managers need to be aware of the ethical challenges confronting those in their workplace and to consider carefully the appropriate organizational responses for their jurisdictions. New technologies, government reform strategies, rising cynicism among citizens, and challenges of community building, along with the more enduring ethical problems of conflict of interest, illegal actions, the appearance of impropriety, reneging on promises, and embellishing claims, accentuate the need for strategic thinking about ethics by public managers. This book discusses a host of practical tools and organizational initiatives that will aid administrators in this general strategic thought process. It is our intent that the articles included here will also assist in resolving specific ethical dilemmas that managers and employees confront as well as in designing ethics management policies and programs tailored to meet the needs of particular jurisdictions.

PART 1

Foundations

The Six Pillars
of Character

Michael Josephson

Editors' Note: Trustworthiness, respect, responsibility, fairness, caring, and citizenship have been identified by the Josephson Institute as "The Six Pillars of Character." These core values and principles, discussed by Michael Josephson here, can be used to improve the ethical quality of decision making.

Trustworthiness

Being trusted is a good thing: we're given greater leeway by those we deal with because they don't feel they need contracts to assure that we'll meet our obligations. They believe us and therefore they believe in us. That's satisfying. But there's a downside: we must constantly live up to the expectations of others and refrain from competitive, self-serving behaviors that tarnish if not destroy relationships, both professional and personal.

Another downside, of sorts: trustworthiness is the broadest and most complicated of the six core ethical values. It is concerned with all the qualities and behavior that make a person worthy of trust—qualities like integrity, honesty, reliability and loyalty.

Honesty   Obviously, honesty is one of the most fundamental of ethical values. We associate honesty with people of honor, and we admire and trust those who are honest. But honesty is a broader concept than many may realize.

Reprinted from Michael Josephson, *Making Ethical Decisions: What Are You Going to Do?* 3rd. ed. Marina del Rey, Calif.: Josephson Institute of Ethics, 1995, pp. 8–17. Reprinted by permission.

Honesty in communications requires a good-faith intent to convey the truth as best we know it and to avoid communicating in a way likely to mislead or deceive. There are three dimensions:

- *Truthfulness*   The obligation of truthfulness precludes intentional misrepresentation of fact (lying). Intent is the crucial distinction between truthfulness and truth itself. Being wrong is not the same thing as being a liar, although honest mistakes can still damage trust insofar as they may be evidence of sloppy judgment.
- *Sincerity/nondeception*   The obligation of sincerity precludes all acts, including half-truths, out-of-context statements, and even silence that are intended to create beliefs or leave impressions that are untrue or misleading.
- *Candor*   In relationships involving legitimate expectations of trust, honesty may also require candor, forthrightness and frankness, imposing the obligation to volunteer information that the other person needs to know.

Honesty in conduct prohibits stealing, cheating, fraud, subterfuge and other trickery. Cheating is a particularly foul form of dishonesty because one not only seeks to deceive but to take advantage of those who are not cheating. It's a twofer: a violation of trust and fairness.

All lies are dishonest, but not all lies are unethical. Huh? That's right, honesty is not an inviolate principle. Occasionally dishonesty is ethically justifiable, as when the police lie in undercover operations or when one lies to criminals or terrorists to save lives. But don't kid yourself: occasions for ethically sanctioned lying are rare and require serving a very high purpose indeed—not hitting a management-pleasing sales target or winning a game or avoiding a confrontation. We're talking about saving a life, that sort of thing.

Integrity   The word *integrity* comes from the word *integer*, meaning "one" or wholeness. This means there are no divisions in an ethical person's life, no difference *in the way* she makes decisions from situation to situation, no difference in the way she acts at work and at home, in public and alone. At one time or another, we all have allowed our behavior to depart from our conscience or to vary according to locale. Even so, almost all of us have lines we will not cross; our challenge is to draw the line around the Six Pillars.

Because she must know who she is and what she values, the person of integrity takes time for self-reflection so that the events, crises, and seeming necessities of the day do not determine the course of her moral life. She stays in control. She may be courte-

There are four enemies to integrity:

Self-interest—Things we want
Self-protection—Things we don't want
Self-deception—A refusal to see a situation clearly
Self-righteousness—An end-justifies-the-means attitude

ous, even charming, but she is never false. She never demeans [her]self with obsequious behavior toward those she thinks might do her some good. She is trusted because you know who she is: what you see is what you get.

Reliability (promise keeping)   When we make promises or other commitments which create a legitimate basis for another person to rely upon us to perform certain tasks, we undertake moral duties that go beyond legal obligations. The ethical dimension of promise keeping imposes the responsibility of making all reasonable efforts to fulfill our commitments. Because promise keeping is such an important aspect of trustworthiness, it is important to:

- *Avoid bad-faith excuses*   Honorable people interpret their contracts and other commitments in a fair and reasonable manner and not in a way designed to rationalize noncompliance or create justifications for escaping commitments.
- *Avoid unwise commitments*   Be cautious about making commitments that create ethical obligations. Before making a promise, consider carefully whether you are willing and likely to keep it. Think about unknown or future events that could make it difficult, undesirable or impossible. Sometimes, all we can do is promise to do our best.
- *Avoid unclear commitments*   Since others will expect you to live up to what they think you have promised to do, be sure that when you make a promise, the other person understands what you are committing to do.

Loyalty   Loyalty is a special moral responsibility to promote and protect the interests of certain people, organizations or affiliations. This duty goes beyond the normal obligation we all share to care for others. Some relationships—husband-wife, employer-employee, citizen-country—create an expectation of allegiance, fidelity and devotion.

Limitations to loyalty   Loyalty is a tricky thing. It is not uncommon for friends, employers, co-workers and others who have a claim on us to demand that their interests be ranked first, even above ethical considerations. Loyalty is a reciprocal concept, however, and no one has the right to ask another to sacrifice ethical principle in the name of a special relationship. Indeed, one forfeits a claim of loyalty when so high a price is put on continuance of the relationship.

Prioritizing loyalties   Because so many individuals and groups make loyalty claims on us, it is often impossible to honor them all simultaneously. Consequently, we must rank our loyalty obligations in some rational fashion. In our personal lives, for example, most people expect us to place the highest degree of loyalty on our family relationships. It's perfectly reasonable, and ethical, to look out for the interests of our children, parents and spouses, even if we may have to subordinate our obligations to other children, neighbors, or co-workers in doing so.

Safeguarding confidential information   The duty of loyalty requires us to keep secrets learned in confidence.

Avoiding conflicting interests   Employees and public servants have an additional loyalty responsibility to make all professional decisions on their merits, unimpeded by conflicting personal interests. Their goal is to secure and maintain the trust of the public, to whom they owe their ultimate loyalty.

Respect
The way one shows respect varies, but its essence is the display of regard for the worth of people, including oneself. We have no ethical duty to hold all people in high esteem or admire them, but we are morally obligated to treat everyone with respect, regardless of who they are and what they have done—even if they don't *deserve* respect. The reason is not because these undeserving souls are human beings, but because we are. We have a responsibility to be the best we can be in all situations, even when dealing with the heinous.

Respect focuses on the moral obligation to honor the essential worth and dignity of the individual. Respect prohibits violence, humiliation, manipulation, and exploitation. It reflects notions such as civility, courtesy, dignity, autonomy, tolerance, and acceptance.

Civility, courtesy and decency   A respectful person is an attentive listener, although his patience with the boorish need not be endless (respect works both ways). Nevertheless, the respectful person treats others with consideration, conforming to accepted notions of taste and propriety, and doesn't resort to intimida-

**Implementation of ethical principles
for public servants**

Ethical principles should be made a part of the work ethic of all government organizations. In order to maximize the incorporation of ethical principles into the day-to-day performance of public service, government organizations should take the following steps:

Exercise leadership
The members of any organization take their cues from the actions of those who hold top leadership positions in the organization. These leaders thus have a special responsibility within their organizations to:

- Advocate the core values and exemplify the guiding principle
- Evaluate their subordinates' performance in the light of these standards
- Seek others with strong ethical values to work in the organization.

Monitor and evaluate
In addition to assessing the ethical performance of individuals, there is also a need to monitor and evaluate the organization itself with respect to:

- How well the values and principles are understood and followed
- The extent to which they influence the organization's ethical climate.

Provide ongoing training
Ethics training should be broadened in focus beyond the current briefings on laws, regulations, and rules. Training sessions should include case studies utilizing the practical precepts. Continuous training is required to keep the core ethical values alive and relevant within a government agency.

Provide sources of advice
Employees with specific ethical dilemmas should have access to established sources of sensible, sympathetic, and reliable advice. These should be easy enough to use so that they can be employed for less than crucial, but still troubling, questions. The means of providing such guidance might include a hot line or off-the-record discussions with peers.

Assure compliance
The organization must be vigorous in insisting upon adherence to its declared ethical standards. It follows that unambiguous failures to observe them must be dealt with firmly.

Source: *Ethical Principles for Public Servants*. The Council for Excellence in Government, 1992. Reprinted with permission.

tion, coercion or violence except in extraordinary and limited situations to teach discipline, maintain order or achieve social justice. Punishment is used in moderation and only to advance important social goals and purposes.

Autonomy   An ethical person exercises personal, official, and managerial authority in a way that provides others with the information they need to make informed decisions about their own lives.

Tolerance   An ethical person accepts individual differences and beliefs without prejudice and judges others only on the content of their character.

Responsibility

Life is full of choices. Being responsible means being in charge of our choices and, thus, our lives. It means being accountable for what we do and who we are. It also means recognizing that what we do, and what we don't do, matters and we are morally on the hook for the consequences.

Responsibility makes demands on us. It imposes duties to do what we can, not because we are being paid or because we will suffer if we don't, but simply because it is our obligation to do so. The essence of responsibility is continuous awareness that our capacity to reason and our freedom to choose make us morally autonomous and, therefore, answerable for how we use our autonomy and whether we honor or degrade the ethical principles that give life meaning and purpose.

Beyond having the responsibility to be trustworthy, respectful, fair, and caring, ethical people show responsibility by being accountable, pursuing excellence, and exercising self-restraint. In other words, they demonstrate the *ability to respond* to expectations of performance.

Accountability   An accountable person is not a victim and doesn't shift blame or credit for the work of others. He considers the likely consequences of his behavior and associations. He recognizes the common complicity in the triumph of evil when nothing is done to stop it. He leads by example.

Pursuit of excellence   The pursuit of excellence has an ethical dimension when others rely upon our knowledge, ability or willingness to perform tasks safely and effectively.

- *Diligence*   It is hardly unethical to make mistakes or be less than "excellent" but there is a moral obligation to do one's best, to be diligent, reliable, careful, prepared, and informed.

- *Perseverance* Responsible people finish what they start, overcoming rather than surrendering to obstacles and excuses.
- *Continuous improvement* Responsible people are on the prowl for ways to do their work better.

Self-restraint Responsible people exercise self-control, restraining passions and appetites (lust, hatred, gluttony, greed, fear, etc.) for the sake of reason, prudence and the duty to set a good example. They delay gratification if necessary and never feel it's necessary to "win at any cost." They realize they are as they choose to be, every day.

Fairness

Most would agree that fairness and justice involve issues of consistency, equality, impartiality, proportionality, openness, and due process. Most would agree that it is unfair to handle similar matters inconsistently. Most would agree that it is unfair to impose punishment that is disproportionate to the offense. Beyond that, there is little agreement. Fairness is another tricky concept, probably more subject to legitimate debate and interpretation than any other ethical value. Disagreeing parties tend to maintain that there is only one fair position (their own, naturally). But while some situations and decisions are clearly unfair, fairness usually refers to a *range* of morally justifiable outcomes rather than discovery of *the* fair answer.

Process In settling disputes or dividing resources, how one proceeds to judgment is crucial, for someone is bound to be disappointed with the result. A fair person scrupulously employs open and impartial processes for gathering and evaluating information necessary to make decisions. Fair people do not wait for the truth to come to them; they seek out relevant information and conflicting perspectives before making important decisions.

Impartiality Decisions should be made without favoritism or prejudice.

Equity Fairness requires an individual, company, or society [to] correct mistakes, promptly and voluntarily. It is improper to take advantage of the weakness or ignorance of others.

Caring

Caring is the very heart of ethics. It is scarcely possible to be truly ethical and not be a caring person, genuinely concerned with the welfare of others. That is because ethics is ultimately about our responsibilities toward other people. If you existed alone in the universe, there would be no need for ethics, and your heart could be a cold, hard stone without consequence to anyone or anything.

It is easier to love "humanity" than it is to love people. People who consider themselves ethical and yet lack a caring attitude toward individuals tend to treat others as instruments of their will. They rarely feel an obligation to be honest, loyal, fair or respectful except insofar as it is prudent for them to do so, a disposition which itself hints at duplicity and a lack of integrity.

A person who really cares feels an emotional response to both the pain and pleasure of others. Oddly enough, though, it is not uncommon for people to be remarkably ungracious, intolerant, and unforgiving toward those they love—while at the same time showing a generous spirit toward strangers and business associates. Go figure.

Of course, sometimes we must hurt those we truly care for and some decisions, while quite ethical, do cause harm. But one should consciously cause no more harm than is reasonably necessary to perform one's duties.

The highest form of caring is the honest expression of benevolence. This is sometimes referred to as altruism, not to be confused with strategic charity. Gifts to charities to advance personal interests are a fraud. That is, they aren't gifts at all. They're investments, or tax write-offs.

Citizenship
The concept of citizenship includes civic virtues and duties that prescribe how we ought to behave as part of a community. The good citizen knows the laws and obeys them, yes, but that's not all. She volunteers and stays informed on the issues of the day, the better to execute her duties and privileges as a member of a self-governing democratic society. That is, she does more than her "fair" share to make society work, now and for future generations. And beyond respecting the law, reporting crimes, serving on juries, voting, and paying taxes, the good citizen protects the environment by conserving resources, recycling, using public transportation, and cleaning up litter. She never takes more than she gives.

When we say something is a civic duty, we imply that not doing that duty is unethical. Yet that can be a harsh and erroneous judgment. If one has a duty to be honest, caring, fair, respectful and responsible, then we mean it is ethically wrong to be the opposite of those things. But does that then mean that if one has a "civic duty" to stay informed that one is unethical if one is ignorant? Certainly we don't have to admire self-absorbed and lazy people who take their citizenship for granted. It is important, however, to make the distinction between what is ethically mandated and what is merely desirable and worthy of emulation. To a great extent, people have to live their own lives, in whatever degree of isolation they choose.

The Insufficiency of Honesty

Stephen L. Carter

A couple of years ago, I began a university commencement address by telling the audience that I was going to talk about integrity. The crowd broke into applause. Applause! Just because they had heard the word *integrity*: that's how starved for it they were. They had no idea how I was using the word, or what I was going to say about integrity or indeed whether I was for it or against it. But they knew that they liked the idea of talking about it.

Very well, let us consider this word *integrity*. Integrity is like the weather: everybody talks about it, but nobody knows what to do about it. Integrity is that stuff that we always want more of. Some say that we need to return to the good old days when we had a lot more of it. Others say that we as a nation have never really had enough of it. Hardly anybody stops to explain exactly what we mean by it, or how we know it is a good thing, or why everybody needs to have the same amount of it. Indeed, the only trouble with integrity is that everybody who uses the word seems to mean something slightly different.

For instance, when I refer to integrity, do I mean simply "honesty"? The answer is no; although honesty is a virtue of importance, it is a different virtue from integrity. Let us, for simplicity, think of honesty as not lying; and let us further accept Sissela Bok's definition of a lie: "any intentionally deceptive message which is *stated*." Plainly, one cannot have integrity without being honest (although, as we shall see, the matter gets complicated), but one can certainly be honest and yet have little integrity.

When I refer to integrity, I have something specific in mind. Integrity, as I use the term, requires three steps: discerning what is right and what is wrong; acting on what you have discerned, even at personal cost; and saying openly that you are acting on your understanding of right and wrong. The first criterion captures the idea that integrity requires a degree of moral reflectiveness. The second brings in the ideal of a person of integrity as steadfast, a quality that includes keeping one's commitments. The third reminds us that a person of integrity can be trusted.

The first point to understand about the difference between honesty and integrity is that a person may be entirely honest without ever engaging in the hard work of discernment that integrity requires: she may tell us quite truthfully what she believes without ever taking the time to figure out whether what she believes is good and right and true. The problem may be as simple as someone's foolishly saying something that hurts a friend's feelings; a few moments of thoughts would have revealed the likelihood of the hurt and the lack of necessity for the comment. Or the problem may be more complex, as when a man who was raised from birth in a society that preaches racism states his belief in one race's inferiority as a fact, without ever really considering that perhaps this deeply held view is wrong. Certainly, the racist is being honest—he is telling us what he actually thinks—but his honesty does not add up to integrity.

Telling everything you know

A wonderful epigram sometimes attributed to the filmmaker Sam Goldwyn goes like this: "The most important thing in acting is honesty; once you learn to fake that, you're in." The point is that honesty can be something one *seems* to have. Without integrity, what passes for honesty often is nothing of the kind; it is fake honesty—or it is honest but irrelevant and perhaps even immoral.

Consider an example. A man who has been married for 50 years confesses to his wife on his deathbed that he was unfaithful 35 years earlier. The dishonesty was killing his spirit, he says. Now, he has cleared his conscience and is able to die in peace.

The husband has been honest—sort of. He has certainly unburdened himself. And he has probably made his wife (soon to be his widow) quite miserable in the process because even if she forgives him, she will not be able to remember him with quite the vivid image of love and loyalty that she had hoped for. Arranging his own emotional affairs to ease his transition to death, he has shifted to his wife the burden of confusion and pain, perhaps for the rest of her life. Moreover, he has attempted his honesty at the one time in his life when it carries no risk; acting in accordance with what you think is right and risking no loss in the process is a rather thin and unadmirable form of honesty.

Besides, even though the husband has been honest in a sense, he has now twice been unfaithful to his wife: once 35 years ago, when he had his affair, and again when, nearing death, he decided that his own peace of mind was more important than hers. In trying to be honest, he has violated his marriage vow by acting toward his wife not with love but with naked and perhaps even cruel self-interest.

As my mother used to say, you don't have to tell people everything you know. Lying and nondisclosure, as the law often recognizes, are not the same thing. Sometimes, it is actually illegal to tell what you know, as, for example, in the disclosure of certain financial information by market insiders. Or it may be unethical, as when a lawyer reveals a confidence entrusted to her by a client. It may be simple bad manners, as in the case of a gratuitous comment to a colleague on his or her attire. And it may be subject to religious punishment, as when a Roman Catholic priest breaks the seal of the confessional—an offense that carries automatic excommunication.

In all the cases just mentioned, the problem with telling everything you know is that somebody else is harmed. Harm may not be the intention, but it is certainly the effect. Honesty is most laudable when we risk harm to ourselves; it becomes a good deal less so if we instead risk harm to others when there is no gain to anyone other than ourselves. Integrity may counsel keeping our secrets in order to spare the feelings of others. Sometimes, as in the example of the wayward husband, the reason we want to tell what we know is precisely to shift our pain onto somebody else—a course of action dictated less by integrity than by self-interest. Fortunately, integrity and self-interest often coincide, as when a politician of integrity is rewarded with our votes. But often they do not, and it is at those moments that our integrity is truly tested.

Error

Another reason that honesty alone is no substitute for integrity is that if forthrightness is not preceded by discernment, it may result in the expression of an incorrect moral judgment. In other words, I may be honest about what I believe, but if I have never tested my beliefs, I may be wrong. And here I mean "wrong" in a particular sense: the proposition in question is wrong if I would change my mind about it after hard moral reflection.

Consider this example. Having been taught all his life that women are not as smart as men, a manager gives the women on his staff less challenging assignments than he gives the men. He does this, he believes, for their own benefit: he does not want them to fail, and he believes that they will if he gives them tougher assignments. Moreover, when one of the women on his staff does poor work, he does not berate her as harshly as he would a man because he expects nothing more. And he claims to be acting with integrity because he is acting according to his own deepest beliefs.

The manager fails the most basic test of integrity. The question is not whether his actions are consistent with what he most deeply believes but whether he has done the hard work of discerning whether what he most deeply believes is right. The manager has not taken this harder step.

Moreover, even within the universe that the manager has constructed for himself, he is not acting with integrity. Although he is obviously wrong to think that the women on his staff are not as good as the men, even were he right, that would not justify applying different standards to their work. By so doing, he betrays both his obligation to the institution that employs him and his duty as a manager to evaluate his employees.

The problem that the manager faces is an enormous one in our practical politics, where having the dialogue that makes democracy work can seem impossible because of our tendency to cling to our views even when we have not examined them. As Jean Bethke Elshtain has said, borrowing from John Courtney Murray, our politics are so fractured and contentious that we often cannot even reach *disagreement*. Our refusal to look closely at our own most cherished principles is surely a large part of the reason. Socrates thought the unexamined life not worth living. But the unhappy truth is that few of us actually have the time for constant reflection on our views—on public or private morality. Examine them we must, however, or we will never know whether we might be wrong.

None of this should be taken to mean that integrity as I have described it presupposes a single correct truth. If, for example, your integrity-guided search tells you that affirmative action is wrong, and my integrity-guided search tells me that affirmative action is right, we need not conclude that one of us lacks integrity. As it happens, I believe—both as a Christian and as a secular citizen who struggles toward moral understanding—that we can find true and sound answers to our moral questions. But I do not pretend to have found many of them, nor is an exposition of them my purpose here.

It is the case not that there aren't any right answers but that, given human fallibility, we need to be careful in assuming that we have found them. However, today's political talk about how it is wrong for the government to impose one person's morality on somebody else is just mindless chatter. *Every* law imposes one person's morality on somebody else because law has only two functions: to tell people to do what they would rather not, or to forbid them to do what they would.

And if the surveys can be believed, there is far more moral agreement in America than we sometimes allow ourselves to think. One of the reasons that character education for young people makes so much sense to so many people is precisely that there seems to be a core set of moral understandings—we might call them the American Core—that most of us accept. Some of the virtues in this American Core are, one hopes, relatively noncontroversial. About 500 American communities have signed on to Michael Josephson's program to emphasize the "six pillars" of good character: trustworthiness, respect, responsibility, caring, fairness, and citizenship. These virtues might lead to a similarly noncontroversial set of political values: having an honest regard for ourselves and others, protecting freedom of thought and religious belief, and refusing to steal or murder.

Honesty and competing responsibilities

A further problem with too great an exaltation of honesty is that it may allow us to escape responsibilities that morality bids us bear. If honesty is substituted for integrity, one might think that if I say I am not planning to fulfill a duty, I need not fulfill it. But it would be a peculiar morality indeed that granted us the right to avoid our moral responsibilities simply by stating our intention to ignore them. Integrity does not permit such an easy escape.

Consider an example. Before engaging in sex with a woman, her lover tells her that if she gets pregnant, it is her problem, not his. She says that she understands. In due course, she does wind up pregnant. If we believe, as I hope we do, that the man would ordinarily have a moral responsibility toward both the child he will have helped to bring into the world and the child's mother, then his honest statement of what he intends does not spare him that responsibility.

This vision of responsibility assumes that not all moral obligations stem from consent or from a stated intention. The linking of obligations to promises is a rather modern and perhaps uniquely Western way of looking at life, and perhaps a luxury that only the well-to-do can afford. As Fred and Shulamit Korn (a philosopher and an anthropologist) have pointed out, "If one looks at ethnographic accounts of other societies, one finds that, while obligations everywhere play a crucial role in social life, promising is not preeminent among the sources of obligation and is not even mentioned by most anthropologists."

The Korns have made a study of Tonga, where promises are virtually unknown but the social order is remarkably stable. If life without any promises seems extreme, we Americans sometimes go too far the other way, parsing not only our contracts but even our marriage vows in order to discover the absolute minimum obligation that we have to others as a result of our promises.

That some societies in the world have worked out evidently functional structures of obligation without the need for promise or consent does not tell us what *we* should do. But it serves as a reminder of the basic proposition that our existence in civil society creates a set of mutual responsibilities that philosophers used to capture in the fiction of the social contract. Nowadays, here in America, people seem to spend their time thinking of even cleverer ways to avoid their obligations, instead of doing what integrity commands and fulfilling them. And all too often, honesty is their excuse.

Moral Compassing

Stephen Covey

When managing in the wilderness of the changing times, a map is of limited worth. What's needed is a moral compass.

When I was in New York recently, I witnessed a mugging skillfully executed by a street gang. I'm sure that the members of this gang have their street maps, their common value—the highest value being "Don't fink or squeal on each other, be true and loyal to each other"—but this value, as it's interpreted and practiced by this gang, does not represent "true north," the magnetic principle of respect for people and property.

They lacked an internal moral compass. Principles are like a compass. A compass has a true north that is *objective and external,* that reflects natural laws or *principles,* as opposed to values that are subjective and internal. Because the compass represents the verities of life, we must develop our value system with deep respect for "true north" principles.

As Cecil B. DeMille said: "It is impossible for us to break the law. We can only break ourselves against the law."

Principles are proven, enduring guidelines for human conduct. Certain principles govern human effectiveness. The six major world religions all teach the same basic core beliefs—such principles as "You reap what you sow" and "Actions are more important than words." I find global consensus around what "true north" principles are. These are not difficult to detect. They are objective, basic, unarguable: "You can't have trust without being trustworthy" and "You can't talk yourself out of a problem you behave yourself into."

Reprinted with permission from Stephen R. Covey, *Principle-Centered Leadership.* Copyright 1990 by Stephen R. Covey.

There is little disagreement in what the constitutional principles of a company should be when enough people get together. I find a universal belief in fairness, kindness, dignity, charity, integrity, honesty, quality, service, and patience.

Consider the absurdity of trying to live a life or run a business based on the opposites. I doubt that anyone would seriously consider unfairness, deceit, baseness, uselessness, mediocrity, or degradation as a solid foundation for lasting happiness and success.

People may argue about how these principles are to be defined, interpreted, and applied in real-life situations, but they generally agree about their intrinsic merit. They may not live in total harmony with them, but they believe in them. And they want to be managed by them. They want to be evaluated by "laws" in the social and economic dimensions that are just as real, just as unchanging and unarguable, as laws such as gravity are in the physical dimension.

In any serious study of history—be it national or corporate—the reality and verity of such principles become obvious. These principles surface time and again, and the degree to which people in a society recognize and live in harmony with them moves them toward either survival and stability or disintegration and destruction.

In a talk show interview, I was once asked if Hitler was principle-centered. "No," I said, "but he was value-driven. One of his governing values was to unify Germany. But he violated compass principles and suffered the natural consequences. And the consequences were momentous—the dislocation of the entire world for years."

In dealing with self-evident, natural laws, we can choose either to manage in harmony with them or to challenge them by working some other way. Just as the laws are fixed, so too are the consequences.

In my seminars I ask audiences, "When you think of your personal values, how do you think?" Typically people focus on what they want. I then ask them, "When you think of principles, how do you think?" They are more oriented toward objective law, listening to conscience, tapping into verities.

Principles are not values. The German Nazis, like the street gang members, shared values, but these violated basic principles. Values are maps. Principles are territories. And the maps are not the territories; they are only subjective attempts to describe or represent the territory.

The more closely our maps are aligned with correct principles—with the realities of the territory, with things as they are—the more accurate and useful they will be. Correct maps will impact our effectiveness far more than our efforts to change attitudes and behaviors. However, when the territory is constantly changing, any map is soon obsolete.

A compass for the times

In today's world, what's needed is a compass. A compass consists of a magnetic needle swinging freely and pointing to magnetic north. It's also a mariner's instrument for directing or ascertaining the course of ships at sea, as well as an instrument for drawing circles and taking measurements. The word *compass* may also refer to the reach, extent, limit, or boundary of a space or time; a course, circuit, or range; an intent, purpose, or design; an understanding or comprehension. All of these connotations enrich the meaning of the metaphor.

Why is a compass better than a map in today's business world? I see several compelling reasons why the compass is so invaluable to corporate leaders:

- The compass orients people to the coordinates and indicates a course or direction even in forests, deserts, seas, and open, unsettled terrain.
- As the territory changes, the map becomes obsolete; in times of rapid change, a map may be dated and inaccurate by the time it's printed.
- Inaccurate maps are sources of great frustration for people who are trying to find their way or navigate territory.
- Many executives are pioneering, managing in uncharted waters or wilderness, and no existing map accurately describes the territory.
- To get anywhere very fast, we need refined processes and clear channels of production and distribution (freeways), and to find or create freeways in the wilderness, we need a compass.
- The map provides description, but the compass provides more vision and direction.
- An accurate map is a good management tool, but a compass is a leadership and an empowerment tool.

People who have been using maps for many years to find their way and maintain a sense of perspective and direction should realize that their maps may be useless in the current maze and wilderness of management. My recommendation is that you exchange your map for a compass and train yourself and your people how to navigate by a compass calibrated to a set of fixed, true north principles and natural laws.

Why? Because with an inaccurate map, you would be lost in a city. What if someone said "Work harder"? Now you're lost twice as fast. Now someone says "Think positively." Now you don't care about being lost. The problem has nothing to do with industry or with attitude. It has everything to do with an inaccurate map. Your paradigm or the level of your thinking represents your map of reality, your map of the territory.

The basic problem at the bottom of most ineffective cultures is the map in the head of the people who helped create that condition. It is an incomplete map, one based on quick-fix solutions and short-term thinking toward quarterly, bottom-line results, and it is based on a scarcity mentality.

The solution is to change from management by maps (values) to leadership by compass (natural principles). A political environment inevitably points to the style of top people—that's supposed to be true north. But the style is based upon volatile moods, arbitrary decisions, raw emotion, and ego trips. Sometimes true north is called an "information system" or a "reward system" and that governs behavior. What grows is what gets watered. Principle-centered leadership requires that people "work on farms" on the basis of natural, agricultural principles and that they build those principles into the center of their lives, their relationships, their agreements, their management processes, and their mission statements.

Strategic orientation

Map-versus-compass orientation is an important strategic issue, as reflected in this statement by Masaharu Matsushita, president of Japan's giant consumer electronic company: "We are going to win and the industrial West is going to lose because the reasons for your failure are within yourselves: for you, the essence of management is to get the ideas out of the heads of the bosses into the hands of labor."

The important thing here is the stated reason for our "failure." We are locked in to certain mind-sets or paradigms, locked in to management by maps, locked in to an old model of leadership where the experts at the top decide the objectives, methods, and means.

This old strategic planning model is obsolete. It's a road map. It calls for people at the top to exercise their experience, expertise, wisdom, and judgment and set ten-year strategic plans— only to find that the plans are worthless within eighteen months. In the new environment, with speed to market timetables of eighteen months instead of five years, plans become obsolete fast.

Peter Drucker has said: "Plans are worthless, but planning is invaluable." And if our planning is centered on an overall purpose or vision and on a commitment to a set of principles, then the people who are closest to the action in the wilderness

---

Universal human values:
Finding an ethical common ground

In a quest to discover core values that are common across cultures, Rushworth Kidder traveled the world interviewing thoughtful individuals from many walks of life. Following are the values that he puts forth as providing a foundation for building goals, plans, and tactics:

Love
The basis of moral behavior is first of all solidarity, love, and mutual assistance. Love is reflected in people helping one another at the personal level.

Truthfulness
We should not obtain our ends through lying and deceitful practices. We have a responsibility to keep our promises. We need to be honest, not lying, not afraid to say our opinion. We converge around and in truth.

Fairness
Treating other people as I would want to be treated. Social justice, fair play, and even-handedness provide common ground.

Freedom
Liberty and the right to express ideas freely. Freedom of expression plus accountability plus equal opportunity.

Unity
Unity embraces a global vision capable of moving humanity from unbridled competition to cooperation.

---

can use that compass and their own expertise and judgment to make decisions and take actions. In effect, each person may have his or her own compass; each may be empowered to decide objectives and make plans that reflect the realities of the new market.

Principles are not practices. Practices are specific activities or actions that work in one circumstance but not necessarily in another. If you manage by practices and lead by policies, your people don't have to be the experts; they don't have to exercise judgment because all of the judgment and wisdom is provided them in the form of rules and regulations.

If you focus on principles, you empower everyone who understands those principles to act without constant monitoring, evaluating, correcting, or controlling. Principles have universal application. And when these are internalized into habits, they

Tolerance
A decent respect for the right of other people to have ideas, an obligation or at least a strong desirability of listening to different points of view and attempting to understand why they are held. There are limits to which you can impose your values on someone.

Responsibility
Responsibility impacts our common future. Responsibility demands caring for others. The principle of responsibility involves not just asserting rights but ensuring that they are protected.

Respect for life
Thou shall not kill. To effectively resolve conflict within the community while protecting killing.

Other shared values

Courage   Stand for what is right.

Wisdom   Attaining detachment, getting away from being too attached to things.

Hospitality   Reaching out to strangers.

Obedience   Respect for higher authority.

Peace   Well-managed conflict.

Stability   Long-term perspective of no problems.

Source: Rushworth M. Kidder, *Shared Values for a Troubled World: Conversations with Men and Women of Conscience* (San Francisco: Jossey-Bass, 1994). Reprinted with permission.

empower people to create a wide variety of practices to deal with different situations.

Leading by principles, as opposed to practices, requires a different kind of training, perhaps even more training, but the payoff is more expertise, creativity, and shared responsibility at all levels of the organization.

If you train people in the *practices* of customer service, you will get a degree of customer service, but the service will break down whenever customers present a special case or problem because in doing so they short-circuit standard operating procedure.

Before people will act consistently on the *principle* of customer service, they need to adopt a new mind-set. In most cases they need to be trained—using cases, role plays, simulations, and some on-the-job coaching—to be sure they understand the principle and how it is applied on the job.

With the compass, we can win

"A compass in every pocket" is better than "a chicken in every pot" or a car in every garage. With moral compassing we can win even against tough competition. My view is that the Japanese subordinate the individual to the group to the extent that they don't tap into the creative and resourceful capacities of people— one indication being that they have had only 4 Nobel Prize winners compared with 186 in the United States. The highest leadership principle is win-win interdependency, where you are both high on individual and high on team.

But once people start to realize that this "compass" is going to be the basis for evaluation, including leadership style of the people at the top, they tend to feel threatened.

The president of a major corporation once asked me to meet with him and his management team. He said that they were all too concerned with preserving their own management style. He said that the corporate mission statement had no impact on their style. These executives felt the mission was for the people "out there" who were subject to the law, but they were above the law.

The idea of moral compassing is unsettling to people who think they are above the law because the Constitution, based on principles, is the law: it governs everybody, including the president. It places responsibility on individuals to examine their lives and determine if they are willing to live by it. All are accountable to the laws and principles.

I'm familiar with several poignant examples of major U.S. corporations telling their consultants, "We can't continue to do market feasibility studies and strategic studies independent of our culture and people." These executives understand what Michael Porter has said: "A implementation with B strategy is better than A strategy with B implementation."

We must deal with people/culture issues to improve the implementation of strategy and to achieve corporate integrity. We must be willing to go through a constitutional convention, if not a revolutionary war, to get the issues out on the table, deal with them, and get deep involvement, resulting in wise decisions. That won't happen without some blood, sweat, and tears.

Ultimately the successful implementation of any strategy hinges on the integrity people have to the governing principles and on their ability to apply those principles in any situation, using their own moral compass.

Ethical Dilemmas: Right vs. Right

―――――――――――――――― Patricia L. Brousseau

A guide for public administrators who must make tough ethical decisions on the job.

The concern of federal officials for integrity in the public sector comes through clearly in a survey conducted by Barry Posner and Warren Schmidt and reported in *Public Administration Review* (1994). When 1,006 federal officials were asked how they view the long-term outlook for ethics in government, 52 percent responded that they are "generally pessimistic" about the future, while only 11.9 percent admitted to being "generally optimistic" (p. 23).

This finding, not surprisingly, echoes a March 1994 *U.S. News & World Report* poll of 1,000 registered U.S. voters. Ninety percent of this sample agreed that "the nation is slipping deeper into moral decline" (p. 56). Given this perspective, how do citizens view the ethics of public policy makers? A study by the Kettering Foundation (Harwood 1991) found that citizens generally do not trust public officials: "Citizens believe that public officials no longer talk straight to them about issues; that public officials regularly dodge tough questions when they know the answers; and that public officials say one thing, only to do another" (p. 33).

On the positive side, Americans believe that values have a place in public policy making. "Our government would be better if policies were more directed by moral values," said 84 percent of the *U.S. News & World Report* poll respondents (p. 51).

Reprinted with permission from *Spectrum: The Journal of State Government* 68, no. 1 (Winter 1995): 16–20. Copyright Winter 1995 by the Council of State Governments.

Public administrators, in their role as guardians of the "process by which a civil society achieves its common good through the agency of the state" (Maritain 1951, pp. 1–27), are aware of citizens' impatience and distrust. But administrators, too, are caught in the dilemma of how to make and effect good policy in an environment where citizens desire reduced government intervention and expenditures on the one hand and maintenance of current levels of service and entitlements on the other (Gallup 1989).

When issues such as abortion, welfare, and the sexual education of our youth divide us along distinct values lines—"ideological dissensus," as Aaron Wildavsky (1988) describes it—what options does a public administrator have? How can public administrators begin to make better, more responsive public policy?

Author and New York Assemblyman Dan Feldman wrote in *Public Administration Review* (1993): "We need some kind of nice, multivariate, decision-making grid, or matrix, that reflects constitutional values [and] confers legitimacy on public administration and public administrators" (p. 239).

Creating a model for ethical decision making, based on the values embodied in the U.S. Constitution (which, we would argue, are the core moral values shared by people of all cultures) and the distilled wisdom of key philosophers through the ages, is possible and practical.[1] The model is built on a series of assumptions and processes designed to provide practical guidance to decision makers in government, business, or personal affairs:

- Identifying shared values—the assumption that there is a discoverable set of core shared moral values and a process called values definition, which identifies this core list
- Analyzing ethical dilemmas—an assumption that ethical dilemmas occur when two values on our core list come into conflict to produce what we call a right-vs.-right dilemma, and a process of analysis based on four right-vs-right dilemma paradigms
- Resolving ethical dilemmas—an assumption that when people make decisions, they are looking for a method that is memorable, balanced in approach and supportive of their desire to make the best decision they can within the purview of their responsibilities, along with a process of decision resolution based on three philosophical frames of reference.

Identifying shared values

Where is there evidence of shared moral values? Rushworth M. Kidder (1994) reports the results of interviews with 24 moral exemplars from 16 countries—individuals such as Nobel laureate Oscar Arias of Costa Rica, Native American tribal chief

Reuben Snake, former First Lady of Mozambique Graca Machel, UNESCO Secretary-General Federico Mayor, and John Gardner, founder of Common Cause. Each interviewee was asked: "If you could formulate a code of ethics for the 21st century, what would be on it?" The list of core values resulting from these conversations was love, truth, fairness, freedom, unity, tolerance, responsibility and respect for life. Is this consensus a fluke of circumstance? In dozens of exercises around the United States, the Institute for Global Ethics has found, empirically, that people with different interests and backgrounds select very similar values to be included on a core list.

Consider, too, the U.S. constitutional tradition. The Declaration of Independence calls for equality, liberty, respect, justice, honor and concern for the public good. The U.S. Constitution emphasizes justice, the common good, freedom from autocratic rule and, in the Bill of Rights, individual rights.

To what extent do citizens feel an attachment to these values? Michael Spicer and Larry Terry refer to the power of this tradition in an article in *Public Administration Review* (1993): "As Irving Kristol (1987) has noted, the Constitution, along with the flag and Declaration of Independence, enjoy an almost sacramental status in the eyes of citizens. Kristol argues that 'there is a spirit of the Constitution, enveloping the text and transforming it in a covenanting document, a pillar of the American civil religion'" (p. 241).

These values also are reflected in professional standards established for public administrators. The Code of Ethics of the American Society for Public Administration (ASPA 1985), for example, identifies a number of ethical values in its list of 12 commitments to the public: integrity (honesty, truthfulness), respect, compassion, responsibility and fairness.

What is the importance of identifying such a list of core values? The reasons reflect in part on our place in time, looking both to the past and to the future—to the past because many citizens believe that we have lost our moral footing in recent years, and to the future because "we will not survive the 21st century with the ethics of the 20th century" (Kidder 1993).

Beginning about 30 years ago, Americans began disassociating from their moral traditions. As an attitude of ethical relativism developed, a common theme arose: "If you don't impose your values on me, then I won't impose my values on you." In 1937, British philosopher Walter T. Stace summarized the nature and effect of ethical relativism this way: "If men come really to believe that one moral standard is as good as another, they will conclude that their own moral standard has nothing special to recommend it. They might as well then slip down to some lower and easier standard" (pp. 58–59).

Where values are not commonly held or understood, and where citizens do not feel the internal moral obligation to evidence them, it may be expected that the law will rush in to fill the resulting void. Lord Moulton, a 19th-century British jurist, once defined ethics as "obedience to the unenforceable." Obedience to the enforceable, he said, is simply obeying the law: If you exceed the speed limit, you will receive a summons and be fined. Obedience to the unenforceable, however, demands self-regulation based on perceived moral principles.

Common values are not only a starting point for making ethical decisions. They also are important to identifying goals, defining objectives, creating a plan of implementation and evaluating results along the way. We must ask, "Is this goal/plan/result consistent with our stated values?" Even when we may disagree as individuals on, for example, the tactics of busing minority children to other school districts, we can probably agree on the value of equal opportunity as a cornerstone to quality education.

"Because they are at the core of people's personality, values influence the choices they make, the people they trust, the appeals they respond to, and the way they invest their time and energy. In turbulent times, values give a sense of direction amid conflicting views and demands" (Posner and Schmidt 1994, p. 24).

Defining and analyzing right-vs.-right dilemmas

The tough ethical dilemmas, it may be argued, involve decisions of a right-vs.-right nature. These dilemmas are markedly different from choices of the right-vs.-wrong sort. For example, if one option in a decision is identified as being "right" and another as being "wrong," then we hope that most people would choose to do what is right. To be sure, there is often the moral temptation to do the wrong thing—"No one will know if I do not pay taxes on this under-the-table income, so I can save myself quite a bit of money." The decision to select an option that one clearly knows is wrong reflects not on one's ability to make decisions, but on one's lack of ethical clarity and moral courage.

Right-vs.-right dilemmas, on the other hand, involve situations where there is a clear moral backing for each option, but where the two are mutually exclusive. The next section discusses ways to select the best option. This section considers the nature of ethical dilemmas. At the Institute for Global Ethics, we have identified four types of right-vs.-right dilemmas:

- Truth vs. loyalty: personal honesty or integrity vs. responsibility and keeping one's promises

- Individual vs. community: the interests of the individual against those of the individual as part of a larger entity, the community
- Short-term vs. long-term: the real and important concerns of the present pitted against foresight and investment for the future
- Justice vs. mercy: fairness and equal application of the rules vs. empathy and compassion.

Because such dilemmas occur in real-life experiences, they are best illustrated by examples. Consider the following: Roberta is the director of the Family Services Division of the State Department of Human Services. She has reopened a position for a child protective services worker despite the recent round of state personnel cutbacks. She is anxious to fill the position. She would prefer a qualified male candidate because her division has many more female workers than male workers, and she feels a more balanced workforce would be healthier for the organization as well as helpful to the clientele. On the other hand, she needs to hire the most competent applicant, given the pressures of the workload and the expertise required when dealing with problem families. The list of prospects she has been given by the State Human Resources Department contains three names—two female and one male. She has completed her first round of interviews with the candidates and has discovered that, while the male candidate is qualified, one of the female candidates has stronger credentials and significantly more experience. What should she do?

In this right-vs.-right dilemma, it is right to hire the female candidate. She is the most qualified and could be expected to do the best job in serving the division. It is also right, however, to hire the male candidate to give him the chance to succeed in the job of his choice. Hiring him also may benefit the organization in the long term.

Justice vs. mercy is the most applicable dilemma paradigm in this case. Justice calls for fairness to all, while mercy calls for compassion for the individual.

The world of public administration is rich with dilemmas such as these. The ASPA Code of Ethics, in its "implementation guidelines," describes many such circumstances in general terms. For example:

- A public administrator may be called upon to withhold certain information from the public even while striving to uphold the highest standards of honesty and integrity.
- A public administrator may be politically appointed and be under the dual pressures of responsiveness to both partisan political objectives and the overall public good.

- A public administrator must, at the same time, "support, implement, and promote merit employment and programs of affirmative action."
- A public administrator must treat the public with sensitivity and receptiveness, remembering, however, that "people have a right to expect public employees to act as surrogates for the entire people with fairness toward all the people and not a few or a limited group."

Applying our dilemma analysis process to these examples, we see that whether to reveal certain information to the public may be seen as a truth-vs.-loyalty dilemma; whether to be responsive to partisan political pressures may be seen as a short-term-vs.-long-term dilemma; whether to hire based on ability or special need may be seen as a justice-vs.-mercy dilemma; and whether to decide on behalf of an individual or the public as a whole may be seen as an individual-vs.-community dilemma. Let's look at a few more examples.

Example   Bob, a recently hired city administrator, is preparing the city's annual budget performance report. It turns out that when the budget was developed by his predecessor and the city council, a major budget item was overlooked. Result: an overexpenditure of many thousands of dollars. The chair of the city council, realizing that the public will react negatively to this discrepancy, asks Bob not to include the overexpenditure in the report. Should Bob insist on presenting a factual budget report, or should he remain loyal to the council chair and, by implication, the rest of the council?

This dilemma pits truth against loyalty and is a common dilemma. This also demonstrates the unfortunate reality that one person's right-vs.-wrong decision often puts someone else in a right-vs.-right situation.

Example   Beth, a senior planner for the State Department of Mental Retardation, is drafting a plan to be presented to the legislature for allocating staff and other resources over the next biennium. The emphasis in recent years has been on moving mentally retarded adults out of institutions and into a community setting. The effort has been highly publicized, and certain advocacy groups have continued to insist upon increasing levels of service for these adults. Beth worries, however, that there will not be adequate resources to work with mentally retarded children who may have more to gain in the long run in terms of independence and self-reliance than do adults.

Beth's dilemma is of the short-term-vs.-long-term variety: It is right in the short term to work toward the successful de-institutionalization of mentally retarded adults; it is also right in the long term to set aside resources to serve the needs of a younger group of mentally retarded individuals.

Example   A low-income housing project in a neglected neighborhood of a major city has been experiencing increasing numbers of violent incidents in recent years, including several deaths from shootings. Residents are afraid to leave the less-than-certain safety of their apartments. Some residents suggest that firearms be prohibited within the project to reduce the likelihood of shootings. Others are afraid of being unable to defend themselves and complain that such a rule would take away their constitutional right to bear arms.

Paul is a member of the three-person authority considering the request. In looking at this individual-vs.-community dilemma, he can see that it is right to uphold the individual's right to bear arms, particularly as a measure of self-defense. It also is right to consider the welfare of the community, where an absence of guns may make a big difference.

Resolving right-vs.-right dilemmas

It is not enough simply to understand that right-vs.-right ethical dilemmas are difficult to resolve or that they may be analyzed in an organized manner. A resolution process is critically important. We suggest three decision rules for thinking through any right-vs.-right dilemma. They are ends-based, rule-based, and care-based. The three decision principles derive from the major strands of moral philosophy that, in turn, derive from everyday experience. This list has been designed to encourage a balanced approach to ethical decision making.

Ends-based thinking   *Ends-based* thinking is concerned with the results of a decision. What will happen? This utilitarian approach is commonly thought of as seeking "the greatest good for the greatest number." It seeks to distinguish right from wrong on the basis of consequences. The administrative standard of "effectiveness" is a form of ends-based thinking. Effectiveness seeks to maximize results and to distribute resources to various groups in direct proportion to their size and ability to affect decisions.

In the ideal pluralistic system, the model decision rule is utilitarian. Unfortunately, the ideal may be far from what transpires, as most U.S. citizens recognize: "Citizens believe the major forces that give form to our politics today—including lobbyists, special interest organizations, expensive and negative campaigns, political action committees, the media, and others—have created an environment where they each pursue their own interests and agendas with little regard for the common good" (Harwood, p. 24).

Rule-based thinking   *Rule-based* thinking seeks to identify and apply the rule that if obeyed, would make the world the kind of world we all would want to live in. It opposes ends-based thinking by denying the possibility that the result or consequence of any decision can in fact be known—or even properly estimated.

The rule-based approach, part of the nonconsequentialist school of thought, seeks to identify a standard to be followed by everyone in similar circumstances. H.J. Paton (1948), in analyzing philosopher Immanuel Kant's work in this area, writes: "A categorical imperative, as we have already seen, merely bids us act in accordance with universal law as such—that is, it bids us act on a principle valid for all rational beings as such, and not merely on one that is valid if we happen to want some further end. . . . We may express this in the formula 'Act only on that maxim through which you can at the same time will that it should become a universal law'" (p. 30).

Care-based thinking   *Care-based* thinking derives from the concept of the Golden Rule: Do unto others as you would have them do unto you. By putting yourself in the other person's position, you are encouraged to take their perspective into account. John Rawls' "veil of ignorance" (1971, pp. 136–142) is another example of the reversibility principle: Imagine that you have not yet been born into the world and you do not know into what station you will be born; what is the decision that will be fairest to you no matter where you end up in the world? The care-based approach is rational, but it is also compassionate and intuitive and thus, unfortunately, may not get adequate consideration in most models of decision making. Camilla Stivers (1993) warns public administrators about relying on reason alone: "As Vaclav Havel has reminded us, the greatest threat to human freedom is not the classic dictator but the phenomenon of impersonal power: power that is rooted in apparently neutral and objective logic. If so, then the responsibility facing public administrators today is to counterpose impersonal power with personal responsibility, conscience, and a politics growing from the heart rather than from a thesis" (p. 257).

In applying the three decision rules to any dilemma, it is important not to become distracted by a natural tendency to be-

The ethical triangle

James Svara discusses three related approaches to resolving ethical dilemmas—virtue, principle, and consequences. Each approach is guided by a question: "What would a person of integrity do in this situation? What principles are at stake in this situation and what actions would follow from these principles? What are the best consequences that could be achieved in this situation, and what actions would be taken to achieve them?" These three elements comprise the "ethical triangle" depicted in the figure below.

As one moves out from the triangle, the ethical basis for action is weakened and unethical actions may seem justifiable. In addition, reinforcement from other bases is decreased. As one moves in toward the triangle, the reinforcement among bases is increased.

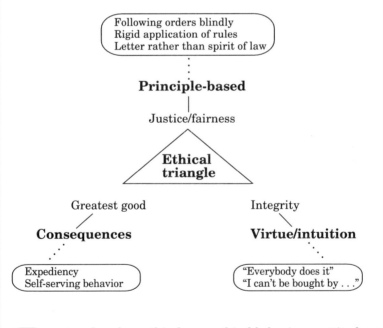

◯ = examples of nonethical or unethical behavior or attitudes resulting from narrow application of the approach.

Source: James H. Svara, "The Ethical Triangle: Synthesizing the Bases of Administrative Ethics." Copyright 1997 by the Council of State Governments. Reprinted with permission from *Public Integrity Annual* 2.

lieve that if two rules suggest one decision and one rule suggests another decision, then the vote is two-to-one and the highest right has been determined by minority vote. Rather, each of the approaches may be seen as equally valid. So the individual who is drawn more to rule-based thinking, for example, is no more or less moral than the individual who prefers ends-based thinking. The value of this process is that it keeps all three decision frames in front of any particular decision maker.

Applications   Consider, once again, Roberta's dilemma as director of the Family Services Division of the State Department of Human Services. In applying each of the three rules, we might come up with the following analysis:

Ends-based: What does Roberta imagine will happen if she hires the male applicant rather than the female applicant? Clearly, from the way she has stated her dilemma, she believes that if she hires him, the organization will work better, he will become comfortable in what has been mostly a female-dominated division and, in the long run, more people will benefit—the organization, the profession, and family members. If she believed, on the other hand, that to hire the male would help him a great deal, but otherwise have no important effect, then she would hire the female because the greatest good would be to hire the most qualified.

Rule-based: This approach denies that the greatest good for the greatest number can be predetermined. Instead, it asks: "What rule should every administrator follow in such cases?" If every public administrator in the world decided to do what I am about to do, would that produce the world I want to live in? One universal rule is "always hire the most qualified person." It may be unfortunate that the male candidate is not the most qualified; on the other hand, it is only fair to hire the female worker because she has earned that right.

Care-based: The key question in this mode of thinking is— who is the other? Is it the male candidate? If so, then you will hire him because he wants to be hired and to be given a chance to prove himself. Is it the female candidate? If so, she also would like to be hired: If the hiring process says look for the most qualified, and she is the most qualified, then she should be hired. Of course, as we have seen, a hiring process may be ambivalent— consider the ASPA guidelines that call for supporting both merit system and affirmative action objectives. In that case, caring will not be of much help unless one can identify the extent to which each of these candidates cares about the job.

In applying this model, Roberta's dilemma has not become suddenly easy to resolve. But she has worked her way through a process of analyzing the nature of the dilemma she faces. The perspective gained from looking at each of the three contribute to the success of this model in promoting learning. The question is: Will training and practice in methods such as these lead to improved ethical decision making on the part of public administrators?

Pedagogical considerations

To many individuals, ethics as a subject of learning conjures up a sense of being impossibly complicated.

But all individuals have meaningful past experiences to draw upon for purposes of discussing the principles of ethical decision making. And it is in the retelling of these experiences that the topic comes alive.

A first principle in promoting learning is: Use real stories to illustrate the principles of decision making and then teach participants how to apply these principles to their own stories. Small group work is an effective way to practice this technique.

A second strategy goes something like this: Put abstract ideas into a simple framework such that they may be readily recalled when needed. One related research finding about adult learning is that, while the ability to retain information in the short-term memory declines very little in the adult years, older adults may experience some difficulties when they are trying to store new information and retrieve old information at the same time. This type of memory loss is not memory loss per se, but "interference from other stored information" (Apps 1981, p. 92). The teaching strategy to address this potential problem involves presenting new information in a way that will help the learner to organize it. One method is to emphasize (1) a short list of core values, (2) four dilemma paradigms, and (3) three decision rules. These can be easily stored in one's memory or even in one's wallet.

John Rohr (1986) has suggested that "the image of a balance wheel best captures the distinctive contribution of the Public Administration" (p. 182). By this, he means that public administrators often have to weigh and choose among conflicting demands from the three branches of government. Similarly, public administrators are subject to differing demands from organized interest groups and from a public opinion that spans a broad spectrum of value systems.

This decision-making method is one practical way to address this important responsibility. Personal moral competence, in our view, is the keystone to more ethical public policy making that, in turn, can provide a basis for improved public support and trust.

Note

1. This process is the original work of Dr. Rushworth M. Kidder, founder and president of the Institute for Global Ethics. Dr. Kidder has completed a book on the topic *How Good People Make Tough Choices,* published by William Morrow & Company.

References

American Society for Public Administration. 1985. *Code of Ethics and Implementation Guidelines.* Washington, DC: ASPA.

Apps, J.W. 1981. *The Adult Learner on Campus: A Guide for Instructors and Administrators.* Chicago, IL: Follett Publishing Company.

Feldman, Daniel L. 1993. "Introduction: Forum on Public Administration and the Constitution." *Public Administration Review* 53 (May/June): 237–239.

Gallup, George Jr. 1990. *The Gallup Poll: Public Opinion 1989.* Wilmington, VA: Scholarly Resource, Inc.

Harwood, Richard C. 1991. *Citizens and Politics: A View from Main Street America.* Dayton, OH: Kettering Foundation.

Kant, Immanuel, as translated by H.J. Paton. 1961. *The Moral Law: Kant's Groundwork of the Metaphysics of Morals.* New York, NY: Barnes and Noble. Originally published in 1948.

Kidder, Rushworth M. 1994. *Shared Values for a Troubled World: Conversations with Men and Women of Conscience.* San Francisco, CA: Jossey-Bass Publishers.

_____. 1993. "There's only ethics . . ." Essay based on a keynote speech presented to the Human Services Council of Northeast Florida on October 1, 1992. Camden, ME: Institute for Global Ethics.

Lord Moulton of Bank. 1924. "Law and manners." *The Atlantic Monthly* 134 (July): 1–5.

Maritain, Jacques. 1951. *Man and the State.* Chicago, IL: University of Chicago Press.

Posner, Barry Z., and Warren H. Schmidt. 1994. "An updated look at the values and expectations of federal government executives." *Public Administration Review* 54 (January/February): 20–24.

Rawls, John. 1971. *A Theory of Justice.* Cambridge, MA: Harvard University Press.

Rohr, John A. 1986. *To Run a Constitution: The Legitimacy of the Administrative State.* Lawrence, KS: University Press of Kansas.

Sheler, Jeffery L., Jerry Buckley, Charles Fenyvesi, and Tarek Hamada. 1994. "Spiritual America." *U.S. News & World Report* 116 (April 4): 48–59.

Spicer, Michael W., and Larry D. Terry. 1993. "Legitimacy, history, and logic: Public administration and the Constitution." *Public Administration Review* 53 (May/June): 239–246.

Stace, Walter T. 1937. *The Concept of Morals.* New York, NY: The Macmillan Company.

Stivers, Camilla. 1993. "Rationality and romanticism in constitutional argument." *Public Administration Review* 53 (May/June): 254–257.

Wildavsky, Aaron. 1988. "Ubiquitous anomie: Public service in an era of ideological dissensus." *Public Administration Review* 48 (July/August): 753–755.

Paradoxes of Government Ethics

Dennis F. Thompson

This article suggests that the larger purpose of ethics standards—the aim that should inform ethics education—is the strengthening of the democratic process. The main business of government ethics should be what may be called education in democracy. Government ethics should be seen as a way of reminding officials that they are accountable to the public, that they primarily serve not their administrative superiors or even their own consciences but all citizens. I shall argue that a failure to appreciate this simple point—to understand what is at stake in setting standards for official conduct—is at the root of some common misconceptions about government ethics. Replacing these misconceptions with a better understanding of the purposes of ethics standards should be the primary aim of ethics education in government.

Three misconceptions are the focus of this discussion. They are those that arise from what I call "the paradoxes of government ethics," because they reflect deep tensions in both political philosophy and practical politics. The misconceptions that they generate are, therefore, neither easy to diagnose nor easy to cure. That is why the educational job of the ethics officers is likely to be difficult.

The priority of government ethics

The following is a version of a common complaint, voiced frequently in many different ways in recent years:

Excerpt from Dennis Thompson, "Paradoxes of Government Ethics," *Public Administration Review* 52, no. 3 (1992): 255–258. Copyright 1992 by the American Society for Public Administration, 1120 G Street, N.W., Suite 700, Washington, D.C., 20005-3885. All rights reserved.

Why are we spending so much time on ethics when there are so many other more important problems that need our attention? Why are we spending our time trying to catch individual officials who accept some $26 gift, when we could be dealing with the conflicts in the Middle East, the condition of the economy, and the drug problem?[1]

This complaint points toward the first paradox, which concerns the relative importance of government ethics. It may be stated in this way: *Because other issues are more important than ethics, ethics is more important than any issue.*

That complaint emphasizes only the first part of the paradox. It contains an important truth—that these and other major public policy problems are not only important but, in a sense, are more important than any problem of government ethics. This truth may be underscored by conducting a simple thought experiment: ask yourself whether you would rather have a morally corrupt government that solved all these problems, or a morally pure government that failed to solve any of them.

If that were the choice, most people probably would sacrifice moral purity. Ethics is not a primary goal of government in the way that, say, national defense, economic prosperity, or public welfare are. These and other public policy goals are intrinsic to government: they are part of the reason that government is established and maintained. Ethics is mainly instrumental to government: its main purpose is to contribute to the other, intrinsic goals of government. This is not to say that government ethics does not have any intrinsic value. Honest government is a good in itself, valuable independently of any good policies that government may make. The value of ethics, however, is still a byproduct of government, not a good at which government directly aims.

From the truth that ethics is mainly instrumental, it does not follow, as many critics seem to think, that ethics is always less important than other issues. Ethics may be only instrumental, it may be only a means to an end, but it is a necessary means to an end. Government ethics provides the preconditions for the making of good public policy. In this sense, it is more important than any single policy because all policies depend on it.

What does it mean to say that ethics provides the preconditions for good government? In the first place, ethics rules, if reasonably drafted and reliably enforced, increase the likelihood that officials will make decisions on the basis of the merits of issues rather than on the basis of factors such as private gain that should be irrelevant.

The point is not to prevent private gain as such. Despite the strong condemnations of private gain in most government ethics codes, there is nothing in itself wrong with personally benefiting from holding public office.[2] What is wrong with private gain is that it often leads to unfairness and partiality.[3] The main point of the rules against private gain should be to prevent the corruption of official judgment—to keep officials' minds concentrated, as far as possible, on the substance of issues, rather than on benefits that their friends or their favorite causes might receive.

Even if officials were able to overcome personal biases in making difficult public decisions, citizens could still have reasonable doubts. This points to the second precondition that ethics helps provide—creating and maintaining confidence in government. This is the stated objective in the first paragraph of the standards proposed by the Office of Government Ethics (OGE), but its meaning often is not fully appreciated. The confidence that ethics rules are supposed to give citizens is not just some general good feeling about government; it is not just to make citizens sleep better. It is supposed to give some reason to believe that officials are making decisions based on the merits. If citizens have this assurance, they are less likely to raise questions about the motives of officials, and are themselves more likely to concentrate on the merits of decisions and on the substantive qualifications of the officials who are making the decisions.

Take, for example, the most prominent scandal in the executive branch in the summer of 1991: the travels of the peripatetic John Sununu. It seems clear that Sununu did not break any law and probably did not violate any ethics rule, as currently written. Yet his actions—accepting free or below-cost trips on corporate jets, using a White House limousine and an air force jet for personal visits—caused many people (including some of his own colleagues in the White House) to raise questions about his judgment (Apple, 1991b). They were right to raise questions because the actions are of a kind that officials in Sununu's position arguably should not take, whether or not they are legally prohibited.

The main point is rather that, in the absence of clear ethics rules on these kinds of activities, the priorities of government business and public debate become distorted. Members of the White House staff spent too much of their time trying to contain the damage of this scandal. Members of Congress, the press, and citizens also had to spend too much of their time questioning Sununu's motives, instead of scrutinizing his role on other decisions, such as the civil rights bill or the choice of a nominee for the Supreme Court.

When ethics are in disorder, or when citizens reasonably believe they are, one should not be surprised that disputes about ethics drive out discussion about policies. Attention needs to be paid to ethics precisely so that ethical controversy does not distract from matters that would otherwise be more important. Ethics makes democracy safe for debate on the substance of public policy. That is why it is so important. That is the sense in which it is more important than any other single issue.

The difference between government ethics and personal ethics

A second paradox derives from the difference between government ethics and personal ethics. The difference is perhaps not so great that one should want to accept the classic maxim, "Private vice is public virtue." The difference is great enough that the paradox can be put this way: *Private virtue is not necessarily public virtue.*

One of the major challenges of government ethics—one of the principal tasks of what I have called education in democracy—is to persuade prospective government officials that, however impeccable their moral character, they still must fill out Form 278. They no doubt wonder: what do disclosure forms and postemployment rules have to do with being ethical?

What they need to understand—what ethics education should try to help them understand—is that personal morality and political ethics are quite different creatures. They are quite different both in their origins and in their purposes. Personal morality originates in face-to-face relations among individuals, and it aims to make people morally better. Political ethics has more modest aims. It arises from the need to set standards for impersonal relations among people who may never meet, and it seeks only to make public policy better by making public officials more accountable.

Some conduct that may be wrong in personal ethics (for example, certain sexual practices) is usually ignored by political ethics, and some conduct that is praiseworthy in personal ethics (returning a favor, or giving preference to a good friend) may violate the principles of political ethics. Also, many of the problems of political ethics (such as the issue of postemployment restrictions) do not arise at all in private life, and others (such as conflict of interest) do not arise in the same form or to the same degree.

It is true that the separation between private and public morality is not quite so sharp as these examples may imply. Some kinds of otherwise private immorality may indirectly affect an official's capacity to do a job. When an attorney general belongs to a private club that discriminates against blacks and women, when the head of the drug agency is addicted to cigarettes, when the enforcement chief of the Securities and Exchange Commission is guilty of wife beating, the public rightly takes notice. The officials in these cases recognized, or were forced to recognize, that their private conduct had too close a relationship to their public role: Griffin Bell quit the club, Bill Bennett evidently stopped smoking, and John Fedders resigned from the SEC.[4]

Even when the private conduct arguably bears some relation to the office the person will hold, public discussions of the ethics of nominees have an unfortunate tendency to dwell on that conduct—to the neglect of conduct more relevant to the office. John Tower's drinking problem may have deserved some discussion during the hearings on his nomination to be secretary of defense, but they surely deserved less than his activities as a consultant for defense contractors (Babcock and Woodward, 1989). Yet because of the public preoccupation with private immorality, and the confusion of private and public ethics, citizens heard little about these financial dealings, which probably would have revealed much more about his capacity to head the Department of Defense.

Some people who may be paragons of virtue in both their personal affairs and their business dealings in private life get into trouble when they go to Washington because they do not realize that government ethics require more, or at least something different. They experience what may be thought of as a reverse spin on *Mr. Smith Goes to Washington*. Instead of finding lower standards of conduct in government, they are shocked to find higher standards, or at least more restrictive ones. Being respectable in their own communities and corporations, they find it hard to understand why they should take these more restrictive standards seriously, especially since they do not have as much respect for government as they do for institutions in the private sector.

This kind of attitude may explain, in part, the epidemic of ethics violations that broke out in the mid-1980s. More than 100 federal officials (mostly political appointees) were indicted or charged with ethics offenses during the early years of the Reagan administration (Lardner, 1988). This outbreak of misconduct was partly the result of the sheer increase in the number and variety of new ethics rules and laws. It also seemed to be partly the product of an underlying attitude of disrespect toward government service—a skepticism about the need for restrictions on upstanding citizens (who, after all, were often accepting significant financial sacrifices to come to Washington).

Recognizing the difference between private and public ethics might go some way toward preventing another wave of misconduct like that witnessed in the eighties. It also might help counteract the continuing complaints about the standards that anyone, whether Mr. Smith or Mr. Sununu, must now satisfy when he or she comes to Washington. In particular, officials need a greater appreciation of the fact that in government they are accountable not to their business partners, their boss, or their board of directors (who probably are already predisposed to trust them). Rather they are accountable to all citizens, as represented by the president and his deputies, and by members of Congress (who cannot be automatically expected to trust officials they do not know well and may never even meet).

Greater appreciation of the difference between personal ethics and government ethics might also help prospective and current officials recognize that they need help in learning how to be ethical in public life. The need for such help is frequently resisted, as officials find it difficult to see why they need to be taught ethics, and perhaps even insulting to be told that they need to learn more about it. Here is one version of the resistance, expressed by a former congressman testifying before the House Task Force on Ethics: "No one learns his ethics in Congress. . . . No one needs to be told by his colleagues what is right and fair and honorable. . . . 'All I Really Need to Know I Learned in Kindergarten.'. . ." (U.S. House, 1989, pp. 35–36).[5]

However precocious a kindergartner might be, he or she is not likely quickly to master the postemployment restrictions. Government ethics standards are complicated and require some careful study because the circumstances with which they deal are complicated and unfamiliar to most people who have not served in government in recent years. Translating basic ethical principles and basic ethical character into ethical conduct in government does not come naturally to most people.[6]

We should not expect the rules of government ethics to be simple or to become simpler in the future. As government has become more complex, government ethics—the standards necessary to assure citizens that those who must cope with this complexity are serving with honor—are also likely to become more complex. As those who serve come from more diverse backgrounds and begin with fewer values in common, the rules of government are likely to become more important and more explicit. Private virtue will not automatically become public virtue.

The importance of appearances

The third paradox concerns the importance of appearances—the so-called appearance standard. Here is a particularly paradoxical way of stating the paradox: *Appearing to do wrong while doing right is really doing wrong.* This paradox could be treated as another instance of the confusion of private and public ethics, but it is the source of some distinct misconceptions and, therefore, deserves separate attention.

Despite the lip service that everyone gives to the importance of avoiding the appearance of impropriety, the appearance standard is often thought of as merely prudential, as a requirement of public relations, rather than as having any ethical significance itself. In this view, appearing to do wrong is not really wrong.

This view is held by many respectable people. One respectable person defending Sununu said, "Nobody likes the appearance of impropriety. On the other hand . . . you shouldn't be judged by appearance. You ought to be judged by fact" (Apple, 1991a). This view of the standard is taken not only by presidents but also by some ethics officials. A former director of the OGE, David Martin, told Congress that: "Our attitude is, when there is an appearance problem, that the persons involved have done no wrong, have committed no improprieties and are presumed to have acted ethically. It is an appearance only" (Roberts, 1988, pp. 181–182).

Whether or not this view is a mistaken interpretation of the ethics standards as they are now written, it is a mistaken basis for the ethical standards government *ought* to have. Officials who appear to do wrong actually do several kinds of moral wrong: they erode the confidence in government, they give citizens reason to act as if government cannot be trusted, and, most of all, they undermine democratic accountability.

The appearance standard expresses principles that are at the heart of our Constitution. The Founding Fathers designed our system of government so that public officials would be deliberately subjected to many different kinds of pressures and would be permitted to act on many different motives. Under these conditions, it is hard enough for any individual official, however conscientious, to find the right balance of these pressures and motives, to sort out the proper from the improper in making any particular decision. It must be virtually impossible for citizens, even well-informed and nonpartisan ones, to judge at a distance whether the official has really done so.

The only reliable way that citizens can judge whether improper actions took place is by looking at the circumstances under which officials act. If the circumstances are of the kind that citizens know from past experience tend to lead to improper actions, citizens are justified in concluding that an action is improper. When an official accepts favors from an interested group, whether or not the official's judgment is influenced, citizens are justified—ethically justified—in believing, and acting on the belief, that the official's judgment has been influenced.

Because appearances are often the only window that citizens have on official conduct, to reject the appearance standard is to reject the possibility of democratic accountability. This was dramatically demonstrated during the Senate Ethics Committee Hearings on the so-called Keating Five. Senator Alan Cranston, along with several others, kept objecting to the idea that his conduct should be judged by how it appears to a reasonable person. That is a "mythical person," he said; the only real person who can judge is the senator himself. "You were not there. I was there. And I know that what I knew at the time . . . convinced me that my [actions] were appropriate" (U.S. Senate, 1991, p. 122).

The logical consequence of rejecting the appearance standard is that only officials themselves would decide whether what appears to be wrong really is wrong. The official who looks bad just says "you have to trust me." Citizens have a right to say that the price of trust in a democracy is that officials have to observe certain standards, which require that they act under conditions that do not give rise to the appearance of wrongdoing. When they violate those standards, they do not merely appear to do wrong; they do wrong.

The main objection that critics raise against the appearance standard is that it is too subjective: what appears wrong to some people does not appear wrong to others, and officials become vulnerable to unfair charges. The appearance standard is, or can easily be made to be, as objective as any other standard. It is a standard based on objective empirical regularities: we have observed in the past that certain kinds of practices (such as accepting free air travel) tend to bring about corruption, and we therefore condemn such practices, whether or not they have been corrupting in this case.

The practices are, or can be, described quite objectively. Indeed, they can be described more objectively than the conduct prohibited by what are usually assumed to be objective standards, such as the criminal law against bribery. The core of a bribery offense is a corrupt intent, an exchange in which the bribe is "the mover or producer of the official act" (18 U.S.C. 201). There are great difficulties in interpreting this standard objectively not only in particular cases but also in more general terms. This difficulty is demonstrated, for example, in the attempts to distinguish bribes from campaign contributions. As one senator admitted, "You can hardly tell one from the other" ("Campaign Contributions," 1978, p. 451; also Lowenstein, 1985).

Another common objection to the appearance standard also rests on a mistaken interpretation. Critics complain that it makes style more important than substance. Politics is already too much dominated by appearances—the world of images, sound bites, and code words. What is needed, the critics say, is more concern with the substantial reality that lies behind these superficial appearances. These are not the kinds of appearances to which the appearance standard refers. The appearances that count in ethics are well-grounded perceptions (what appears to be the case to a reasonable, well-informed citizen), not the images and illusions that the critics correctly condemn. The standards proposed by OGE are a further move in this direction; for the first time, they refer to "the perspective of a reasonable person with knowledge of the relevant facts."[7]

Rather than reinforcing the superficiality of political debate, appearances in the sense assumed by the appearance standard are the source of substantive criticism. It is mainly on the basis of this kind of well-grounded appearance that politicians can be criticized for being superficial, for failing to deal with the substance of issues. By the same token, it is mainly on the basis of appearances in this sense that one can and does legitimately criticize public officials for failing to act ethically. Appearances matter ethically, not just politically.

Conclusion

A large part of the educational responsibility of ethics officers, then, is persuading other public officials, and those who would become public officials, that the rules of government ethics are an integral part of our democratic process. They must come to appreciate the paradoxes of government ethics discussed here and to see that misconceptions of government ethics to which they can give rise stand in the way of making government more democratic. That is why this responsibility is appropriately understood as education in democracy.

If this rendering of the role of government ethics officers is accepted, their responsibility may be even greater than it has been in the past. Among the several ways in which that responsibility might grow, three are especially important.

Because education is a continuous process, the job of the ethics officer is not finished when a new employee has been helped to fill out the forms and put through the first training session. Not only because the law changes, but also because circumstances change, new lessons have to be learned. (Some of the tedium of this might be reduced by enlisting colleagues who are not ethics specialists to serve as teaching assistants. They may be surprised at how much they learn themselves.)

Another consequence is that, because the lessons that educators impart should be constructive, some of the instruction ethics officers provide will have to be positive—more positive, for example, than one of the OGE's most popular publications, *How to Keep Out of Trouble.* (This handbook answers, with unusual directness, the question: "Can You Gamble While on Duty?"

The answer, in case there is any doubt, is: "No" [U.S. OGE, 1956, p. 6].) This kind of handbook is certainly necessary and important, but ethics education should go further. It should not only be about how to stay out of trouble but also how to make democracy work better.

Third, to be effective educators, ethics officers will not only have to be accessible but will also have to establish a strong presence throughout the government. It is no longer likely that many officials are unaware of their Designated Agency Ethics Officer or the functional equivalent, and the annual training sessions should help increase that awareness. The DAEOs will have to be available for consultation on a daily basis and will have to be willing to serve as a general adviser on proper conduct in the democratic process, whether or not the advice is directly related to the ethics regulations.

The rules of government ethics sometimes seem (and indeed sometimes are) mundane in content and suspicious in tone. Ethics officials have to keep reminding their colleagues (and perhaps themselves) that the purposes of government ethics are important and honorable—as important as the confidence of democratic citizens they are meant to sustain and as honorable as the vocation of democratic public service they seek to strengthen.

Notes

1. The complaint is a composite of many different comments; see, e.g., the testimony of former congressman Otis Pike: "You weren't . . . sent here to appear ethical. You were sent here to write laws and resolve problems. Your preoccupation with each other's ethics is preventing you from doing your jobs" (U.S. House, 1989, May 3, p. 2).

2. See *Federal Register*, 1991, 2635.101 (b)7 and 2635.702 (a)–(e), p. 33788. An example of what seems an excessive effort to prohibit private gain is the proposed restriction on the use of one's title when engaged in teaching, speaking, or writing (2635.807 [3][b]).

3. That fairness is a significant part of the rationale for prohibiting compensation for outside activities is evident in the justification for the exception allowed for teaching: "there is little possibility that [anyone] will unfairly benefit from their government positions" (*Federal Register*, 1991, p. 33790).

4. For a discussion of the relevance of private conduct in judging public officials, see Thompson (1987, ch. 5).

5. Congressman Pike did concede that we could stand to learn *something* more about ethics: "We don't know how to define ethics, and we aren't sure whether the word is singular or plural" (U.S. House, 1989, pp. 35–36).

6. Skepticism about the need or possibility of teaching ethics to adults is widespread in many of the professions and even in colleges and universities. For an early and influential effort to quell this skepticism, see Bok (1976).

7. *Federal Register*, 1991, 2635. 101(b)(14). If the phrase "with knowledge of the relevant facts" is interpreted too strongly, however, the appearance standard is in danger of collapsing into an actual conduct standard. The regulations also establish a procedure by which an agency ethics officer may authorize officials who have an appearance problem in

particular cases not to disqualify themselves. This procedure is a "means to ensure that their conduct will not be found, as a matter of hind-

sight, to have been improper" and thus provides a further objective basis for the appearance standard (2536.502 [d], p. 33786).

References

Apple, R.W., 1991a. "A Sununu 'Appearance Problem' Is Conceded by a Still-Loyal Bush." *New York Times* (June 20), p. D22.

_____, 1991b. "Sununu's Power Wanes in Furor over His Travel." *New York Times* (June 24), pp. 1, A12.

Babcock, Charles R., and Bob Woodward, 1989. "Tower: The Consultant as Advocate." *Washington Post* (February 13), p. Al.

Bok, Derek, 1976. "Can Ethics Be Taught?" *Change,* vol. 8, pp. 26–30.

"Campaign Contributions and Federal Bribery Law," 1978. *Harvard Law Review,* vol. 92.

Federal Register, 1991. Part II, Office of Government Ethics, vol. 56 (July 23). Washington: Government Printing Office, pp. 33778–33815.

Lardner, George, Jr., 1988. "Conduct Unbecoming an Administration." *Washington Post National Weekly Edition* (January 3), pp. 31–32.

Lowenstein, Daniel H., 1985. "Political Bribery and the Intermediate

Theory of Politics." *UCLA Law Review,* vol. 32 (April), pp. 784–851.

Roberts, Robert N., 1988. *White House Ethics.* New York: Greenwood Press.

Thompson, Dennis F., 1987. *Political Ethics and Public Office.* Cambridge, MA: Harvard University Press.

U.S. Office of Government Ethics, 1986. *How to Keep Out of Trouble: Ethical Conduct for Federal Employees in Brief* (March). Washington: Government Printing Office.

U.S. House of Representatives Bipartisan Task Force on Ethics, 1989. *Congressional Ethics Reform.* 101st Cong., 1st sess., Hearings (May 3, 24, July 12, September 20). Washington: Government Printing Office.

U.S. Senate, Select Committee on Ethics, 1991. *Preliminary Inquiry into Allegations Regarding Senators . . . ,* Open Session Hearings, 101st Cong., 2d sess., part 1 of 6. Washington: Government Printing Office.

PART 2

Implementation

Institutionalizing Ethics in Government

 Gary B. Brumback

Ethics in the workplace cannot be left solely to each person's conscience for two obvious reasons. First, temptations and pressures in the workplace may overcome conscience. Second, a person's unethical behavior invariably affects other people. Ethics, therefore, must be an organizational as well as an individual responsibility.

In this article[1] we shall put ethics into a practical as opposed to a philosophical perspective, briefly examine the nature of unethical behavior, and selectively discuss some elements of a program for institutionalizing ethics in a particular workplace, government.[2] In doing so, we shall draw somewhat upon a survey conducted and three papers written for a panel session we organized and moderated at the 1989 national conference on government ethics sponsored by the American Society for Public Administration.[3]

The bottom line of ethics

Our practical perspective here is the ethical behavior of public servants. We have drawn in Figure 1 a line to differentiate ethical from unethical behavior. We call it the bottom line of ethics. The hatched area around it represents the gray area of ethics. It is a relatively small area. Disagreements over whether behaviors there are ethical or unethical do not preclude an operational, or behavioral, definition of ethics (a congressman at the ASPA conference said it was impossible for him to define ethics). Nei-

Reprinted with permission from *Public Personnel Management* 20, no. 3 (1991):353–363, published by the International Personnel Management Association, Alexandria, Virginia. 703/549-7100, http://www.ipma-hr.org.

Figure 1. The bottom line of ethics versus the law.

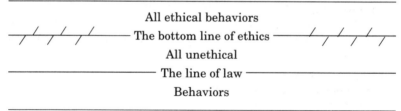

All ethical behaviors	
The bottom line of ethics	
All unethical	
The line of law	
Behaviors	

ther does it warrant the disproportionate attention often given to it (e.g., the belaboring of case studies of ethical dilemmas).

Figure 1 conveys a vertical ordering of behavior. There is undeniably a descending order below the bottom line. But is there an ascending order above it, and if there is, are there any practical implications? We are unsure, even after a large corporation showed us its scale, three levels of which are positive, for rating their managers on an ethics factor.[4] What impressed us was not the scale, but the simple fact that here was an organization that made ethics an appraisal factor. Few organizations do that. As we shall see, this approach to ethics accountability is an essential element of a government ethics program and does not require differentiation above the bottom line.

The nature of unethical behavior

Figure 1 shows two kinds of unethical behavior, the illegal and the legal. The former gets more publicity, but is vastly outnumbered by the latter.[5] That is why the legal threshold is drawn so far below the bottom line. A government program that does nothing more than keep behavior legal, while no small accomplishment, would not be a bona fide ethics program. It would be more of a law enforcement program. Laws and regulations are not the answer to keeping behavior above the bottom line of ethics.[6]

If you have looked at any codes of conduct, you know why we stress the difference between ethics and law. A case in point is the pamphlet "How to Keep out of Trouble—Ethical Conduct for Federal Employees—In Brief," published by the Office of Government Ethics (OGE).[7] Our immediate reaction, of course, is that there is more to ethics than staying out of trouble. Inside the pamphlet, the foreword reads:

The laws and regulations that make up those government-wide standards are found in Title 18 of the United States Code, sections 202 through 209, and Executive Order 11222, as implemented by Part 735 of Title 5 of the code of Federal Regulations.[8]

With due respect to OGE, do we need to say more on this particular matter? One reason ethics is much easier said than done is that the legal kind of unethical behavior has become so very ordinary, as we can see from these generic examples:

- Embellishing claims
- Scapegoating personal failures
- Shirking distasteful responsibilities
- Knowingly making unreasonable demands
- Stonewalling questions
- Acting disingenuously
- Reneging on promises
- Dissembling
- Making consequential decisions unilaterally
- Using chicanery in budgeting
- Loafing and loitering.

None of these behaviors is scandalous. But each nonetheless violates a sense of what is the morally correct behavior (e.g., the behaviors of personal responsibility, honesty, fairness, etc.), abets cynicism and distrust, undermines integrity, and can be a stepping-stone to egregious behavior.

The fact that unethical behavior has various origins, and each is a mix of personal and situational conditions, also makes ethics more difficult to institutionalize. One mix guaranteed to produce wrongdoing is given in this "prescription":

Put a moral rationalizer
Hurrying to succeed
In a seductive position
Give him/her ignoble expectations
And upside-down incentive
And walk away.[9]

While there may be additional conditions, such as personal insecurity and the best and worst of times, the six identified above must be targeted if any government ethics program is to be effective. Each is briefly explained below.

1. Rationalizations. When there are corrupting situations like the ones characterized above, people in them may behave unethically and rationalize their behavior as ethical. This "mind-over-manner" tendency (see Table 1) is a big reason why good people sometimes behave badly.[10]
2. Impatient ambition. Short-term success is valued in our society. As a federal budget director put it, "We seem on the verge of a collective now-now scream 'I want my Maypo; I want it NOWWWWWW!'"[11] And wanting it now can drive people to cut ethical corners.

Table 1. Mind over manner: Excuses for wrongdoing.

Denying or trivializing its significance
- "Show me a victim."
- "It's not illegal."
- "You can't legislate morality."
- "It's just a technicality."

Invoking the double standard
- "Morality is a personal matter."
- "I don't mix business with my personal feelings."

Arguing necessity
- "It's cutthroat out there."
- "If I don't do it, someone else will."
- "It's my job."
- "It will save some jobs."

Arguing relativity
- "It's not illegal elsewhere."
- "In the U.S., ideals are turned into laws."
- "No act is inherently illegal."
- "We are no worse or better than society at large."

Professing ignorance
- "I wasn't told."
- "Ethics is a gray area."
- "The rules are inscrutable."

3. Seductive positions. Any position that gives its holder power, considerable discretion, and/or access to funds is seductive. Such a position tests moral character.

4. Ignoble expectations. Behind every great performance is usually a great expectation. Unfortunately, ignoble expectations also have a considerable influence on behavior. An ignoble expectation accentuates achievement of results *and* is either silent on the manner of pursuing them (typically the case when MBO is used), gives implicit approval to unethical means (e.g., "wink-and-nod management"), or gives explicit approval or even an order.

5. Upside-down incentives. As influential as expectations are, incentives are often tacked on for added emphasis. Sometimes they are tacked on upside down. A common example is giving bonuses based on inflated performance ratings. The bonuses further reinforce the dishonesty behind the ratings.

6. Unguarded trust. Ethics clearly cannot be taken for granted when any of the other conditions exist. Unguarded trust, or a laissez-faire posture, in these circumstances will be counterethic.

The elements of an ethics program

We had asked people at the ASPA conference to rate the importance of several approaches to institutionalizing ethics in government.[12] The approaches were then ordered into three categories of relative importance. The results are presented in Table 2.

Implementation of the approaches in the first category would attack all of the causes of unethical behavior. The whole category should thus be part of any government ethics program. So too should the second category since its approaches were not rated unimportant and are already part of some ongoing programs. The third category probably could be excluded, although we would take one of its approaches, certification, and put it into the oath of office and the performance management process (to be discussed shortly).[13]

We cannot discuss here all of the important approaches. Instead, we shall discuss just a few in the first category that are of greatest interest to us.

The ethics factor in hiring

First, hire the right people. Employees who are included to be ethical are the best insurance you can have.[14]

—CEO of a management consulting firm

Table 2. Rated importance of some ways to put ethics to work.

Most important
- Moral leadership
- Make ethics a qualification requirement
- Conduct ethics training
- Establish, monitor, and enforce a code of ethics
- Factor ethics into performance management process
- Spot and control vulnerabilities to wrongdoing
- Eliminate PACs and honoraria

Moderately important
- Have ethics counselors available
- Regularly communicate on ethics
- Establish hot line
- Require financial disclosures
- Survey employees' opinions about ethics
- Narrow personal immunity law

Least important
- Lengthen budget cycle and elected terms of office
- Require certification of adherence to code
- Use a table of penalties
- Require approval of outside activities
- Reward whistle-blowers for valid disclosures
- Pay higher salaries

That, like being ethical, is easier said than done. There are some hurdles:

- The polygraph is not a good predictor and its use is severely restricted.[15]
- Paper and pencil integrity tests are not much better and their use is increasingly being restricted.[16]
- Job applications tempt dishonesty, and one in every two applicants tends to lie on them.[17]
- Most people are fooled most of the time by lies.[18]
- Surreptitious screening (e.g., covert questions) is unethical.

Not screening for ethics, on the other hand, seems to call for too much unguarded trust. Moreover, there are a growing number of cases in which employers have been sued for negligent hiring.[19] We suggest several ways out of this Catch-22.

1. Review background investigation policies and procedures to determine if they are ethical, can be improved, and are used for the right (seductive) jobs.
2. Build the agency's reputation for integrity by implementing the other important approaches in Table 2. Then stress that reputation to recruits.
3. Do not use surreptitious screening and explain the policy to recruits.
4. Ask new hires to pledge a commitment to ethics in government in the oath of office.

The ethics factor in performance management Managing performance is the only sure way to get desired results consistently (we know what the two alternative approaches, aimless performance and crisis management, tend to produce). Factoring ethics into the process of managing performance is the best way to ensure that work objectives are achieved in an ethical manner, and that other on-the-job behaviors are ethical.[20] People are sensitized to the fact that ethical behaviors are valued and expected, and that there will be an accountability for unethical behavior. No ignoble expectations. No upside-down incentives.

Illustrated in Table 3 is one version of the appraisal part of the process. It is the version we advocate. It is extremely simple, yet would account for both results and behaviors, and would provide a basis for performance bonuses.[21]

Note that there would be no chance for dishonest ratings. They are, incidentally, so common in practice because little lies are so easy to make and accept (e.g., a level 5 rating when level 4 is much closer to the truth).[22] Being dishonest about a yes/no appraisal, on the other hand, would require making and accept-

Table 3. A simple but complete performance appraisal.

	Yes	No	Explain in addendum
Did you meet all objectives?	☐	☐	x
*Was your manner of performance positive:			
On the managerial factor?	☐	☐	x
On the professional/technical factor?	☐	☐	x
On the general conduct and ethics factor?	☐	☐	x
Is there clear evidence you significantly exceeded one or more objectives? (If yes, describe below, attach or reference)	☐	☐	
Reviewer's concurrence?	☐	☐	x
Employee and reviewers' signatures and dates:			
*See Manner of Performance Handbook.			

ing boldfaced lies ("yes" and "no" is the truth, or vice versa). A "yes" on the ethics question, as we alluded to earlier, would be tantamount to a recertification of the commitment to ethics.

Note also that the appraisal would be self-made, albeit with the concurrence of someone else. Self-appraisals epitomize a guiding principle of ours, "in the performer we trust."[23] The trust should be guarded, of course, when preconditions exist for unethical behavior. When they do, closer monitoring and review by someone else is in order.

Note finally the reference to the handbook. It would contain examples of negative behavior in the three categories and guidance on how to use them in making yes/no judgments on manner of performance. The examples would have been generated through a consensus-building exercise by people within the agency. The examples for the third category would be, in effect, the organization's code of conduct. No legalese or regulatese, please. Just behavioral examples. And by being part of the performance management process, the code would not be out-of-sight, out-of-mind.[24]

Unfortunately, the ethics factor is not commonly factored into the performance management systems of business and government. Arguments we have heard for its exclusion are given in Table 4 along with our rebuttals. Presumably, our survey people would side with us. Would you?

Ethics training   A member of the audience at our panel session rose and said, "Most ethics training is deadly." After the session, someone told us about a particular pedagogical exercise that was "highly entertaining and hardly useful."

Table 4. Debate on the ethics factor in performance management.

- "Ethics is not performance"
- "Ethics is behavior, and behavior and results are the two parts of performance"

- "Ethics is too subjective to be measured"
- "Ethical behaviors can be appraised"

- "It's Orwellian big brother"
- "Not if done right, like self-appraisal with exceptions"

- "It makes ethics confrontational"
- "Unethical behavior needs to be confronted"

- "We hold people accountable in other ways"
- "What ways and how well?"

- "It's implicitly understood"
- "Ethics and its communication are too important to be left to mind reading"

We wonder if ethics training is frequently overdone and/or poorly done. Here is what we would recommend doing:

1. Don't overdo ethics training. Its value is limited. Most of the preconditions for unethical behavior are situational, not personal. A trained person back in the wrong situation is one-half a solution.
2. Trim case studies. Overdoing them and gray-area deliberations turn ethics into an intellectual exercise and ethics training into a placebo. Case studies are only good for increasing job knowledge and problem solving and planning skills.[25]
3. Use small group exercises in which behaviors are role played. Such exercises are the best way to confront rationalizations and change attitudes and motivation.[26]
4. Above all, tell people what the preconditions of unethical behavior are, what the bottom line of ethics is, and what the agency and each individual can do to make ethics a work habit.

Auditing the program   A government ethics program needs to be audited periodically to see if all its elements are fully in place and working well. The audit should include a survey of members' opinions and perceptions of the program and the agency's ethical climate. Besides being diagnostically useful, a survey is another way to communicate the importance of ethics.

The survey should include questions about each of the program's elements. Here are a few illustrative questions:

- If you were hired within the last two years:
was the importance of ethics communicated clearly to you during the selection interview?
- Was the pledge of ethics done properly (e.g., in neither an authoritarian nor cavalier way)?
- To what extent do you think self-appraisals are truthful?
- To what extent if any do you think unethical behavior is being rewarded?
- How useful has last year's ethics training been to your _____work _____thinking about ethics?

Besides programmatic questions, there should be questions aimed at the agency's ethical climate. Here we suggest consideration of questions like those in the "Organizational Integrity Perception Audit" developed by a midwestern ethics center.[27] This survey has 40 questions on overall ethical motivation and habits, ethical responsiveness of the organization's mission and structure, ethical sensitivity in problem solving, etc.

The survey should be administered anonymously with everyone given an opportunity to respond, at least in the inaugural round. People should be told the findings for their own major division of the agency and for the agency overall. The findings should be used by the ethics program office to fine-tune the program. The findings should not be used to reward or punish individual division managers.

Conclusion

It is not an oxymoron to say that ethics needs to be institutionalized in government. Although each public servant must be personally responsible for his or her own behavior on the job, given the fragility of the human conscience, government must also be responsible for a workplace that is conducive to ethical behavior.

Government scandals notwithstanding, corruption is not the primary problem. The problem is more serious, because most unethical behavior is legal, and government ethics programs tend to be more like law enforcement programs. Most unethical behavior, whether in government or in business, is more ordinary than scandalous, more than a routine response to routine situations in the workplace. The enemy of ethics, in other words, is us and the situations we create or find ourselves in.

Criminalizing more unethical behavior is clearly not the answer to making ethical behavior more habitual in government. Government can contribute most of this goal by implementing a comprehensive ethics program that addresses the basic personal and situational causes of unethical behavior. The elements of such a program are known, but some of them are either missing or inadequately implemented in ethics programs of today.

Notes

1. Opinions expressed in this article are the personal ones of the author.
2. Singling out government does not mean we think business is on higher moral ground.
3. Brumback, G.B. (Chair). Institutionalizing ethics: How to make ethics real. Panel session at the ASPA national conference on ethics in government, Washington, D.C., November 14, 1989. The panelists were Dr. Loretta Cornelius, assistant professor, Graduate School of Business and Public Affairs, Old Dominion University; Dr. Thomas Donaldson, John A. Largay Scholar and professor, School of Business, Georgetown University; James Keogh, formerly executive director, Business roundtable, now retired author; and Thomas McFee, assistant secretary of personnel administration, U.S. Department of Health and Human Services.
4. The five levels are "nonsupportive," "minimally supportive," "supporter," "practitioner," and "leader."
5. Brumback, G.B. Unethical behavior in government: More than you thought? Paper presented at the ASPA conference, op. cit.
6. Josephson, M. Limitations of ethics laws. *EthNet Newsletter*, 1989, 3, p. 2.
7. Office of Government Ethics. How to keep out of trouble—Ethical conduct for federal employees—In brief. March, 1986.
8. OGE, ibid.
9. Brumback, G.B. It takes two to do wrong. Paper presented at the ASPA conference, op. cit.
10. Gellerman, S.W. Why "good" managers make bad ethical choices. *Harvard Business Review*, 1986, 64, 85–90.
11. Dentzer, S. The Maypo culture. *Business Month*, 1989, 134, 26–34.
12. About 50 conferees answered our survey.

13. Although some of the approaches in the third category are in use, they have serious drawbacks. For instance, salary inducements to be ethical are regarded by some as either a bribe and/or ineffective.
14. Quoted from *Ethics: Easier said than done*, 1988, 1, p. 51.
15. Sackett, P.R., Burris, L.R., and Callahan, C. Integrity testing for personnel selection: An update. *Personnel Psychology*, 1989, 42, 491–529.
16. Sackett, et al., op. cit.
17. *Ethics: Easier said than done*, op. cit.
18. Ekman, P. Would a child lie? *Psychology Today*, 1989, 23, 62–65.
19. Bureau of National Affairs, Inc. Negligent hiring torts are resulting in more cautious selection procedures. *Current Developments*, 1988, no. 214.
20. Brumback, G.B. Putting ethics to work by adding a new bottom line. Paper presented at the ASPA conference, op. cit.
21. To see how much an approach could support bonus decisions, we refer to G.B. Brumback, Sequelae: Ten years after reform and new models of performance management, in *Readings in performance management*, Alexandria, VA: IPMA, 1988.
22. As one line manager told us, "There are office pockets of honesty where the number of outstanding ratings don't outnumber the rest. These offices pay dearly for their honesty when bonus allocations are made throughout a pool of offices."
23. See, e.g., T.S. McFee and G.B. Brumback, Reforming performance management: Ten years unfinished. Invited paper presented at the tenth anniversary review and assessment of the Civil Service Reform Act of 1978, Washington, D.C., May, 1988; also, G.B. Brumback, Quality of service and employment empowerment. Paper

presented to the U.S. Office of Personnel Management, 1989.

24. In 1979, the U.S. Supreme Court could not get 12 copies of a color poster of the government's code of ethics. The negatives had been destroyed in 1972 by the government's printing office.

25. Carroll, S.J., Paine, F.T., and Ivancevich, J.J. The relative effec-tiveness of training methods—Expert opinion and research. *Personnel Psychology,* 1972, 25, 495–509.

26. Carroll, et al., op. cit.

27. Center for Ethics, Responsibilities, and Values. Organizational integrity perception audit. College of St. Catherine, St. Paul, MN, 1987.

Creating an Ethical
Work Environment

Stephen J. Bonczek

Today's public managers face increasingly complex ethical dilemmas, often having to weigh personal and professional values
against current public opinion and the law. In a climate of expanded concern over ethical conduct in government institutions—
heightened by a decade of well-publicized cases of both willful
and negligent abuses of public trust—administrators confront
new challenges in the practice of public service. There is a growing realization among local governments of the cost of unethical
behavior and, conversely, of the benefits of ethical behavior.

The various aspects and complexities of ethics in government
are an intricate web. Correspondingly, for organization members,
the process of resolving ethical situations is like a tangled fish-
ing line: the more you attempt to unravel it, the more tangled it
becomes. It is clear that a substantial commitment of leadership
is needed to enhance organizational effectiveness in dealing with
the ethical issues of the 1990s.

Enhancing ethical awareness in the workplace

To promote ethical decision making in public organizations by
establishing ethics guidelines that reflect the organization's well-
defined value system is an excellent approach for local governments. The ethical dilemmas facing public service in the 1990s
warrant serious policy action by elected and appointed officials.
The creation of an ethics policy and guidelines provides the organizational foundation for employees to evaluate actions that
have ethical implications. The strengthening of the ethical frame-

Reprinted by permission from *Public Management* magazine (October 1991):
19–23.

work of the organization is a critical first step in improving the ethical consistency of its actions.

After establishing an ethics policy and presenting it to members of the organization, how does management create increased ethical awareness in the work environment? Can you teach ethics through a standard employee training development program? Largo, Florida, is a medium-sized city of 70,000 population that had successfully created ethics guidelines based on the administrative value system. As Largo's city manager, I had particular interest in exploring the areas of measuring ethical awareness in the organization and the effectiveness of formalized ethics training in employee attitudes and behavior.

Ethical climate survey

To assess accurately the efficacy of ethical initiatives, a benchmark of the ethical beliefs, attitudes, and behavior of employees must be established.

An ethical climate survey can be accomplished efficiently by surveying all employees or by a random employee selection representative of the different personnel classifications and organizational units. To achieve a random selection, every third employee was selected to participate in the survey. A representative sample from the different organizational levels and job classifications enhances accuracy. The number surveyed from each compensation plan—executive management, operational management, supervisory/confidential, union contacts—should reflect the composition of the total workforce. If a particular employee group comprises 10 percent of the total employees, then the employees selected from this group should equal approximately 10 percent of the total surveyed. In order to achieve substantial participation, the following is recommended:

1. Send participating employees a letter of explanation from the city manager requesting cooperation and emphasizing the purpose of the project—to develop an educational program on ethical decision making.

2. Make participation voluntary, but emphasize the importance of the issue and the need to assess ethical awareness at all levels of the organization.

3. Assure the employees that they were selected randomly and not for any assumed predisposition to unethical behavior.

4. Inform survey participants that they will remain anonymous throughout the process.

5. Facilitate the employees' participation by having several survey sites available at convenient times during normal work hours.

6. Share the survey results with employees when they are final, presenting them as part of the basis for an ethics training program.

The actual questions asked must be selected carefully to increase the validity of the process. (Refer to Figure 1 for sample questions.) The intent of the questions is to determine employees' perceptions of the ethical standards of both the organization and the individuals in it. The survey should request response to such statements as: It is not unusual for members of my department to accept small gifts for performing their duties; I trust my supervisor; and My supervisor sets a good example of ethical behavior. It is also useful to have an open-ended question that asks if there are any practices or behaviors in local government that create ethical problems for the employee. This may indicate an area which should receive particular attention in a training program.

The initial survey is essentially a "pretest" to establish a level of ethical awareness and understanding to compare with a

Figure 1. The ethical climate survey: Sample questions.

The 10 questions listed below are an example of what can be included in an ethical climate survey. These questions have been excerpted from a 61-question survey conducted by City Manager Steve Bonczek of Largo, Florida. A sampling of Largo employees were asked to respond to the questions using the categories of strongly agree, agree, disagree, or strongly disagree. Their responses were used to design a training program on ethical decision making.

*   Members of my department have misused their position to influence the hiring of their relatives and friends in city government.
*   Quality is given a high priority in my department.
*   There is nothing wrong with accepting gifts from persons who do business with the city so long as those gifts do not influence how I do my job.
*   We don't rely too heavily on individual judgment; almost everything is checked.
*   My superiors set a good example of ethical behavior.
*   I have a large say in decisions that affect my job.
*   Members of my department sometimes leak information that benefits persons who do business with the city.
*   Public employees like myself should be held to a standard of conduct that is higher than the standard of conduct expected of elected officials.
*   During the past 12 months I have observed on-the-job unethical behavior by members of my department.
*   Are there any practices or behaviors in city government that are ethical concerns for you? If yes, briefly describe those concerns.

"posttest" done after completion of ethics training and other initiatives. If the training efforts are successful, there should be a measurable difference in employees' sensitivities to the ethical implications of the way they fulfill their responsibilities. An analysis of the survey results also will reveal any differences between the perceptions of executive management and those of lower-level workers.

Ethics training that works

Many public organizations have recognized the need to do more than establish standards of ethics by giving employees an understanding of why ethical behavior is necessary. There is increased effort by local governments to take the initiative to instill ethical values in employees and to provide them with some form of ethics training. But there are misconceptions about what ethics training should do. Consequently, organizations often find that such training fails to meet their expectations.

Ethics training for all levels of the workforce is necessary to ensure that everyone has the same principles, understandings, and resources to assist in responding to ethical dilemmas. The design of training is critical in addressing the needs of different levels of employees and the specific responsibilities of their positions.

Establishing an ethical basis

Successful ethics training will equip employees with the knowledge and understanding to:

- Recognize the ethical implications of issues as they arise
- Examine ethical dilemmas objectively and apply reasoned judgment to their resolution
- Correct unethical practices that previously may have been unrecognized or ignored
- Handle diplomatically ethical dilemmas that could affect personal relationships
- Communicate the need for applying ethical principles at all levels of the organization.

The initial effort to increase ethical awareness should occur at the orientation session for new employees. A discussion of the mission, administrative vision, and values will facilitate an understanding of ethics guidelines in employee behavior and decision making. When the administrative leadership successfully identifies the goals and values of the organization and adheres closely to those goals through effective communication and control, it is easier for employees to recognize ethical difficulties and to bring problems into the open.

Basic information on the ethical practice of government is critical in helping new employees begin public service with the understanding and confidence that will support their decisions in the public interest. The following are areas to be addressed in new employee orientation and training:

1. A clear and concise statement by the chief administrator on expectations concerning the ethical behavior of all employees
2. The statutes, ordinances, formal code of ethics, regulations, rules, and procedures within which they must operate and the penalties for not observing them
3. The organization's management philosophy—mission and values—and rules, how the rules are enforced, what safeguards exist against groundless accusations or unfairness, how disciplinary codes are enforced, and what are the appeals procedures
4. What constitutes ethical practice in government and what are the dilemmas most commonly faced by employees of the city, conflict of interest, outside employment, gifts and favors, information that may or may not be disclosed, political activity, whistle-blowing, and so forth, and the resources available to discuss and receive advice about potential ethical dilemmas or clarification about the above areas.

A commitment to empower employees to take action at their level to further organizational goals and values certainly includes the ethical dimension of their work environment.

What should ethics training do?

If ethics training and initiatives should not focus primarily on promoting ethical behavior, what is their purpose? Certainly employees' ethical behavior is a desirable goal. The aim, however, of highly effective ethics training and related actions is to provide employees with the tools they need to identify ethics issues and to work out how to resolve them.

Employees are recognizing the need for assistance in identifying potential ethical problems that can be hidden in situations faced daily. Having the tools for identifying and shaping ethical issues may mean simply knowing the right questions to ask. A useful tool is a set of structured questions such as, "What, if any, are the aspects of this situation that might have ethical consequences for me personally, for my supervisor, for the members of my work group or department, for my organization, and for society as a whole?"

The ethics training should provide a process for resolving ethical issues, one that can be demonstrated using case studies on dilemmas. The following steps can be taken in dealing with ethical problems:

1. Define the problem, considering the organization's expressed values and guidelines. What are the facts involved? Are your values in conflict with the policies of the government? With other individuals with whom you must work? With those of the groups or individuals who are most affected by the decision?
2. Determine whether it is an ethical problem or a straightforward administrative decision.
3. Define the desired outcome for the entire situation where ethical issues have been identified. Who will be affected by the decision? Who else needs to be involved in determining a course of action?
4. Identify those elements of the problem that are ethical concerns.
5. Identify difficult obstacles to resolving the ethical issues and determine how to overcome them.
6. Develop alternative solutions to the problem and determine their acceptability from legal, moral, and sound business practice perspectives. Does the solution support the organization's mission and values and the image it wishes to have with elected officials, employees, and citizens?
7. Select the best solution that can be implemented at reasonable cost, both short- and long-term, with a minimum of disruption and with a high probability of success.
8. Resolve the ethical issue.

There are excellent diagnostic tools available in discussing ethical issues and raising awareness of staff through ICMA and the American Society for Public Administration (ASPA) publications that provide analysis of ethical dilemmas and explore various aspects of ethics: *Applying Professional Standards and Ethics in the Eighties; Combatting Corruption / Encouraging Ethics* (ASPA); and *Ethical Insight / Ethical Action: The Ethics Factor Training Program* (ICMA).

How ethics training can succeed

Successful ethics training requires the support of executive management. Ethics programs work best from the top down. First, high-level managers are trained to identify and resolve ethical issues. They then are able to reinforce the training their employees receive.

The most effective ethics initiatives are comprehensive and pervasive. Periodic reinforcement is important, using such methods as follow-up training and statements from executive management stressing the importance of paying attention to ethical issues.

An "ethics audit" is another means of letting employees know the positive effects of their efforts and emphasizing the desirability of such efforts. Managers are encouraged to review with their employees all decisions on ethical issues, asking, "What did we do right? What did we not do that we should have done? What should we do in future, similar situations?"

Management staff has the responsibility to develop more ethical environments. It is essential that managers be models of the kinds of behavior they expect from their employees. Nothing is more powerful for employees than seeing their managers behave according to their expressed values and standards; nothing is more devastating to the development of an ethical environment than a manager who violates the organization's ethical standards.

The executive staff also can legitimize the decisions about ethical issues in their own departments or divisions. An executive may need to take the initiative in raising ethical issues whenever decisions have to be made. Executives can encourage others to raise these issues and ensure that employees' questions always are given fair hearings.

It is advantageous to use weekly staff meetings to review all discussions and decisions for ethical implications. When a potential problem is identified, a staff member can be assigned to clarify the issue and develop a strategy for resolving it at the next meeting. The staff meeting is also a useful forum for using the diagnostic tools from ICMA and ASPA for discussion and evaluation of ethical issues.

The management staff who are effective in creating ethically aware work environments are clear about the priority given to ethical concerns. They ensure that the goals set for their departments are not in conflict with the ethical values of the organization. Managers also keep employees continuously aware that ethical considerations are an integral part of their job responsibilities. The performance appraisal can be used to review employee work behavior and results in relation to the organization's expectations regarding ethics. It also is important to address consistently and fairly violations of ethical standards and to acknowledge publicly examples of ethical conduct.

Another important aspect of ethics training is reinforcing the importance of communication and listening to employees. Executive management must have the courage to listen in order to monitor where the organization is to determine where it should be going, and to provide the necessary leadership to move it in the right direction ethically. The grapevine provides an excellent source of information that enhances and complements the more formal methods of communication. It is a good source to determine employee perceptions of the ethical implications of management decisions and the level of acceptance of organization values. To ensure accuracy, the manager must give the grapevine attention so that any misinformation can be corrected.

Through specialized training

An aggressive approach to establishing an ethical work environment through specialized training and related initiatives to reinforce the ethical values of the organization will yield positive results. The ethical climate of an organization can affect the performance and productivity of its employees and their willingness to support such important values as efficiency, effectiveness, quality, and teamwork.

It is clear that ethical awareness can be enhanced through the development of ethics guidelines that reflect organizational values and individual accountability. A training program that focuses on preparing employees through case studies, diagnostic reviews, periodic ethics audits, and consistent dialogue at staff meetings and in organization newsletters will increase chances for success. The challenge for executive management is to increase employees' understanding of ethical implications in the workplace and their ability to use a structured process to resolve ethical dilemmas.

An ethical organization, in perception and in fact, is a fundamental requirement of a democratic government. If public managers are to fulfill the leadership responsibility of serving the public interest in a way that inspires confidence and trust, then ethics initiatives and training are essential.

The First Step in the Reinvention Process: Assessment

Montgomery Van Wart

The age-old dictum, "know thyself," applies to organizations as well as people. The penalty for lack of self-understanding is usually failure in crisis and an inability to plan realistically for the future. Because the need and desire to change is becoming commonplace in public sector organizations, causing innumerable organizational planning initiatives and probably as many crises, organizations must be very careful to understand their current values and problems before lunging toward "new" values and solutions. Yet ironically, it is amazing how many organizations do not know themselves and flounder in a sea of conflicting values when hastily initiating organizational changes. Organizations are usually far wiser to proceed thoroughly through the first step in the reinvention process, assessment, rather than discovering later that fundamental disagreement or misunderstanding exists about the problems of and solutions for organizational maladies.

This article briefly focuses on values changes in society and in public sector organizations. It notes that social and organizational values are in a period of unusual change. The bulk of the article then looks at the strengths and weaknesses of seven types of assessment strategies being used by organizations today. This inventory is meant to provide an overview for practitioners confronted with "reinvention" challenges and for scholars studying those organizations.

Reprinted with permission from *Public Administration Review* 55 (September/October 1995): 429–438. Copyright 1995 by the American Society for Public Administration, 1120 G Street, N.W., Suite 700, Washington, D.C., 20005-3885. All rights reserved.

Distinguishing value shifts and value adjustments

Value shifts are substantial changes in social systems that consequently affect subsystems such as public administration (Kanter, Stein, and Jick, 1993). In stable societies, major shifts only occur every few generations. In the United States, it seems to result in a 50-year cycle, epochal changes that have occurred in the 1930s move to activist government, the 1880s progressivism, the 1830s Jacksonian patronage-responsiveness movement, and so on (Lan and Rosenbloom, 1992; Rosenbloom and Ross, 1994).[1] This infrequent level of substantial value changes is particularly important for us now because we are in the midst of a substantial value shift (T. Peters, 1992, 1994; Ingraham and Romzek, 1994).

Value adjustments are the intermittent adaptations made by institutional subsystems such as churches, civic organizations, and public agencies as a result of value shifts. Value adjustments often do not occur in a direct linear relationship with value shifts because of internal traditions, priorities, rigidities, and critical mass issues. Value adjustments occur more like the pressure that builds up for earthquakes; sometimes the pressure produces a number of small earthquakes and at other times, a big earthquake with aftershocks. In the private sector, organizations that cannot make appropriate value adjustments usually go out of business. In the public sector, many agencies are not allowed to die, but they may remain in a state of suspended malaise for decades if they are unable proactively to adjust priorities and values.

There are three responses to the need for organizational value adjustments. The first response is not to make any adjustments at all. In many instances, this is the correct response. In a stable era, value adjustments may be so few and infrequent that for all important purposes they are unnecessary and inappropriate because things are functioning well. Because we are currently *not* experiencing a stable era in public administration, this is rarely an appropriate response for organizations today.[2]

The second type of response is to make minor value adjustments. Such value adjustments can be implemented for two reasons. One reason is that the *stated* values in formal organizational aspects such as personnel rules, organizational procedures, and executive directives do not match *actual* values as demonstrated by performance. Another reason to make minor value adjustments is that both the current values and actual performance (whether or not they are aligned with each other) are out of alignment with the environment.

The third type of response is to make major value adjustments or to reinvent organizational values in order to achieve different performance standards. This response is similar to the last except in degree. Many public sector organizations are seeking to reinvent organizational values today (Osborne and Gaebler, 1992; West, Berman, and Milakovich, 1993). Reasons seem to vary. Lack of funding is one strong motivator. Some organizations are trying to improve lagging performance. Others are trying to shatter dysfunctional organizational rigidities. Some organizations have aligned values and performance for today's environment but want a set of values and a performance system that will propel them into the future and make them "world-class" today.

Because so many public sector organizations are moving from a rigid culture of making no values adjustments, they often lack the tools to assess current values or lack a perspective to use them in a dynamic manner. The next section looks at the range of assessment tools for use by organizations that feel they are "awash in a sea of values."

Considerations in assessing stated, actual, and future values

Few strategies call for the assessment, at one time, of the stated values of the organization (what it says it does and values), the actual values (demonstrated or perceived performance), and the future values (the values that the organization chooses to adopt with the purpose of changing current actual values over time). Because organizations are complex entities, it is wise to have numerous types of assessments before trying either to align current values better or adopt new values. The following seven types of assessment strategies are discussed here:

1. Mission, values, and planning and vision statement assessments
2. Ethics assessments
3. Customer and citizen assessments
4. Employee assessments
5. Performance assessments
6. Benchmarking
7. Quality assessments.

Although most organizations have performed some of these assessments within the last four or five years, few organizations have conducted all of them, and until recently, organizations often analyzed assessment information without acting on the information. Selection of a few new or revised assessment strategies is generally preferred over the use of all of the strategies because of the resources required to administer them and analyze the results. Which assessment strategies to use is largely an executive decision based on informal criteria. In practice, public sector executives are turning more and more to customer, employee, and quality assessments for fresh perspectives.

The executive (or executive team) trying to decide what assessment strategies to use should consider at least five rules of thumb before undertaking the process. First, the executive should assess her or his appetite for change. If the executive has little expectation of substantial change, then it is counterproductive to undertake numerous assessment strategies that heighten organizational expectations and then disappoint those expectations and lead to increased cynicism. Second, executives should be careful to match the assessments with their demand for organizational resources. Third, it is critical that prior to the assessment a commitment is made that the data will result in changes, no matter how minor. This ensures an action-oriented philosophy. Fourth, it is important to commit to rapid feedback of the data to those from whom the data were collected or the organization at-large, depending on the circumstances. Coupled with a commitment to make changes, this reduces cynicism that senior managers want information but neither give information nor do anything with it. Fifth, the assessment strategies used should be selected for the fresh outlook that they can bring to bear.

Mission, values, and planning and vision statement assessments Organizations generally have formal statements of what they do, what they value, and how they plan to achieve their goals. Organizational value adjustments usually begin with a review of these statements. In the public sector, this area seems deceptively simple, but as Levin and Sanger note, "public organizations have diverse and multiple goals, defined for them by external elements; private firms have far fewer and can define their goals themselves" (1994; 69).

Mission statements represent the global purpose of an organization or system. Organizational missions generally change slowly, although it is useful to revisit them from time to time for clarity and currency, even in stable times. In the public sector, mission statements can be found in the authorizing legislation. Mission statements are also found in published documents as a part of the budget process, for public education, and for internal training purposes. So profound are many of the current organizational value changes in the public sector that some organizations are seeking or experiencing changes in their authorizing legislation that fundamentally change their core purpose.[3] For example, many operational units in the federal government have functioned as control mechanisms for other agencies. Today, there is much interest in changing some of them to service units that in some cases would compete with private sector organizations. An example supplied by the National Performance Review was the recommendation to allow federal agencies to purchase printing services outside the Government Printing Office (Gore, 1993; 78–80; Gore, 1994).

Values statements express the principles by which members of an organization will operate. Because values had changed little for a long time, such statements were relatively uncommon in the past, but they have become much more common in the last decade. Traditional values are largely implicit and may be best explored by comparing them to values that are being adopted by many contemporary organizations. Generation of a values statement has been widely hailed as a highly useful tool for those organizations changing their values set. Some of the general values adjustments occurring in many organizations today are shown in Table 1.

As indicated in Table 1, the range of values shifting is startling. At the macro level, new emphasis is on competition, market incentives, continuous improvement, weeding out programs, and reengineering processes. Values about structure are now emphasizing decentralization, teamwork, flattened organizational structure, multidimensional jobs, and multiple versions of service provision. Values about work now generally emphasize customer (citizen) focus, innovation, creativity, measurement as a positive stimulus, bottom-line productivity, maximization of worker potential, and prevention of problems rather than reaction to them. Values about employees have stressed their needs, employees as assets, shifting management functions to frontline workers, and increasing employee development generally.

These overall trends are the result of many factors, and thus they do not form a single, coherent, intellectual model (B.G. Peters, 1994). Quite the contrary, at least two separate models are competing with the recent traditional bureaucratic model. While they frequently overlap in their recommendations, they do so for different intellectual rationales. More problematic for the practitioner, sometimes the trends listed in Table 1 are contradictory. One set of driving forces is contained in an organizational model based on *competition*. The competitive model emphasizes public choice (customer focus and multiple versions of service), entrepreneurial leadership (competing with other public and private providers), and flexibility of structure and workforce (process reengineering and a flat organization). This model implicitly encourages midmanagement reductions, significant employee redeployment initiatives, and often employee downsizing when redeployment is insufficient. The *empowerment* model is based on organization democracy (decentralization of leadership),

Table 1. *A comparison of traditional public sector values with those competing for emphasis.*

Traditional	New
Macro-level values	
Monopoly	Competition
Regulation	Market incentives
(organization for control)	(organization around mission)
Reduction v. growth	Continuous improvement
Adding programs	Changing programs
Values about structure	
Centralized	Decentralized
Supervisor as controller	Supervisor as helper
Nondemocratic	Participative
Individual work	Teamwork
Hierarchical organization	Flat organization
Simple jobs	Multidimensional jobs
Single service	Multiple versions of service
Values about work	
Expert focus	Customer focus
(internally driven)	(externally driven)
Focus on tradition (status quo)	Focus on innovation (change)
Problem analysis	Seeing possibilities
Measurement is feared	Measurement is an opportunity
Protective	Productive
Performance	Ability
Inspection and control	Prevention
Values about employees	
System indifference	Employee needs
Employee as expense	Employee as asset
Manager focus	Employee focus
Appraisal/sanction/ranking	Development/learning/recognition

Partial source: James Flanagan, City of Phoenix.

worker creativity (continuous improvement by workers and employee development), and worker commitment (focusing on employee needs and employees as assets) in order for them to willingly be more flexible and make sacrifices when necessary. This model implicitly encourages reducing management by devolving much decision making to the line, returning many managers to the line, and full employment despite work downturns. Although some trends such as the flattening of the organization and the reductions of midmanagement are common to both, the ultimate driving force in the competitive model is the customer/ citizen, and in the empowerment model, it is the employee.

Planning statements are nearly as common as mission statements. They are efforts to define planned achievements. Planning and vision statements are found as a part of strategic plans, the budget process, and public relations materials. The planning elements have traditionally included goals and objectives in highly rational blueprints. Because of this, strategic plans have received much criticism as being sterile planning rites that led to large tomes that sat on shelves. This may have been partially due to the tedious and mechanical quality that they often assumed. They may also have been susceptible to exaggerated assertions based on excessively optimistic assumptions. Vision statements are also future oriented but tend to be more global, less detail oriented, more inspiring, and realistic about the challenges that inevitably face achievement. Contemporary planning has tended to deemphasize and reduce inflexible, long-term strategic planning models and integrate popularly held vision elements. For example, planning models are increasingly allowing for learning and change as a natural part of the project cycle (Hamel and Prahalad, 1994; T. Peters, 1992, 1994).

Ethics assessments   Ethics assessments, also sometimes called ethics audits (Lewis, 1991), may either determine what the stated legal norms are and/or probe the gap between the stated legal values and the actual performance of the organization. The former is best done by an ethics audit structural assessment and the latter by an ethics audit perceptual assessment.

An ethics audit structural assessment is usually conducted by one or a few people. The researchers determine, through document review, interviews, and expert analysis, what general ethics controls exist (such as conflict of interest), how operational areas that commonly lead to ethical breaches are controlled (such as travel), and what types of support for ethical norms exist (such as through training).

An ethics audit perceptual assessment focuses on what employees perceive rather than on the controls and stated policies themselves. This is important because some organizations have few ethics policies and are nonetheless perceived to be highly ethical environments, and other organizations have many rules but are considered unethical environments. Perceptual assessments may survey overall ethical issues, select operational issues, and types of support and inspiration. Perceptual assessments should either survey a large sample or the entire agency. Although responses must be anonymous, responses can be color coded by division for better follow-up. For an example of an ethics audit perceptual assessment, see Table 2.

Table 2. Perceptual assessment of ethical conduct.

I. Explicit ethical issues:
1. How well do you think the individuals in your agency (as a whole) do in complying with the letter and the spirit of ethics legislation, ethics policies, and informal standards of conduct expected of the public sector?[a]
    Conflict of interest
    Competitive bidding
    Disclosure of confidential information
    Discrimination (hiring/promotion)
    Employment of relatives
    Gifts, favors, or extra compensation
    Political activity by employees
    Conducting meetings open to public
    Public records access
    Use of public equipment, personnel, or facilities for personal use
    Safeguards of whistle-blowers

2. (a) How good and clear are ethics legislation and ethics policies?[a]
    (b) How well are the informal standards explained through handbooks, training, and administrative explanation?[a]

II. Operational ethics issues:
3. How well do you think the individuals in your agency (as a whole) do in complying with the standards of conduct expected of the public sector in the following categories?[a]
    Financial allocation and expenditure
    Procurement
    Equipment
    Personnel
    Travel

4. Do you have an inspector general, designated ethics ombudsman, ethics hot line, or ethics office? (Yes, No, Don't know)
    If yes, do they seem to make a difference? (No, Some, or Big)

III. Personal ethics issues:
5. Is there an organizational credo which promotes aspirational values? That is, is there a statement or part of a statement that talks about ideal or model behavior for employees? (Yes or No)

    If yes, do you think that it provides a useful ideal for you? (Yes or No)

    Where is it located and in what format is it? (open-ended question)

6. Rate the professional ethics of employees at-large in your organization in each of the five areas below:[a]
    (a)   Service to the public is considered beyond service to oneself.
    (b)   There is respect, support, and understanding of the Constitution and laws of the land.
    (c)   The highest standards of personal integrity are demonstrated at all times.
    (d)   Strengthening organizational capacity to operate efficiently and effectively is a goal.
    (e)   There is an effort to strengthen individual capacities and to encourage professional development.

[a]Respondents were asked to reply on a five-point scale, 1 being "very poorly" and 5 being "very well."

Quality experts warn that quality initiatives cannot be successful if the system is "out of control." Likewise, ethical norms are part of the bedrock of the organization, and egregious or common breaches of ethical standards must usually be addressed prior to other organizational values adjustments occurring. For example, if petty theft, disclosure of insider information, or vehicle use for private purposes is common, these conditions create an environment of cynicism, distrust, and anger. However, if ethical controls are already tight and commonly internalized, executives may decide to place assessment resources elsewhere.

Customer and citizen assessments   An explosion of interest in values related to customer and citizen preferences has led to an immense expansion in assessment use in this area in the public sector. Previously, the tendency was to rely on experts to analyze and recommend from their experience. More recently, the tendency has been to seek out direct input from customers and citizens and to use this direct data in problem selection and decision-making processes. Customer assessments are considered by many the single most powerful tool in assisting government organizations to make value adjustments today. Five types of customer/citizen assessments are discussed: customer identification, citizen surveys, customer focus groups, customer complaint resolution, and community visioning.

Customer identification (similar to what was formerly called stakeholder analysis) is a popular tool in quality improvement initiatives. The assumption is that many organizations and units have become so process oriented and legalistic, and so captured by self-interests and territoriality, that they have forgotten just who their customers (stakeholders) are. Customer analyses can be powerful tools for discussion and for focusing more sophisticated assessment strategies which succeed them.

Citizen surveys are generally more expensive but reliable ways to tap into contemporary citizen values. They are more common at the local government level: 74 percent of all local governments implementing quality improvement initiatives recently reported some sort of customer satisfaction survey (West, Berman, and Milakovich, 1993). These surveys can serve two functions. First, they rate perceptions of past services. Second, they rank perceptions of future expenditures. For example, the city of Phoenix has a professional survey research company review citizen attitudes toward city services every two years. Interviewees are first asked to rate the *past* performance of 27 services on a 1 (low) to 10 (high) scale. Services include police, fire, traffic enforcement, garbage collection, street repair, handicap access, bus service, park maintenance, housing for the elderly, homeless care, and the like. Next, interviewees are asked to rank the services as deserving more, the same, or less funding in the *future* (Table 3 as an example).

Customer focus groups are a less expensive and ambitious assessment strategy but are nonetheless time-consuming to conduct properly. Focus groups can be selected at random but are more often selected based on prior experience. They can range in size from 3 to 50 but 5 to 15 is generally recommended for manageability. If focus groups precede other customer assessments, their aim is generally broad and exploratory. If they follow other customer assessments such as citizen surveys, they often concentrate on one or two issues that have been targeted as problems, but they look at those issues in great depth.

Customer complaint resolution in the public sector has generally been handled by relatively legalistic dispute systems (administrative law) in the past. Several new trends are emerging. One is a trend to track complaints by type over time. This provides valuable information about systemic problems that are more efficiently handled by process changes or improvements rather than as individual problems to resolve. Another trend is to be more proactive in getting point of service evaluations (which assist in complaint tracking). Sometimes these evaluations are cards that are placed on service counters. In other cases, evaluation cards are sent periodically to every nth customer. Many police departments have begun sending every 20th ticketed speeding "customer" an evaluation form asking about the officer's courtesy, informativeness, and accuracy.

Community visioning is a process that encourages citizen input about ideal futures of tLeir locality. By envisioning an ideal future and unifying behind it, community members contribute ideas, direction, and enthusiasm to the political process that normally tends to be rather divisive in today's environment. Such a process simultaneously reflects and molds community values as citizens envisage ideals to achieve, rather than solely focusing on problems to solve and conventional implementation issues (Peirce, Johnson, and Hall, 1993; Chrislip and Larson, 1994). The challenge is to relate these community "feelings" to tangible organizational value adjustments.

Employee assessments   A long-time emphasis (and many would now assert imbalance) placed on the issues and values of management has recently veered toward a new focus on employee input and values as organizations become flatter and many management issues are decentralized to self-managing employee teams. Because of this trend, assessments of employee opinions and values have become much more common and more

Table 3. Citizen assessment of services (by telephone) with ratings of current and future preferences.

Questions 9–62: As you know, the City of Phoenix provides various services to the community ranging from fire protection to street maintenance. On a scale of one to ten, where one means you think the city is doing a poor job and where ten means you think the city is doing an excellent job, how would you rate each of the following?

Questions 63–89: Now let's go through the list again quickly, but this time, for each service, tell if it is one on which the city should be spending more money, less money, or about what it spends today.

Rating	Service	More	Same	Less	OK
6.8	Police protection in your area 54%		43%	2%	1%
8.1	Fire protection in your area 27		71	1	2
6.5	Endorsement of traffic laws 40		53	6	1
4.6	Juvenile crime prevention and youth programs . 82		14	1	4
7.7	Garbage collection 15		81	2	2
5.6	Frequency of uncontainerized trash collection .. 47		49	1	3
5.3	Controlling and cleaning up illegal dumping . 61		34	1	4
5.6	Protecting our water supply from pollution ... 73		24	1	3
6.1	Helping citizens understand how to conserve water 49		47	3	1
5.6	Street repair and maintenance 44		50	6	1
5.8	New street construction 37		52	9	2
6.2	Providing bus services for the handicapped and elderly 54		37	1	7
6.3	Providing regular scheduled bus service in your area 40		55	1	4
6.0	Preventing street flooding during rains in your area 41		54	4	2
6.8	Providing adequate parks in your area 30		65	4	1
6.0	Providing adequate recreation programs in your area 44		49	3	4
5.1	Providing housing for the elderly 66		25	1	8
4.2	Providing housing for the poor 71		21	3	5
4.0	Caring for the homeless 74		19	3	4
7.3	Library services in your area 20		74	4	2
5.6	Attracting new employers to the community ... 57		34	5	4
5.2	Helping existing employers to grow 60		33	3	4
5.6	Requiring homeowners to maintain their properties to minimum standards 49		44	5	2
8.0	Ambulance and paramedic service 25		72	1	2
5.9	Preserving the character of residential neighborhoods 44		49	4	2
5.0	Providing facilities for recycling 64		31	3	2
6.1	Providing art and cultural events 31		57	10	3

Question 90: Would you say that you are very satisfied, somewhat satisfied, somewhat dissatisfied, or very dissatisfied with the overall performance of the city in providing services to Phoenix residents?

Very satisfied	Somewhat satisfied	Somewhat dissatisfied	Very dissatisfied	Not sure/OK
15%	64%	16%	5%	0%

important in helping organizations make value adjustments. Three types of assessments are discussed here: employee opinion surveys, employee focus groups, and employee value sorts.

Employee opinion surveys can be administered internally or by an external consultant, whose experience and neutrality may improve confidence in the results. Employee opinion surveys tend to focus on the factors and levels of job satisfaction and evaluations of organizational effectiveness in various areas. Although a strict sense of confidentiality must be maintained, results can be identified by division so that feedback can be more specific and follow-up action can be more targeted. As with other survey data, it is useful to see results compared on a longitudinal basis. (Figure 1 is an example from a county government.)

Employee focus groups are relatively easy to assemble. They usually are used either to identify the detailed aspects of an already-articulated problem (such as a general problem identified in an employee opinion survey), brainstorm alternate strategies, or critique a revised process. Employee focus groups bring not only employee values to bear but employee creativity as well.

One important use of employee value sorts is to gather employee perceptions of organizational values. Such a profile can be useful when new values are being considered for the organization. Because high-performing organizations tend to have similar organization value clusters, a wide range of perceptions of this type of values sort should lead to sustained employee discussions about organizational value adjustments in order to enhance loose consensus (Katzenbach and Smith, 1993; Drucker, 1993). Employee value sorts can also be used to identify specific employee values about their preferred work environment.[4] Because employees rank aspects of work differently, a profile of those values can assist management in meeting those needs better as well as enhancing employee understanding of alternate priorities. For example, those in a research unit may place a high value on a creative work environment, freedom, and support. However, the administrative and clerical elements of that same unit may place a low value on those elements and instead select structure, security, and financial rewards as the most important values. Preferred work environment value sorts should not be used to try to change personal preferences, but can be used to enhance mutual respect of alternate priorities.

Performance assessments   Every organization and unit has its own performance standards. In the public sector, performance standards traditionally have suffered from at least six problems: weak comparability with other similar units, lack of unit costs, lack of rewards for efficiency, inability to measure true effective-

Figure 1. Assessment results from an employee survey.

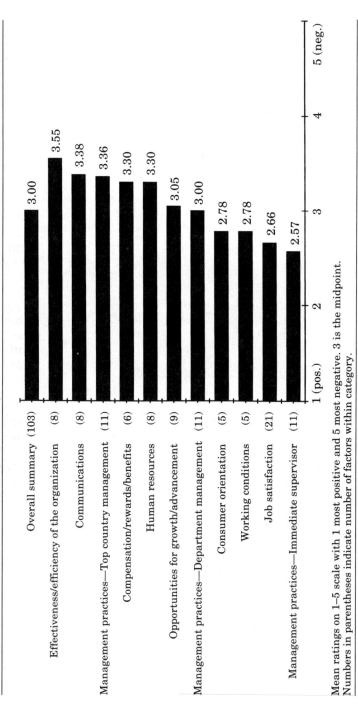

Overall summary (103)	3.00
Effectiveness/efficiency of the organization (8)	3.55
Communications (8)	3.38
Management practices—Top country management (11)	3.36
Compensation/rewards/benefits (6)	3.30
Human resources (8)	3.30
Opportunities for growth/advancement (9)	3.05
Management practices—Department management (11)	3.00
Consumer orientation (5)	2.78
Working conditions (5)	2.78
Job satisfaction (21)	2.66
Management practices—Immediate supervisor (11)	2.57

Mean ratings on 1–5 scale with 1 most positive and 5 most negative. 3 is the midpoint.
Numbers in parentheses indicate number of factors within category.

ness, inability to measure team and system performance, and a deficiency in identifying and correcting systemic errors. Because of the tremendous importance of performance standards in a competitive environment, much work has been done in this area in the last decade (Hatry et al., 1990; Harris, 1995; and others), but the results are still rudimentary. Without improvement in performance assessment that remedies traditional weaknesses, organizations will have difficulty in tying their value adjustments to concrete goals. This section looks at three major areas of performance assessments: traditional, evaluation, and new.

Traditional performance standards include those that focus on individuals, organizational units, and the overall organization. Individuals have workload requirements such as the amount of work that must be produced, the size of the budget to be managed, the number of employees to supervise, and so forth. They also have performance criteria, which have recently been enhanced with the new emphasis on quality such as error rates, timeliness, customer relations, service and product appearance, expertise, ease of use and access, and problem-solving ability. Organizational units have similar performance standards aggregated at the next higher level but must also consider whether customer needs are being met overall, whether the services provided are in statutory compliance, and what constitutes unit and individual success. Some other traditional performance measures include productivity per employee, safety (accidents), absenteeism, and turnover. At the highest level, the organization monitors its operating and capital costs against authorized expenditure estimates. At this level, there is attention to shifting legislative and executive priorities, emergencies with financial implications, and legal accounting issues such as funds separation. Weak performance at any of these levels with any of these standards can be highly problematic. A police officer who uses an incorrect arrest protocol may necessitate the release of a high-visibility criminal, leading to public anger. A child protective services unit with weak management practices and poor public relations may find itself frequently attacked in the newspaper because strict confidentiality requirements prevent immediate explanation when abused or neglected children die. A county government with multiple elected officials, numerous funding sources, and a weak accounting system may suffer a severe loss of public confidence if budget overruns occur. Because of technological advances in tracking systems, traditional performance assessments are being improved, as well as added to, in many organizations today.[5]

Evaluation and audit performance measures are internal mechanisms that monitor performance. Internal comptrollers and auditors monitor expenditure requests and fund balances.

Management monitors worker compliance with statutes and policies. Cash disbursements are generally dually controlled; special units monitor inventory, vehicles, and fixed assets; and auditors pay special attention to the completeness and accuracy of data. In the past, most of the attention was devoted to stopping poor or illegal practices after they had occurred, and thus a legalistic inspection approach was adopted. Value adjustment has occurred in many organizations with more interest in preventive and educational approaches in regulatory areas as well as a search for market-based incentives to replace legal mandates in service provision areas. For example, because of the broader and deeper assessment strategies that many public sector organizations have recently adopted, they are able to pinpoint weak systems and proactively bring numerous organizational resources together to fix them rather than critiquing isolated problems or specific individuals in periodic, *a posteriori* audit reviews. In another example, there is a value adjustment toward market-based incentives to deregulate services such as stores, vehicle maintenance, printing, garbage collection, training, facility maintenance, and so forth, and to require those units to compete with private sector companies. Finally, it should be noted that much recent attention has been given to improving efficiency measurement through the expansion of cost accounting and unit cost practices, and effectiveness measurement by focusing as much on outcomes as outputs.

While some of the newer trends in performance measurement have been mentioned, other trends are also worth noting because they are likely to complement major value adjustments. Although team performance measures are still nearly nonexistent, there is a tremendous interest in bringing them into individual performance evaluations. Additional progress will need to be made as self-managed teams become more commonplace in the public sector. Continuous learning and continuous improvement are almost entirely unmeasured in most public sector organizations, but this type of productivity must be captured quantitatively much like the Japanese companies that routinely record thousands of improvements by thousands of workers. Measures of reengineering (Hammer and Champy, 1993) or massive systems redesign (Fiorelli and Feller, 1994) tend to be conjectural or nonexistent. Organizations also need to ensure that routine failure associated with experimentation is not penalized in traditional microanalytic performance assessments as individuals and units systematically search for better ways of doing things (Light, 1994). Supplier and "partner" performance is currently moving from an adversarial approach to a more proactive, mutual problem-solving approach. Measuring this value adjustment will be challenging. Finally, there is a new interest in system integration. This is leading toward a rethinking of rigid and impersonal personnel functions, a reworking of cumbersome and antiquated data management systems, an inclusion of more stakeholders in the administrative decision-making process, and a more aggressive attitude toward process and procedure streamlining and improvement.

Because performance assessment is where "the rubber meets the road," it is critical that the reshaping of organizational values take this complex area into consideration. The adoption of new values invariably means the deemphasis of other values that are deemed excessive in the current environment. For example, the extreme statutory and legalistic approach to performance measurement common in the past is being softened so that systems have greater flexibility to experiment, inspire rather than intimidate, and capture the synergy of collective thinking.

Benchmarking Benchmarking is defined by Bogan and English (1994) as seeking out superior performance through the systematic search for and use of best practices, including innovative ideas, effective operating procedures, and successful strategies. Today, one tends to think of benchmarking primarily in its most sophisticated form, the analysis and use of practices adapted from world-class leaders. However, Bogan and English point out a seven-level hierarchy of benchmarking, including learning from past internal successes, borrowing good ideas without regard to their origin in the organization, developing internal best practices, matching average or standard practices, establishing leadership through industry best practices, targeting national best practices without regard for industry, and matching or exceeding world-class practices. Benchmarking is the science of using internal and external comparison assessments to stimulate higher performance. Although the focus of benchmarking is on changing practices, process, and procedures, these frequently require concomitant value adjustments to implement.

Benchmarking types vary. Process benchmarking focuses on specific work processes and operating systems such as citizen complaints, lengthy procurement processes, cumbersome recruitment procedures, and excessive interview eligibility protocols. Process benchmarking identifies the best operating practices from many organizations that perform similar work functions. This form of benchmarking seeks rapid improvements. Performance benchmarking examines comparable positions by focusing on technical quality, cost, service or regulatory features, and other parameters. Strategic benchmarking scrutinizes the successful strategies that have enabled high-performing organizations to flourish. Yet all types of benchmarking require several elements to work: a well-designed performance measurement and benchmarking process, senior management support, training for the project team, useful information systems, cultural practices that encourage learning from others, and resources such as time and financial support.

Benchmarking has been hampered in the public sector by lack of data, especially unit costs for citizen and regulatory services, lack of comparable services because of varying local conditions (such as the different weather conditions affecting road maintenance), and fear of public misuse of comparison data. Ironically, the only benchmarking historically done in the public sector has tended to be by auditing organizations who have used the benchmark data to judge and critique agencies. Such an after-the-fact and critical usage gives little assistance to the fostering of an internal desire to improve and learn. However, it is likely that benchmarking will be better received as a proactive organizational assessment strategy in the future because of other value adjustments toward measurement, continuous improvement, and reengineering.

Quality assessments   There are numerous types of quality assessments today. They share a number of features: they are all relatively comprehensive and stress customer satisfaction, employee involvement and development, continuous learning and improvement, prevention over inspection, and supplier partnerships far more than was done in past organizations. Taken seriously, quality assessments inevitably cause numerous substantial values adjustments because the principles promoted are at variance with the operational values of most organizations today. Because of its renown, the Malcolm Baldrige National Quality Award is discussed first. Other quality award systems are also briefly mentioned.

The Malcolm Baldrige Awards are given on the basis of an assessment of seven formal categories: senior executive leadership, information and analysis, strategic quality planning, human resource development and management, management of process quality, quality and operational results, and customer focus and satisfaction (Malcolm Baldrige National Quality Awards, 1994). The different categories receive different weights, with customer focus and satisfaction being substantially more emphasized than the other categories. For example, one of the six customer focus and satisfaction subcategories, customer satisfaction results, receives nearly as much or more weight than leadership, information and analysis, or strategic quality planning. To score well on the Malcolm Baldrige criteria, it is assumed that the organization has conducted numerous assessments and, in fact, has institutionalized assessment as a part of its organizational life, especially in the areas of customer satisfaction, customer satisfaction comparison (benchmarking with other corporate leaders), operational results (especially gains in productivity), comparison of operational results, quality results (especially gains in timeliness, product value, ease of use, etc.), employee satisfaction, and employee involvement. The awards do not insist on a particular assessment strategy, but they do suggest that routine assessment is the foundation of management by fact. Therefore, the types of assessment discussed in earlier sections of this chapter are consistent with Malcolm Baldrige Award criteria and implicitly expected of world-class organizations. Some of the awards' outstanding strengths are their comprehensiveness and their rigor.

The Malcolm Baldrige Awards, for all of their virtues, do have a number of weaknesses that are useful for organizations to be aware of before embarking on systematic use of them. First, for the organization new to quality management, the comprehensiveness of the award criteria can easily lead to confusion and conceptual overload. If there are many areas to work on, which ones should an organization start with? Some organizations seeking highly ambitious change agendas have failed to make any lasting changes at all. Second, the rigor of the award system and the technical nature of the language of the award criteria can be daunting to those new to quality improvement initiatives. Third, the awards currently are intended for and limited to the private sector. Also, some of the assumptions occasionally show a strong private sector orientation, such as market-based competition and the drive for market share and profits. These assumptions apply weakly or not at all to most of the public sector, which tends to be oriented toward publicly derived mandates, due process, and social equity. For example, despite its comprehensiveness for the private sector, the Malcolm Baldrige Awards have no equivalent for the ethics assessments discussed earlier in this article that take into account the legal compliance and norms critical in the operational mechanisms of a constitutional democracy.

The Malcolm Baldrige Awards are not the only relatively comprehensive quality assessments. Although they dominate, others are of note. Since 1988, the federal government has conducted the President's Award for Quality and the Quality Improvement Prototype (QIP) Awards. These award programs currently use the same criteria, with the highest scoring applicant receiving the Presidential Award and the runners-up receiving the QIP Award. The award criteria have always been modeled on the Malcolm Baldrige Awards but with language more accessible to the novice quality initiates and more consistent with the public sector. There are plans to integrate these federal awards with the Malcolm Baldrige system in the next few years (Office of Personnel Management, 1994). Many states have initiated quality award programs for state government agencies. Numerous states have adopted the Senate Productivity Award that allows local government applications. Of course, the prototype for quality awards was invented in Japan with the Deming Award. The Europeans use a system called ISO 9000, which is a quality assurance system rather than a quality awards system. "ISO is the International Organization for Standardization, and its objective is to promote the development of standards, testing, and certification" (Hutchins, 1993; 1). As Juran has noted, "Certification to ISO 9000 has become a de facto license to market in Europe" (1994; 14).[6] Although ISO does not yet apply to governmental entities, the worldwide trend to emphasize rigorous standards and high quality will clearly have an effect on value adjustments in the public sector as well.

Conclusion

The environment in which organizations exist occasionally undergoes major changes or shifts which result in significant adjustments in values and practices in those organizations. We are currently responding to a major value shift in the public sector in the United States. In order to be able rationally and intelligently to adopt (or reject) "new" values, organizations must have a clear sense of what their current values are. This is much more difficult than it would seem because we take values for granted much the way we do the air we breathe, which is invisible, tasteless, and everywhere, but nonetheless critical to existence. Therefore, almost all change strategies begin with an assessment phase. If the assessment phase is too hurried or badly done, it is likely that the changes will be unsuccessful or superficial.

This article focused on the different types of assessments that are possible: mission, values and planning and vision statement assessments, ethics assessments, customer and citizen assessments, employee assessments, performance assessments, benchmarking, and quality assessments. Although quality assessments are worthy goals because of their comprehensiveness and the integrated-systems critique that they require, they demand extensive resources, commitment, and expertise. Because most public sector organizations have traditionally been weak in organizational assessment, most would do well to target just a few areas that have a *prima facie* need in order to strengthen some of their inferior areas and build their assessment capabilities.

It is important to remember that a deep understanding of current values and performance practices does not fully articulate which values to embrace *in the future* although a lack of such understanding does preclude sound adoption of new values and practices. Inevitably strong assessment strategies are the primary drivers of strong change processes. The rigorous investigation of values and practices leads to a genuine understanding about the need for new values. Furthermore, some of the assessment strategies discussed enhance the forward aspects of assessment, such as vision statements and visioning, customer surveys identifying future desires, employee surveys identifying strategic opportunities, benchmarking, and quality assessments. The task of distinguishing traditional and new value emphases in order to make rational decisions about what value adjustments to make can only be made after balanced assessment has been done.

Notes

1. Of course, the dates represent only an approximate beginning of amorphous trends that took decades to form and mature.
2. In a survey of participants in an executive program in which they were asked about the degree of change occurring in their organizations, 90 percent responded that their organizations were experiencing substantial or massive amounts of change.
3. Of course, missions can change without changes in the authorizing legislation as well.
4. For a review of public employee values, see deLeon (1994; 135–142).
5. There are two caveats. First, all measurement is expensive, and substantial value should be provided that would lead to changes if the data indicated problems. Second, that which gets measured gets attention. Therefore, it is important to measure things that you want to get attention.
6. However, Juran is rather critical of the omissions in the European system because they fail to address adequately "personal leadership by the upper managers, training the hierarchy in managing for quality, quality goals in the business plan, a revolutionary rate of quality improvement, and participation and empowerment of the workforce" (Juran, 1994).

References

Bogan, Christopher E., and Michael J. English, 1994. *Benchmarking for Best Practices.* New York: McGraw-Hill.

Chrislip, David D., and Carl E. Larson, 1994. *Collaborative Leadership.* San Francisco: Jossey-Bass.

deLeon, Linda, 1994. "The Professional Values of Public Managers, Policy Analysis and Politicians." *Public Personnel Management,* vol. 23, no. 1, 135–142.

Drucker, Peter F., 1993. *Managing for the Future: The 1990s and Beyond.* New York: Plume.

Fiorelli, Joseph, and Richard Feller, 1994. "Re-engineering TQM and Work Redesign: An Integrative Approach to Continuous Organizational Excellence." *Public Administration Quarterly,* vol. 18, no. 1, 54–63.

Gore, Al, 1993. *Creating a Government That Works Better and Costs Less: The Report of the National Performance Review.* New York: Plume.

_____, 1994. *Creating a Government That Works Better and Costs Less: The Status Report.* Washington,

DC: U.S. Government Printing Office.

Hamel, Gary, and C. K. Prahalad, 1994. *Competing for the Future.* Boston: Harvard Business School Press.

Hammer, Michael, and James Champy, 1993. *Reengineering the Corporation: A Manifesto for Business Revolution.* New York: Harper Collins.

Harris, Jean, 1995. "Service Efforts and Accomplishments: A Primer of Current Practice and an Agenda for Future Research." *International Journal of Public Administration,* vol. 18, nos. 2 and 3, 253–276. See these volumes for a symposium of articles on service measures.

Hatry, Harry P., et al., 1990. *Service Efforts and Accomplishments Reporting: Its Time Has Come.* Norwalk, CT: Governmental Accounting Standards Board.

Hutchins, Greg, 1993. *ISO 9000: A Comprehensive Guide to Registration, Audit Guidelines and Successful Certification.* Essex Junction, VT: Oliver Wight Publications.

Ingraham, Patricia W., and Barbara Romzek, eds., 1994. *New Paradigms for Government: Issues for the Changing Public Service.* San Francisco: Jossey-Bass.

Juran, Joseph, 1994. "The Upcoming Century of Quality." Address for the 1994 ASQC Annual Quality Congress. Las Vegas, May 24.

Kanter, Rosabeth Moss, Barry A. Stein, and Todd D. Jick, 1993. *The Challenge of Organizational Change.* New York: The Free Press.

Katzenbach, Jon R., and Douglas K. Smith, 1993. *The Wisdom of Teams: Creating the High-Performance Organization.* Boston: Harvard Business School Press.

Lan, Zhigong, and David H. Rosenbloom, 1992. "Public Administration in Transition?" *Public Administration Review,* vol. 52, no. 6, 535–537.

Light, Paul C., 1994. "Creating Government That Encourages Innovation."

In Patricia W. Ingraham and Barbara S. Romzek, eds., *New Paradigms for Government: Issues for the Changing Public Service.* San Francisco: Jossey-Bass, pp. 63–89.

Levin, Martin A., and Mary Bryna Sanger, 1994. *Making Government Work: How Entrepreneurial Executives Turn Bright Ideas into Real Results.* San Francisco: Jossey-Bass.

Lewis, Carol W., 1991. *The Ethics Challenge in Public Service: A Problem-Solving Guide.* San Francisco: Jossey-Bass.

Malcolm Baldrige National Quality Award, 1994 Award Criteria.

Office of Personnel Management, 1994. "President's Quality Award Program Will Move to Baldrige." *Federal Quality News,* vol. 2, no. 6, 1, 9.

Osborne, David, and Ted Gaebler, 1992. *Reinventing Government.* New York: Addison-Wesley.

Peirce, Neal, Curtis Johnson, and John Hall, 1993. *Citistates.* Washington, DC: Seven Locks Press.

Peters, B. Guy, 1994. "New Visions of Government and Public Service." In Patricia W. Ingraham and Barbara S. Romzek, eds., *New Paradigms for Government: Issues for the Changing Public Service.* San Francisco: Jossey-Bass, pp. 295–321.

Peters, Tom, 1992. *Liberation Management.* New York: Alfred A. Knopf.

———, 1994. *The Pursuit of Wow! Every Person's Guide to Topsy-Turvy Times.* New York: Vintage.

Rosenbloom, David, and Bernard H. Ross, 1994. "Administrative Theory, Political Power, and Government Reform." In Patricia W. Ingraham and Barbara S. Romzek, eds., *New Paradigms for Government: Issues for the Changing Public Service.* San Francisco: Jossey-Bass, pp. 145–167.

West, Jonathan, Evan Berman, and Mike E. Milakovich, 1993. "Total Quality Management in Local Government." *The ICMA Year Book.* Washington, DC: ICMA.

Achieving the Ethical Workplace

━━━━━━━━━━ Stephen Bonczek and Donald Menzel

For local government managers, an important responsibility and challenge is to enhance ethical awareness through the organization by providing systems that support employees in doing the right things. Managers who use shared leadership—the concept of leadership as an activity engaged in by different people at different times—to establish the necessary support systems will improve their chances of creating an ethical workplace. Developing an organizational vision, mission, values, ethics guidelines, ethics committee, and ethics dialogue, as well as initiating a training program on ethical decision making, will result in a work environment that motivates employees to exercise ethical judgment with confidence. With that empowerment will come responsibility and accountability.

This increased emphasis on and attention to ethics can improve communications, resolve disagreements, and set high standards for employee/management relations. As more local governments adopt such management techniques and processes as continuous quality improvement, the concepts of openness, trust, and allowing employees to take risks gain in ethical importance. Doing the right things right the first time incorporates the universal ethical principles of fairness and honesty with the derivative organizational values of efficiency and effectiveness.

The Government Ethics Center of the Josephson Institute of Ethics supports five ethical principles of public service: public trust, objective judgment, accountability, democratic leadership, and respectability (*Principles of Public Service Ethics: Standards*

Reprinted by permission from *Public Management* magazine (March 1994): 13–17.

of Conduct and Guidelines for Government Decision Making; see reference listing at end of article). These principles of public service ethics reflect moral obligations that exist independently of and transcend obligations imposed by law and formal codes of conduct.

In the process of developing organizational values from ethical principles, a clear picture arises of what is critically important to an organization and its members. Such values as customer service, employee empowerment, professionalism, and integrity provide the parameters for ethical decision making.

Dr. Robert Denhardt's 1993 book, *The Pursuit of Significance*, focuses on highly effective public managers and the reasons for their success—namely, a clear focus on mission and a values-driven organization. A strong ethical foundation becomes institutionalized in the organization if employees are given the responsibility to handle the ethical dimension of their jobs and if organizational values are made an integral part of the workplace, creating both an ethical and a productive organizational climate. The development of an ethical environment is essential to facilitating decision making in the public interest.

Talking about the need for and desirability of an ethical workplace is an important first step that local government managers can take toward infusing their organizations with an ethical perspective. It is, however, just that—a first step. As most significant decisions are made by employees on the front line of service delivery, they need to know that their ethical judgments are supported by the manager, higher-level supervisors, and peers. Employees committed to doing the right thing deserve organizational leadership that encourages an ethical climate sustained by effective ethical systems.

Easier said than done? Probably. Indeed, employees and the public often make erroneous assumptions about ethics in the local government workplace that can hinder the most determined efforts of managers to foster an ethical environment. These misperceptions must be recognized, understood, and overcome.

Ethical assumptions in the workplace

The following false assumptions undermine efforts to enhance ethical awareness in public organizations. Managers who recognize and address these assumptions through education, leadership, and employee empowerment will strengthen their organizations' capacity to act ethically. The restoration of deficient (or absent) ethical systems or strategies will result in much higher levels of trust among employees and citizens. The authors would like to share eight false assumptions with readers, along with their personal reflections on them.

1. Ethical values are personal and are not expressed within the organization   False! Just as it is a misconception to believe that public organizations are plagued by ethical problems, it is also a mistake to believe that ethical problems are rare or do not exist at all. This assumption is a dangerous one because many members of government, including chief executives, may earnestly want to believe that problems do not exist. Indeed, succumbing to this misconception may well breed ethical complacency.

Inherent conflicts exist in the workplace between, on one hand, personal and organizational values and, on the other, their expression in actions and in decision making. In less defined areas, sometimes rationalization prevails over ethical reflection, causing incongruent action. We may believe, for example, that honesty is essential and that we would never steal our public employer's resources, but *we use the city car to run personal errands while doing project site visits.* Because we observe working hours scrupulously and often put in overtime, *it seems innocent enough to tell our supervisors we got caught in traffic when we actually overslept.* Or, we may know that our coworker is operating a small business of her/his own on the side, using the office telephone, copier, typewriters, paper, and time. *But we have been friends for years, and she/he is a single parent with a son in college. It is unlikely that she/he will be caught if we do not inform anyone, so we do not.*

Wanting to be ethical and consistently being ethical are two different things. Clearly, conflicting loyalties, fear of failure or of being fired, and systems that force us to compromise ethical principles threaten the establishment and maintenance of an ethical workplace.

An ethical dilemma can create conflicts among competing loyalties to country, state, community, constituency groups, government organization, peers, supervisors, family, and self. The challenge is to develop a process to determine which loyalty or loyalties prevail when resolving ethical issues. In prioritizing loyalties, the Josephson Institute emphasizes the primacy of serving the public interest, the reputation of the government, and the integrity and efficiency of the department, even at the cost of injuring a supervisor, peer, or friend. To avoid inappropriate expectations when situations of ethical concern occur, the placement of institutional loyalty above individual loyalty should be made clear to members of the organization.

2. Ethical people always act ethically regardless of what goes on in the organization   False! Most people want to do the right thing, but they occasionally find themselves in ethically compromising situations. Good people can make bad judgments when organizational ethical support systems are not in place. Hiring ethical people is an important first step in fostering an ethical organization, but it is hardly a last step. Ethics is an individual responsibility and opportunity—one person, one decision at a time. Managers need to develop strategies to inform, inspire, and encourage individuals to act ethically and to hold them accountable if they do not.

Ethics is a force in government organizations that supports such values as accountability and commitment to serving the public interest. Ethics in government is the basis for formulating effective and responsive public policy. A government's ethical foundation must instill confidence in those served; it is not just a matter of feeling good. With every contact between the government and the public, the government should give citizens a reason to believe that officials are making decisions based on the public's interest rather than on personal benefit.

3. Ethics discussions in public organizations contribute little, if anything, to productivity, morale, or problem solving   False! Many managers likely believe that it is nice to talk about ethics in the workplace but that such talk matters little when it comes to getting the job done. Indeed, time devoted to ethics discussions or formal training might be viewed as a major distraction from time that could be devoted to providing public services in a more cost-effective fashion. But the evidence, though limited, suggests that the opposite is true. A 1993 study by this article's coauthor, Dr. Menzel, found significant correlations between the presence of a strong ethical climate in local government and the emphasis placed on such values as efficiency, effectiveness, quality, excellence, and teamwork (*Ethics and Public Administration,* pp. 191–204; see reference listing).

As managers, it is important to develop strategies that encourage dialogue on issues with ethical implications and to provide an approach to establishing an ethical workplace. The creation of a shared value system based on ethical principles requires meaningful and serious dialogue through an inclusive, not an exclusive, process. Ethics guidelines set the parameters for appropriate behavior and help translate values into action. The involvement of employees in ethics training and development seminars that allow for questions and confrontations will give individuals the greater confidence they need to take action, resolve problems, and raise productivity.

4. Ethics cannot be learned, taught, or even discussed in any meaningful way   False! The argument that the only way in which one can acquire ethics is through the crucible of personal experiences, although intuitively appealing, is specious. Ethical persons and ethical workplaces are not simply the products of life or of organization-driven "pinball-like" experiences. Although published data regarding the effects of ethics training on individuals and organizations are accumulating, there is no compelling reason to take a "naturalist" view of how an ethical sense is acquired or transmitted. Rather, ethical behavior is learned behavior, and practice improves performance.

The challenge to managers is to build organizational processes and strategies of ethical reflection and discourse that will encourage employees to take risks toward improving decision-making outcomes. Ethics initiatives and training may not create ethical employees, but they should facilitate decisions that reflect organizational values and purpose. The authors believe that serious ethical contemplation and discussion challenge employees and increase responsiveness to democratic principles. When ethics training is successful, employees become aware of ethical choices and have the knowledge and resources to choose and carry out the right choices.

5. Only employees who have greater opportunity for ethical failings or shortcomings should be encouraged or required to attend ethics training   This assumption, too, is false. A successful ethics training initiative must start at the top of the organization, but it is not a real success story until it includes all employees. When employees understand that ethical principles must be the basis for making decisions and that ethical obligations extend beyond compliance with the law or with agency rules, the organization will be known and trusted for its integrity.

Many employees who regard themselves as ethical often lose sight of the fact that their daily work—their treatment of others within and outside the organization—is more than doing things right. It also is doing the right thing!

Ethical decision making involves employees knowing their organization's values and its definitions of right and wrong. With this knowledge, workers can act on what is right. It is essential to set up an educational process that increases employees' understanding of the principles of complex situations and that enhances their ability to rank conflicting ethical obligations. Enhanced success comes from infusing into the organization the principles of honesty, integrity, fairness, caring, respect, and accountability as the ground rules for decision making.

**6. Creating and distributing a written ethics policy elimi-
nates any further responsibility of the organization or its
leaders**   False! While it is important to have ethics guidelines
and to provide those guidelines to employees, this action alone
will likely fall short of guiding behavior, and can do little toward
changing it when such change is needed. An ethics training initiative is necessary to enhance ethical decision making through
a structured problem-solving process. Ethics training must have
substance and must address more than just methods of staying
out of trouble. It also needs to focus on making government work
better in serving the public interest.

As Frank Navran argues, when there is no respect by employees for the organization, sabotage can occur. Such sabotage
takes several forms:

- Scapegoating—blaming other people, groups, or departments
  for missed commitments, bad decisions, or poor results
- Allowing the manager to fail by withholding information and
  not pointing out risks
- Playing budget games—padding the budget in anticipation
  of cuts, or going on end-of-the-year spending sprees to match
  estimates to actual figures
- Generating endless meetings and memos to ensure that you
  are covered or that you can distance yourself from a bad
  decision
- Avoiding risks—not doing what is needed to succeed because
  the organization punishes for failure more than it values
  success.

These behaviors result in low morale, personal stress, and
high employee turnover. Such ethical deficits must be addressed
by managers if productivity, high-quality services, and satisfied customers are to be the benchmarks of effective local
government.

**7. Appearing to do wrong and actually doing wrong are
different matters**   False! The belief that a person's ethics
should be judged not by appearance but by facts does not reflect
the power of perception. Appearing to do wrong when we actually have done nothing improper may have the same negative
impact as doing wrong, or an even greater one. The appearance
of impropriety erodes public trust and confidence in government
and weakens the principles of accountability, exactly as if the
deed had been done. It may, for example, be legal for managers
to own investment property in the jurisdictions they manage,
but they will have difficulty convincing a skeptical public that

they are not using the power of their position for personal gain. The appearance of impropriety is inescapable, regardless of the reality.

8. An ethical workplace can be achieved quickly False! For managers, there can be no more important public service endeavor than working with organization members to establish an ethically aware and sensitive work environment. A fundamental change in the way the organization conducts its affairs will not be achieved by decree. Time, effort, and consistent ethical leadership are necessary.

Ethics management is a leadership task that depends heavily on the ability of the manager to influence, to provide guidance and direction on ethics as a fundamental basis for action. By encouraging employees to concentrate their creative energies, managers can make the organization's ethical vision a reality. Management is needed to take responsibility for, to conduct, and to accomplish the administrative activities necessary to implement ethics initiatives.

Clearly, ethics leadership is a shared organizational responsibility that has profound implications for the democratic processes of government.

A continuous process

The achievement and maintenance of an ethical workplace is a challenge for all members of the public organization. The establishment of ethical standards in an age of tolerance and diversity requires shared leadership and commitment throughout the organization. It is important to be alert to false assumptions that act as barriers or obstacles to a work environment that is ethically sensitive.

Public managers must involve themselves continuously, positively, and visibly in educating and empowering employees to act on their democratic responsibilities. Ethical action and commitment to public service by local government managers and employees must be consistent and reflected throughout the organization. It is from shared leadership and dedication that an ethical workplace is created and maintained in appearance and in fact.

References

Bonczek, Stephen J., "Creating an Ethical Work Environment: Enhancing Ethics Awareness in Local Government," *Public Management*, International City/County Management Association, Vol. 73, No. 10, October 1992.

Denhardt, Kathryn G., "Ethics in the Workplace," a presentation to the Suncoast chapter of the American

Society for Public Administration, Tampa, Florida, April 28, 1993.

Denhardt, Robert B., *The Pursuit of Significance: Strategies for Managerial Success in Public Organizations*, Belmont, California: Wadsworth Publishing Co., 1993.

Josephson Institute for the Advancement of Ethics, *Preserving the Public Trust; Principles of Public Service Ethics: Standards of Conduct and Guidelines for Government Decision Making*. Marina del Rey: Government Ethics Center, 1990.

Karp, H.B., and Abramms, Bob, "Doing the Right Thing," *Training and Development*, American Society for Training and Development, Vol. 465, No. 8, August 1992.

Lewis, Carol W., *The Ethics Challenge in Public Service*, Washington, D.C.: Jossey-Bass, 1991.

Maddox, Robert B., and Maddox, Dorothy, *Ethics in Business: A Guide for Managers*, Los Altos, California: Crisp Publications, Inc., 1989.

Menzel, Donald C., "The Ethics Factor in Local Government: An Empirical Analysis," in H. George Frederickson, ed., *Ethics and Public Administration*, Armonk, New York: M. E. Sharpe, Inc., 1993.

Thompson, Dennis F., "Paradoxes of Government Ethics," *Public Administration Review*, American Society for Public Administration, Vol. 57, No. 3, May/June 1992.

Ethical Decision-Making in Business and Government

Anita Cava, Jonathan P. West, and
Evan M. Berman

Organizations, public and private, are attempting to improve the decision-making skills of employees. One way of achieving this goal is to underline the importance of core values to the institution, and to emphasize the significance of such values in the decision-making calculus (Robin et al. 1990; Vogel 1988; Dean 1992). The proliferation of internal codes of ethics or standards of conduct might be seen as an example of this effort. Not surprisingly, a code of ethics is perceived to increase the accountability of employees and organizations to ethical norms (Gellerman 1989).

Typically, these documents address potential problem areas that might not be equally obvious to all. In some cases, code provisions simply outline the requirements of law. In many instances, however, codes give guidance: Can one accept a holiday gift from a long-time client? Should a bank employee's family use that institution's services? Does it matter if the employee is a loan officer or a teller? Should a state building inspector attend a party in honor of an influential developer?

These questions stimulate another set of queries: Do managers really need a code that specifically addresses these situations? Might it not be better to rely upon ethical principles to guide decision-making, and invite managers to employ some common sense in thinking through these dilemmas? Do we discourage initiative and individual responsibility by setting out decision-making strategies that appear paternalistic?

Reprinted with permission from *Spectrum: The Journal of State Government* 68, no. 2 (Spring 1995): 28–36. Copyright Spring 1995 by the Council of State Governments.

Similar issues confront managers in both the public and the private sectors. The challenge is to adopt the strategy that is most likely to improve ethical decision-making. This article suggests that two main strategies address these common concerns. An organization may choose to utilize a formal approach and create codes of ethics or standards of conduct. Alternatively, the entity may rely on an informal approach, where general ethical principles are used to promote ethical decision-making. These differ in form and substance and provide a frame of reference for the strategies currently in use.

Formal strategies: Codes of conduct

As a society, we seek guidance from rules that prescribe acceptable conduct. Generally, such rules exist as laws, comprehensive announcements of unacceptable behavior. Obviously, the general law of the land may not be sufficiently precise to address organizational concerns. Accordingly, organizations have undertaken the task of writing codes of conduct to fill the gap. These might be seen as a formal, written expression of the internal law of the land.

Organizational codes of ethics tend to address common issues—for example, the propriety of giving or accepting gifts, the importance of respecting the property and proprietary information of the enterprise, and the significance of avoiding even the appearance of a conflict of interest in public and private affairs (Menzel 1992). Indeed, in many such circumstances, there is law relevant to the proscribed conduct, but it is subject to interpretation depending on the particular facts at hand. In such cases, the code becomes a species of formalized "in-house law" and operates to minimize legal liability to an irate customer or citizen (Ettore 1992; Laverty 1989).

Sometimes these standards of conduct instead promote adherence to broad ethical principles: "be honest and trustworthy in all relationships" (McDonnell Douglas); "our first responsibility is to . . . [those] who use our products" (Johnson & Johnson), and the like (Osborne 1991; Berenbeim 1987). Such codes, although more general in nature, nevertheless represent a formal attempt by the organization to communicate and promote ethical values. Whether they are specific enough to provide real guidance is the subject of some debate (DeGeorge 1991; Raiborn and Payne 1990). At least one company, J.C. Penney, has undertaken a combined approach, where general ethical principles are announced and then case scenarios are used to apply them to difficult situations (Berenbeim 1987).

The application and assistance of such explicit codes of conduct is easily demonstrated. Consider the following hypothetical situation.

State building inspector Frank Stone is invited to the wedding of his best friends' daughter, who has been like a child to him. She is marrying Tony Toddson's only son, and Mr. Toddson, local manager of an international cruise line, has arranged a day trip for the wedding ceremony and reception. Many influential business people are invited, including some influential developers. Mr. Stone guesses that they will not hesitate to try to "talk to him" regarding some decisions he has to make next month, which will affect development in the state capital for the next several years. What should he do?[1]

This scenario raises the issue of conflicts of interest, an area of concern for all organizations. One need not have evil intent to create the appearance of favoritism toward an individual or organization that may have the real or perceived opportunity to profit from such favoritism. Accordingly, codes of conduct tend to mention the importance of avoiding the appearance of a conflict of interest, and even give explicit guidelines on dealing with such situations.

Our building inspector might consult the model legislation developed by the Council on Governmental Ethics Laws (COGEL), which offers general guidance under the "intent and purpose" section of the act. Other model state ethics laws have been developed by the Government Ethics Center (GEC) affiliated with the Josephson Institute of Ethics and by the National Municipal League (NML). Alternatively, the building inspector might consult the American Society for Public Administration (ASPA) code of ethics, which offers broad provisions that are a relatively informal version of the formal strategy under consideration. Each statement in the COGEL, GEC and NML model laws and in the ASPA code, however, is followed by detail, commentary or implementation guidelines that explain the intended meaning. Relying exclusively on the COGEL and ASPA resources, relevant provisions of each are:

The proper operation of democratic government requires that . . . the public have confidence in the integrity of its government and public officials and employees. (COGEL)

Demonstrate the highest standards of personal integrity, truthfulness, honesty and fortitude in all our public activities in order to inspire public confidence and trust in public institutions. (ASPA)

Mr. Stone might be compromised by being on this cruise with some, but not all, parties with an interest in the decisions.

. . . a public official or employee [must] not use public office to obtain a private benefit. (COGEL)

Serve in such a way that we do not realize undue personal gain from the performance of our official duties. (ASPA)

In this particular scenario, this is not a problem. Mr. Stone can go on the wedding cruise.

. . . a public official or employee [must] be independent and impartial. (COGEL)

Avoid any interest or activity which is in conflict with the conduct of our official duties. . . . To strengthen resistance to conflict of interest, public employees should avoid frequent social contact with persons who come under their regulation or persons who wish to sell products or services to their agency or institution. (ASPA)

If Mr. Stone's contacts with these people are not frequent, he may go on the trip.

A more developed code for public managers is that adopted by the International City/County Management Association (ICMA), which also provides sanctions for violations of the code. Similarly, several states have enacted their own ethics laws affecting public officials and employees. If our building inspector were to consult the ICMA document, he would discover the following guidelines:

Public Confidence. Members should conduct themselves so as to maintain public confidence in their profession, their local government, and in their performance of the public trust.

Mr. Stone should consider not attending the wedding party, because to do so would undermine public confidence.

Impression of Influence. Members should conduct their official and personal affairs in such a manner as to give the clear impression that they cannot be improperly influenced in the performance of their official duties.

Mr. Stone should avoid this trip, which would tend to create the impression of influence by the developers.

Gifts. Members should not directly or indirectly solicit any gift or accept or receive any gift—whether it be money, services, loan, travel, entertainment, hospitality, promise, or any other form—under the following circumstances: (1) it could be reasonably inferred or expected that the gift was intended to influence them in the performance of their official duties; or (2) the gift was intended to serve as a reward for any official action on their part.

Mr. Stone can go because this is not a gift of the prohibited kind.

Personal Relationships. Members should disclose any personal relationships to the governing body in any instance where there could be the appearance of a conflict of interest.

This might be wise advice because the public would certainly support the manager's right to attend a close friend's wedding reception, and to publicly disclose the event and its ramifications lessens the appearance of impropriety. Nevertheless, Mr. Stone must be careful as the guidance above reveals several pitfalls in choosing to attend this event.

At the state level, the COGEL, GEC and NML model laws represent an ideal approach to crafting ethics provisions. But what kinds of assistance do decision makers get from the actual laws in effect? Some state ethics laws provide guidance on these matters.

Tennessee's ethics law, for example, addresses the **public confidence** issue by stating that "inherent in the concept of public office as a public trust is the principle that persons refrain from using or attempting to use their governmental position to attain: . . . undue personal benefits, advantages or privileges not available to the public at large, either for themselves or their immediate families."

The **impression of influence** concern is reflected in state-level legal restrictions on accepting financial compensation, gifts, favoritism, or services of value. State-level officials and employees are typically obligated to disclose gifts (e.g., property, automobile or transport, works of art, or perishable goods) which might influence decisions or create the appearance of doing so. State ethics statutes frequently require the disclosure of any hint of conflict of interest such as "personal relationships" where there are benefits to be derived by the public employee, his or her family, business associates, or businesses owned by the employee resulting from the conduct of official business (Goodman, et al. 1994).

Another approach is that adopted by J.C. Penney in its policy statement, which leaves little to the imagination. It offers a comprehensive aspirational definition similar to the above, and an accompanying page of examples of problematic situations. The reader is explicitly educated as to the official policy:

Each Associate shall avoid any activity, interest, or relationship . . . which would create, or might appear to others to create, a conflict with the interests of the Company.

An explanation of the purpose follows:

To assure that all Company Associates, at all levels, wherever located are able to perform their duties and exercise their judgments on behalf of the Company without impairment, or the appearance of impairment by virtue of a non-Company activity, interest or relationship.

Then, an elaboration of the statement points out that the company shall determine whether a conflict exists, not the employee. Gifts, loans and entertainment are specifically discussed in full paragraphs that mention bribery, improper (other than nominal) gift-giving, and appropriate business-related social functions. It specifies that business-related *outings*—including tickets to theater or sports events and golf trips—*may be accepted only if it is practicable for an Associate to reciprocate at an appropriate time.* If such will not be possible, the employee is asked to get a supervisor's permission.

This type of comprehensive approach has its pitfalls. Some might assume that, if not strictly prohibited, a particular personal quandary might be permissible. Moreover, situations do not always fit neatly into a formula. For example, what if Mr. Stone in the hypothetical above were a manager at Penney's and the future father-in-law were also a major supplier to the company? Do the rules explained above suggest a course of action? Does one really have to get supervisory permission to attend the wedding party of a close family friend? Nonetheless, the guidance exists as an aid to decision-making and assists the manager in his or her own job and in assisting others to do theirs.

Informal strategies: Ethical principles

Decision-making can be improved through informal mechanisms, as well. These include maxims such as the Utilitarian principle, "promote the greatest good for the greatest number of people"; the Theory of Justice, "benefits and burdens should be distributed impartially"; the principle of Equal Freedom, "respect individual freedom consistent with the rights of others"; the Reversibility Rule, be "willing to change places with the person affected by your decision"; or the Intuition Ethic, "do what one feels is right" (Vogel 1991; Bowie and Beauchamp 1990). Such guidelines are part of our ethical culture, are often used to make decisions in personal life, and can be understood to constitute a scheme of personal values (Fritzche 1991). When brought into the organizational context, these ethical principles can stimulate the kind of questions that are the hallmark of critical thinking (Osborne 1991).

A scheme for organizing these questions to be effectively used by managers is offered by Badaracco (1992). He proposes a set of four questions that capture the essence of different philosophical approaches to ethical decision-making. A manager who asks these questions and attempts to reach rigorous answers will have considered many of the less obvious facets of difficult issues. The four questions, modified to apply to a broad organizational context, are:

1. Which course of action will do the most good and the least harm?
2. What plan can I live with, which is consistent with the basic values and commitments in my organization?
3. Which alternative best serves others' rights, including stakeholders' rights?
4. Which course of action is feasible in the world as it is?

If one expands the list of explicit issues embraced within each of the questions above, one might come up with a list of ethical principles and guiding questions such as proposed in Figure 1. Note that these are grouped by principles of consequences, integrity, rights and practicality, all of which are genuine and sometimes conflicting considerations in making any decision. Once again, a hypothetical provides the vehicle for illustrating the analysis.

Mary Pound is a state-level purchasing agent. She recently concluded negotiations for a large order of furniture with Anthony Able of Furniture City. Unbeknownst to Ms. Pound, Mr. Able's wife works for Tony Toddson and can readily make certain arrangements, especially if a ship is not filled to capacity. Today, Able offers Pound a pair of tickets for a weeklong Caribbean cruise at a 35 percent discount. "Use them; the ship is half empty and we need to fill it up. Besides, these aren't a gift because you're paying me." Pound recalls having seen this discount advertised in the papers, but is not certain whether the promotion is in effect at the moment. In any event, she sends Able a check for the discounted price, but two months have gone by and the check has not been cashed. The cruise is supposed to be next week and her husband is really looking forward to it. What does she do?

While each of the 16 principles outlined in the figure would assist in understanding all the ramifications of the decision, one can illustrate the usefulness of these questions by posing any set of four. For example, using a sample from each of the basic four groups, the following analysis emerges:

Proportionality ethic: "What are the good and bad results of this decision and do the good outweigh the bad?"

The benefit/harm calculation requires one to go beyond the impact on the budget and even beyond an "innocent mind." In keeping with the utilitarian emphasis on intangible effects of a decision upon such ideals as reputation, harmony, and trust, the negative effects of going on this cruise must be assessed. Will other bidders for this contract jump to conclusions? Will the bid-

Figure 1.

Consequences	What course of action will do the most good and the least harm?
Utilitarian ethic	What course of action brings the greatest good for the greatest number of people?
Proportionality ethic	What are the good and bad results of this decision and do the good outweigh the bad?
Theory of justice	Does this action apply impartially to each employee and organizational unit?
Golden rule	If I were in the position of another person affected by my decision, would my actions be considered fair by that person?
Reversibility rule	Would I be willing to change places with the person affected by my contemplated action?
Protect health, safety, welfare	What course of action will best protect the health, safety and welfare of others?
Integrity	*What plan can I live with, which is consistent with the basic values and commitments in my organization?*
Virtuous character	Would this action be undertaken by someone of exemplary or virtuous character?
Disclosure rule	What course of action would I be comfortable with if it was examined by my friends, family and associates?
Professional ethic	Can my action be explained before a committee of peers?
Intuition ethic	Which course of action feels right to me?
Rights	*Which alternative best serves others' rights, including stakeholders' rights?*
Principle of equal freedom	Will my contemplated action restrict others from actions that they have a legitimate right to undertake?
Rights ethic	Will my action deprive any person affected by it of a right that must be respected?
Practicality	*Which course of action is feasible in the world as it is?*
Conventionalist ethic	What action will further my self-interest without violating the law?
Darwinian ethic	What course of action will enable me to succeed and survive in this organization?
Organizational vs. personal ethic	Is this action consistent with both organizational ethics and personal ethics and do organizational considerations override personal ones?
Organizational loyalty	What are the organizational goals and what can I do that is good for the organization?

Copyright Jonathan West

ding process be tainted in the future? Must the decision to go be explained if the check is never cashed? Obviously, one simple question generates 10 more, some of which might not have been on the table were it not for the initial inquiry.

On balance, it appears that the good results of having a delightful cruise with one's spouse are outweighed by the possible bad effects of doing so under these conditions.

Professional ethic: "Can my action be explained before a committee of peers?"

Although the traditional definition of a professional is limited to members of the clergy and those who practice medicine, law, and post-secondary school education, the term today is used in a broad context and implies the right to self-regulate (DeGeorge 1990). An assessment of the opinion of peers gives pause, whether or not a formal code of conduct has been adopted. In this case, it appears clear that accepting any gift from a vendor puts one in a compromising position, despite explanations that reveal no evil intent.

Rights ethic: "Will my action deprive any person affected by it of a right that must be respected?"

On first blush, the answer appears to be no. Who else is affected by Ms. Pound's decision to pay for and go on this trip? But, upon further reflection, the same questions arise. Will not other vendors believe that there is some connection between the contract and the trip? Will they understand the underlying facts, or will they simply focus on the appearance of the facts? Is there a difference between believing one has been deprived of the right to freely compete in business and actually being deprived? Notice the questions that arise without much effort. The action is not advisable.

Conventionalist ethic: "What action will further my self-interest without violating the law?"

Certainly, Ms. Pound's self-interest lies in going on the trip, at least in the short term. However, the fact that no law forbids this behavior should be scant solace. Our legal system is almost infinitely flexible in declaring illegal that which is not, but perhaps should be. Moreover, one's interest in keeping one's job should be considered. Nonetheless, the application of this rather Machiavellian principle is the strongest to support Ms. Pound if she were to decide to take the trip.

Although the analysis is ultimately a personal one, the principles of ethical decision-making offer guidance for pursuing critical thinking, and by extension, improved decision-making. Their utility seems obvious, even if the practicalities of the situation cannot always accommodate the preferred result. The real issue is how managers can bring these principles, and the questions they raise, to the workplace. In this regard, a variety of strategies has been suggested: (1) training, (2) ethical leadership by example from top leaders, and (3) regular communication on matters of ethics.

First, training often involves the use of cases for the purpose of increasing awareness about specific ethical problems that may occur in the workplace, such as conflict of interest or misuse of property or position (Williams 1982; Menzel 1992). Training also provides employees with appropriate guidance in recognizing and responding to ethics problems in ways that are in accordance with the organizational guidelines and purposes. Ethics training helps employees stay out of trouble, while clarifying the ethical culture and principles used to guide conduct (Hoffman 1986).

In the case of state government, for example, reference to the specific principles discussed above in the context of ethics training serves to reinforce the mission of the organization. Arguably, ethics training should be conducted on a regular basis, perhaps as often as four times each year. Each session would then provide an opportunity to highlight different ethical issues and deal with emerging problems.

Second, the importance of high-level management in providing an ethical climate is increasingly recognized (Enderle 1987). Senior management sets the tone of acceptable and expected conduct in agencies. It does so forcefully in the eyes of employees, through its own examples of minimizing wrongdoing (e.g., by avoiding conflict of interests), and by undertaking actions which do the most good to the agency's stakeholders (proportionality ethics), which are professional, and which respect the rights of all parties affected (rights ethic). For top managers, ethical conduct is a criterion and modus operandus for achieving an agency's objectives. Conversely, agencies that do not require ethical conduct from their top leadership should expect that their actions will be challenged and that their employees will become demoralized and less than fully committed to agency priorities.

Third, to ensure an ethical climate, regular communication about ethics is important. Communication is necessary, for example, to explain the rationale behind leadership policies and actions: such communication is necessary in the case of Mary Pound's trip, lest her actions be interpreted as constituting conflict of interest. Communication takes place in many different settings, such as staff meetings and newsletters. Communication on matters of ethics also occurs through management decisions affecting hiring, promotion and performance appraisal. When an employee with a dubious ethics record is not hired or promoted, an unambiguous message is sent to all.

Although no empirical data are available regarding the use of different ethics strategies in state government workplaces, previous research by the authors suggests that in local governments a wide range of such strategies is available (Berman, West and Cava 1994). Responding to a national survey among personnel directors, 73 percent of respondents indicated that they rely on exemplary moral leadership of senior managers to ensure an ethical climate in their organizations. In addition, 41 percent of jurisdictions use voluntary ethics training courses and 29 percent provide regular communication to employees about ethics. Mandatory training courses exist in 29 percent of jurisdictions, and 41 percent adopt formal codes of ethics. These data suggest that ethics implementation strategies are not generally available. With regard to specific ethics principles, respondents selected the following as most important:

1. Protect the health, safety and welfare of the public (97%)
2. Respect individual freedom consistent with the rights of others (88%)
3. Act with empathy and understanding toward others (87%)
4. Do what feels or is known to be right (84%)
5. Conform to professional codes (83%).

On the other hand, the following emerged as the least useful principles in the public sector:

1. Whoever survives is right (rejected as not important by 75% of respondents)
2. Pursue self-interest without violating the law (47%).

While comparable data have not yet been collected on state ethics laws, research by Goodman and his colleagues (1994) suggests that state employees are subject to similar provisions. For example, these authors did a content analysis of state ethics laws and determined that the most common categories addressed in legislation are: use of official position (found in 81% of the states reporting), receipt of gifts or incentives (70%), conflicts of interest (65%), use of public resources (54%), and restrictions on representation (22%). COGEL's *Blue Book* provides state-by-state reporting of ethics-law provisions, which are consistent with the categories used by Goodman and his associates. The provisions in state laws referred to by these two sources as well as the COGEL Model Law give greater emphasis to negative injunctions ("thou shalt nots") than to positive, aspirational statements.

More affirmative injunctions are included in the Government Ethics Center Model Law.

The data in Figure 2 are adapted from the COGEL *Blue Book*, noting caveats and reservations expressed within that document.

These data provide the beginning bits of useful information on the target of specific yet informal strategies that might be appropriate in government. Further research in this area would be necessary to design the actual content of effective training and implement the most appropriate ways of communicating about the many ethical dilemmas that confront public managers.

Conclusion

In today's complex world, managers face an increasing need for guidance in recognizing and handling ethical dilemmas. A formal strategy for addressing this need seems to be emerging albeit slowly: developing and implementing an official or formal code of ethics or standard of conduct. Less official, but nonetheless important strategies also assist in emphasizing ethical principles in decision-making. These include training, ethical leadership by example that creates an organizational culture supportive of ethical decision-making, and regular communication on matters of ethics that maintains that supportive environment.

Formal codes have the appeal of offering a more standard and objective set of guidelines useful to any decision-maker. These guidelines essentially attempt to ensure that the many facets of a decision are explored and resolved. Although many codes offer positive, aspirational guidelines, others provide specific illustrations of the application of the provisions, which is

Figure 2. Percentage of states with restrictions on the following activities.

Item	Percent of states
Use of public position to obtain personal benefits	92%
Providing benefits to influence actions	89
Outside activities	80
Use of confidential information	80
Competitive bidding	78
Receiving gifts by officials	76
Financial conflicts of interest	73
Representation of private clients	71
Fees by public officials	69
Nepotism	67
Travel payments	62
Political activities	57
Prohibitions on post-government employment	53

probably most helpful to individuals genuinely in a conundrum. Sanctions for violation of code provisions ensure their legitimacy and acceptance.

Ethical principles also have a place in decision-making, one that may be in place of or alongside of formal codes or standards. These principles can be translated into questions, which offer the decision-maker important assistance in considering all facets of a decision, similar to the process referred to above. Assessing the consequences of a decision, the extent to which the decision furthers one's personal and organizational sense of integrity, the extent to which the alternative preserves the rights of all affected, and the extent to which the decision is feasible requires an analysis of numerous issues, many of which may not be obvious at first blush. This analysis, a process of critical thinking, is one that might be profitably encouraged in the workplace. Training with case study scenarios not only teaches the usefulness of this technique, but also communicates the importance of such questions to the organization (Menzel 1992).

Note

1. This scenario is adapted from a hypothetical created by Jorn Roesler for a graduate course in Politics and Ethics.

References

Badaracco, J. Jr. 1992. "Business Ethics: Four Spheres of Executive Responsibility." *California Management Review,* Spring 64–79: 74–77.

Beauchamp, T., and N. Bowie. 1990. *Ethical Theory and Business.* 4th ed. Prentice Hall, NJ: 1–48.

Berenbeim, R.E. 1987. Corporate Ethics: Research Report No. 900. New York City, NY: 1–48.

Berman, E., J. West, and A. Cava. 1994. "Ethics Management in Municipal Governments and Large Firms: Exploring Similarities and Differences." *Administration and Society* 26, 2: 185–203.

Council on Governmental Ethics Laws. 1991. *A Model Law for Campaign Finance, Ethics, and Lobbying Regulation.* Lexington, KY: The Council of State Governments.

Council on Governmental Ethics Laws. 1993. *Blue Book.* Lexington, KY: The Council of State Governments.

Dean, P.J. 1992. "Making Codes of Ethics Real." *Journal of Business Ethics* 9: 285–290.

DeGeorge, R. 1990. *Business Ethics.* 3rd ed. New York: MacMillan: 381–396.

Enderle, G. 1987. "Some Perspectives of Managerial Ethical Leadership." *Journal of Business Ethics* 6: 657–663.

Ettore, B. 1992. "The Buck Had Better Stop Here." *Management Review,* April: 16–21.

Fritzche, D. 1991. "A Model of Decision-Making Incorporating Ethical Values." *Journal of Business Ethics* 10: 841–852.

Gellerman, S.W. 1989. "Managing Ethics from the Top Down." *Sloan Management Review* 30, 2, Winter: 73–79.

Goodman, M.R., T.J. Holp, and E.W. Rademacher. 1994. "State Legislative Ethics: Proactive Reform or Reactive Defense?" Unpublished paper delivered at the Midwest Political Science Association meeting, Chicago, Illinois.

Hoffman, W. 1986. "What is Necessary for Corporate Moral Excellence." *Journal of Business Ethics* 5: 233–242.

Laverty, E. 1989. "The Ethical Context of Administrative Decisions: A Framework for Analysis." *Public Affairs Quarterly*, Fall: 375–387.

Menzel, D. 1992. "Ethics Attitudes and Behaviors in Local Governments: An Empirical Analysis." *State and Local Government Review* (forthcoming).

National Municipal League. 1979. *Model State Conflict of Interest and Financial Disclosure Law*. New York: National Municipal League.

Osborne, R. 1991. "Core Value Statements: The Corporate Compass." *Business Horizons*, September-October: 28–34.

Raiborn, C., and D. Payne. 1990. "Corporate Codes of Conduct: A Collective Conscience and Continuum." *Journal of Business Ethics* 9: 879–889.

Robin, D., M. Giallourakis, F.R. David, and T.E. Moritz. 1990. "A Different Look at Codes of Ethics." In P. Madsden and J. Shafritz (eds.), *Essentials of Business Ethics*. New York: Meridian: 212–228.

The Government Ethics Center. Nd. *Model State Legislative Ethics Act*. Marina del Rey, CA: Joseph & Edna Josephson Institute of Ethics.

Tennessee Enacted House Bill 1349, Section 19: 25.

Williams, O. 1982. "Business Ethics: A Trojan Horse?" *California Management Review* 24, 4:14–24.

Vogel, D. 1991. "Business Ethics: New Perspectives on Old Problems." *California Management Review* 10, Fall: 102–104.

Vogel, D. 1988. "Ethics and Profits Don't Always Go Hand in Hand." *Los Angeles Times*, 28 December: 7.

Strategies and Tactics for Managerial Decision Making

Picture the scene: as personnel director, you learn at a top-level staff meeting that the municipality's retrenchment plan calls for reorganization and cuts in managerial staff. The tentative blueprint has the city's Department of Community Services absorbing the small elderly services unit, whose program director, a close friend of your family, is slated for termination. The city manager, whose judgment you respect, mentions the program director's poor performance and as the meeting adjourns reminds everyone that the discussion is confidential as usual. As you leave, you remember that your friend is about to make a substantial down payment on a new home. *How would you handle this?*

Reviewing the decision-making checklist shown in Exhibit 1 is a good beginning. By putting ourselves in the personnel director's role, we can use the checklist to elicit acute considerations.

Facts. Does the city manager know about the imminent down payment?—No. Is the city manager aware of the friendship?— Yes. Is your friend aware of prospective termination?—No. Are you sure your friend depends upon her municipal salary to finance housing?—Yes.

Is information confidential just because the city manager says so? Is a strictly legalistic view right or an excuse? You strike a middle ground by asking yourself, "Is this privileged information, known to me through my job but not known generally?"— Yes. A draft model ordinance (designed to aid municipal attorneys

Reprinted with permission from Carol Lewis, *The Ethics Challenge in Public Service: A Problem Solving Guide,* pp. 110–115. Copyright © 1991 by Jossey-Bass, Inc., Publishers. All rights reserved.

Exhibit 1. Decision-making checklist.

☐	1. Facts (including law)
☐	2. Empathy and inclusion
☐	3. Underlying causes and precedents
☐	4. Stakeholders and responsibilities
☐	5. Motives and objectives
☐	6. Possible results and rationality
☐	7. Potential harm (stakeholders)
☐	8. Participation
☐	9. Long-term time frame and anticipated change
☐	10. Disclosure and publicity
☐	11. Appearance and communication
☐	12. Universality and consistency

in drafting municipal ethics codes) defines confidential information as "all information, whether transmitted orally or in writing, which is of such a nature that it is not, at that time, a matter of public record or public knowledge" (National Institute of Municipal Law Officers, 1990, p. 3).

Does your jurisdiction prohibit using public office for *anyone's* personal gain and divulging confidential information?—Perhaps. But either way, you know confidentiality is a widely accepted administrative value because federal standards (see Exhibit 2) and state law in more than half of all states forbid the use of confidential government information.

Empathy. How would you feel if financial ruin threatened you? Can you put yourself in the city manager's shoes? How important is confidentiality in *your* job? How are other people in the community affected by your helping or not helping your friend?

Causes. Thinking about causes helps you define the problem and solutions. Your friend brought on termination herself through poor performance but not the retrenchment's coinciding with the new house. Therefore, the problem is not keeping the job but avoiding financial disaster.

Stakeholders. Friendship does make ethical claims on you, but the difficult part of public service is that personal friendship is rejected as a legitimate basis of action: it is nontransferable from the personal to the public realm. You must weigh responsibilities and obligations to *all* affected parties, including the city manager, who unknowingly put you in a difficult position; your family friend; yourself, spouse, and family; the municipal organization; and residents and taxpayers.

Objectives. The city manager's motives are not clear, but because he did not know about the down payment, because confi-

Exhibit 2. Judge Nebeker's memorandum.

The following information is excerpted from a September 12, 1988, memorandum from the director of the U.S. Office of Government Ethics on the independent counsel's 1988 report concerning the activities of Attorney General Edwin Meese III. Reference is to Section 201(c) and Section 205 of Executive Order 11222, still in force in 1988.

Assisting a friend is not in and of itself prohibited by the Executive Order. But, assisting a friend in a manner which misuses official position for the friend's private benefit, which gives that friend preferential treatment not properly afforded, which causes a Government decision to be made outside official channels, which affects the public's confidence in the integrity of its Government, or which leads an informed and reasonable person to believe that any of these things have occurred, is what this section was in part intended to prohibit. . . .

Section 205 states "[a]n employee shall not directly or indirectly make use of, or permit others to make use of, for the purpose of furthering a private interest, official information not made available to the general public."

This provision of the standards of conduct is directed not only to information which is by statute confidential or classified, but also to the large amount of information which is neither, yet clearly not information generally available to the public . . . [which may mean preferential treatment or its appearance].

dentiality is standard procedure at these staff meetings, and because you trust his judgment, you assume he intends to act for the best. You even may feel that he knowingly put you on the spot and ought to do something about it. The obligation to prevent injury emerges from checklist items 2 and 3, above, but what about *your* objective? Are you acting to protect a friend through special treatment?

Universality and consistency. At this point you skip to checklist item 12 because you realize that you happen to have specific information that warrants consideration on behalf of *anyone* in a precarious situation, not only your friend. Your intention is *not* to use privileged information from public office solely to protect a friend.

Possible results. What happens if your friend loses her job and cannot make the mortgage payments? How can you face her accusation of betrayal? What happens if she learns about the retrenchment plan from you, does not buy the house, but then does not lose her job? If you were to betray a trust for friendship's sake and your friend knows you have other friends too, can she ever trust you again? Can you be effective in your job without the city manager's trust? What if everyone disclosed confidential information at whim? Can government function if public trust takes second place to employee needs? To personal friendship?

Potential harm. Your friend faces financial harm. The city manager's trust is at issue. You also realize that the organization is at risk: do you want to work in an organization that would allow something like this to happen to an employee, even one being fired? Does the city deserve an administration like this? You decide something should be done to prevent injury.

Participation and Appearance. Because of the friendship, you conclude it would be best for communication to come from someone else. Given the fact-finding in checklist item 1 above, you begin to think about bringing the city manager into the picture.

Change and Disclosure. You do not see these items as directly applicable to the problem you face.

Next, you turn to assess the options stimulated by your thinking:

1. Do nothing; say nothing.
2. Tell your spouse, who is not bound by confidentiality.
3. Tell your friend immediately and directly.
4. Inform the city manager of your friend's impending down payment.
5. Say nothing but be prepared to help your friend financially.
6. Casually hint to your friend about impending shake-ups.
7. Leak the retrenchment plan to the media.
8. Tell your friend and other municipal employees that budget cuts mean that a shake-up is imminent and suggest that they avoid new commitments at this time.
9. Say nothing, and help your friend get another job when the time comes.

Can you stand by and do nothing? Is this your problem? The obligation to keep confidentiality (involving legal compliance, loyalty, and trust) clashes with another top-ranking obligation—to refrain from doing harm. Although you are not directly causing the problem, inaction or silence could result in serious injury. Therefore, your obligation is reduced but still compelling. You may remember the story about George Washington refusing to help a job-seeking friend: "As George Washington, I would do anything in my power for you. As President, I can do nothing" (Bailey, 1964, p. 241). You feel that *his* obligation of affirmative help was lighter than the one you face, the obligation to avoid doing harm.

Pragmatism affects your choice among alternatives. Given your municipal salary, the remedy or relief of supporting your friend's new home is not realistic; financing your own mortgage is hard enough each month and soon both families would be insolvent. Helping in the job hunt does not mean omitting the friendship or poor performance appraisal from a reference, but you know of many publicly advertised openings and your expertise can really help a friend here.

You can think of no way to sidestep the conflict. Embroiling your spouse unties no ethical knots and is itself unethical. Even a hint or two to your friend ("cutbacks in towns across the region counsel postponing life choices") abides by the letter more than the spirit of the obligation. Even worse, ignoring other employees possibly in comparable positions results in favored treatment for a friend. Leaking the story as an unidentified source means breaking confidence on a grand scale plus trying to escape responsibility. A general tip-off to employees personally or through the media still breaks confidence, stimulates gossip, and would cause anxiety and distress. Inflicting minor injury on many, including the innocent (those with good job performance) to protect a friend from more serious harm makes you uncomfortable.

Using the threshold test, you determine that there is a need or problem, you do know something, you are capable of helping but at either some professional or personal cost. However, you are *not* the last resort, and this realization along with considerations of participation and appearance lead you to speak with the city manager. You request that he inform your friend and the others targeted in the retrenchment plan.

Now comes the hard part. Assume that the city manager, whose judgment you respect, declines to make the retrenchment plan public, citing potential employee demoralization and not giving advance notice for affected agencies to undercut the plan by eliciting citizen opposition. He explains that the decision is still tentative, and he does not feel that widespread employee stress is a reasonable price for your friend's financial security. He also refuses to give *your* friend special treatment. Empathically, you reconsider obligations and options from the city manager's perspective.

If you still believe that his response fails to meet the ethical claims that are emerging from your analysis and you genuinely believe that anyone should be told, not just your friend, then you decide to go further. You try to persuade the city manager and explain your ethical posture. Your task is to convince him that the information should be disclosed to those at severe risk; the city has a responsibility to employees, too. You point out that your professional code (that of the IPMA [International Personnel Management Association]) bids you "to insure that full and early consideration is given to the human aspects of management plans and decisions." You argue that information deeply affecting people ought to be made public or at least available to directly affected parties, especially when withholding it causes serious harm.

If that fails, you acknowledge that the city manager's ethical preference or lapse does not absolve you of the responsibility that you already determined is yours. You then reassess capability in terms of *excessive* risk to yourself (job, integrity, family, friendship, professional identity) and the values and principles associated with all participants, including your good friend, the municipal organization, city residents, the profession, and others.

Presuming an authentic assumption of ethical responsibility in this case, you decide that legal compliance and avoiding the conflict of interest represented by respecting privileged information are preeminent obligations in public service. IPMA's code reinforces your commitment to "treat as privileged, information accepted in trust." You decide to say nothing, to help your friend in her job search, and to initiate an outplacement program for all municipal employees. (This last idea illustrates inventive resolution—Cooper's "moral imagination"—at work.)

You conclude by asking, "Can I live with this?" You test the emotional components of your decision and assess the likelihood that you will follow through. To find out, you decide to let the decision sit for a time, but you feel pushed by the pace of events. Your personal anguish is sincere, and you ask yourself, "Am I right?" Insofar as you attempted to use reasoned, unbiased judgment in an informed, systematic way, yes. Does everyone agree with your resolution? No; that is why this is a dilemma that recurs with different faces and different choices at all levels of public service.

City Manager Perceptions of the ICMA Code of Ethics

————————— Lloyd A. Rowe and Richard W. Hug

This article presents the results of a study of the perceptions of municipal managers on the influence of the International City/County Management Association (ICMA) Code of Ethics and Guidelines on their professional roles.[1] Specifically, the article reports on perceptions of (1) the influence of the code in several categories of managerial responsibilities, (2) its influence as a source of ethical guidance in comparison with other potential sources, (3) the importance of the individual tenets of the code, and (4) its overall impact.

The ICMA Code of Ethics has been a centerpiece of professional municipal management since its creation in 1924. It has been amended through the years as managers sought to shape their roles appropriately within the political system, meet the needs of their communities, and maintain their professionalism (Stillman 1974). Scholars frequently give it a prominent place in their discussions of public sector codes of ethics because of ICMA's pioneering role in creating and sustaining such a code, the code's inclusion of a system of enforcement, and the seriousness with which the code is viewed by ICMA (Pugh 1991). One scholar refers to the ICMA code as a "cherished artifact" for public administration (Plant 1994, p. 229).

Despite this, scholars generally remain skeptical of codes of ethics. In a review of public administration literature on codes, Plant (1994) notes that codes have been characterized as a "low road" to ethical behavior designed to keep bureaucrats out of trouble (Rohr 1978), belaboring the obvious (Gortner 1991), not

An earlier version of this paper was presented at the 1996 Southeast Conference on Public Administration (SECOPA), Miami, Florida, October 3–5, 1996.

taken seriously by top management and not generally used in daily management decisions (Bowman 1990), not fundamental in understanding the ethical problems of public administration (Denhardt 1988), and of marginal interest to most scholars in public administration (Rohr 1990). On the other hand, Plant notes how some have argued that codes can go beyond laws in projecting ideals (Cooper 1990) and can set a tone and create expectations for public administrators (Chandler 1989). Generally, however, scholars seem skeptical because it is unclear that codes of ethics actually provide the premises of decision making and moral reasoning where significant administrative discretion is involved.

One reason for the skepticism of the impact of such codes on decision making may be the small number of studies undertaken on the topic. The study reported here was conducted to explore this question further.

Methodology

Questionnaires were mailed in the spring of 1994 to 605 ICMA member municipal managers in the United States in municipalities of 5,000–99,999 population and to all ICMA member managers in municipalities of more than 100,000 population, selected randomly from ICMA's *Who's Who in Local Government* (ICMA 1993). Replies were received from 315 managers. These responses allow estimates of ±5 percent with 95 percent confidence.[2]

The questionnaires came from 37 states and were distributed as shown among municipalities of the following population sizes: 5,000–9,999: 20 percent; 10,000–24,999: 25 percent; 25,000–49,999: 21 percent; 50,000–99,999: 16 percent; and 100,000 and up: 17 percent. Eighty-nine percent came from council-manager municipalities and 11 percent came from general management municipalities. About 80 percent of those responding had master's degrees, and 77 percent majored in public administration or a related field. Their years of service were distributed as follows: up to 5 years: 6 percent; 6–10 years: 17 percent; 11–15 years: 26 percent; 16–20 years: 23 percent; and 21 years and up: 27 percent. Ninety-six percent were men and 95 percent were white.

The ICMA code as guidance for managerial responsibilities

Without question, city managers have complex roles that involve many responsibilities. Whether defined as POSDCORB (Planning, Organizing, Staffing, Directing, Coordinating, Reporting, and Budgeting) (Gulick 1937); as such core administrative functions as political, program, and resource management (Starling

1993); or as a complex sharing with local elected officials of the mission, policy, administration, and management roles of the council-manager form of government (Svara 1985), city managers engage in a variety of tasks related to the maintenance and development of their communities and local governments. Many of these tasks undoubtedly involve ethical considerations.

For this reason, managers were asked to indicate the extent to which the ICMA code in practice extended into and provided guidance for their responsibilities as professional managers. They were first asked the degree to which the code extended into the broad range of their responsibilities and then asked the degree to which it extended into specific areas of responsibility—namely, (1) relationships with the governing body, (2) relationships with those outside the municipal government, (3) relationships inside the municipal government, (4) policy and program development, and (5) day-to-day implementation of policy and programs.

Table 1 shows that a large majority of managers believe that the code extends into a broad range of their responsibilities. Eighty-seven percent indicated that it applies to either most or a high percentage of what they do.

Table 2 shows that managers also believe that the code provides guidance in the five specific areas of responsibility. The importance of the guidance appears to be greatest for relationships with the governing body, with 86 percent indicating that it is either very important or important. Relationships with outsiders and insiders are next in importance, with 79 percent and 73 percent, respectively, indicating that the code is either very important or important. Guidance in policy and program decision making and in day-to-day implementation appears to be last in importance, with 68 percent and 63 percent of the managers, respectively, indicating that the code is either very important or important.

Other areas reported by managers in which the code provides guidance generally fit into the above categories; however, some managers cited the code as important in personal affairs and as a reminder of professionalism. Although some mentioned common sense and personal ethics as being more important, the overall results suggest that managers believe that the code is embedded in much of what they do.

The ICMA code as a source of ethical guidance

Local government managers faced with ethical decisions may look to the ICMA code as a source of guidance. But despite its long history and prominent place among public professional codes of ethics, the code is only one of many potential sources of guidance for these managers. One purpose of this study was to deter-

Table 1. *Manager perceptions of applicability of ICMA Code of Ethics and Guidelines to manager responsibilities* (n = 255).

| | Applicability to how much of what I do | | | | |
	Most No. (%)	A high percentage No. (%)	About half No. (%)	A small percentage No. (%)	Very little No. (%)
Degree to which code/guidelines extend into a broad range of my responsibilities	84 (33)	138 (54)	26 (10)	4 (2)	3 (1)

Table 2. *Manager perceptions of importance of ICMA Code of Ethics and Guidelines in specific areas of responsibility* (n = 315).

Area of responsibility	Very important No. (%)	Important No. (%)	Somewhat important No. (%)	Of limited importance No. (%)	Not important No. (%)
Relationships with governing body	151 (48)	120 (38)	25 (8)	10 (3)	9 (3)
Relationships with those outside the local government	117 (37)	133 (42)	51 (16)	6 (2)	8 (3)
Relationships with those inside the local government	99 (31)	133 (42)	62 (20)	14 (4)	7 (2)
In policy and program development decision making	85 (27)	130 (41)	76 (24)	16 (5)	8 (3)
In policy and program implementation[a]	70 (22)	129 (41)	84 (27)	22 (7)	9 (3)

Note. Percentages may not add to 100 percent because of rounding.
[a] For this area only, the base was 314 rather than 315.

mine how the code is valued in comparison with other ethical influences.

Several scholars have suggested the likelihood of there being large numbers of such potential influences. Waldo (1980), for example, identified twelve ethical obligations for public servants: obligations to the Constitution; law; nation or country; democracy; organizational-bureaucratic norms; profession; family and friends; self; middle-range collectivities such as party, class, race, union, church, and interest groups; public interest or general welfare; humanity or the world; and religion or God.

The potential for competing claims among such a variety of ethical obligations is, of course, quite obvious. Lewis (1991) states explicitly that public managers have multiple roles—personal, humanity oriented, professional, agency, and jurisdictional—and that each involves more or less separate obligations. Cooper (1990) argues that those who work for the public have the dual obligation of both serving the public and being a member of the public—that is, a citizen. The potential for competing ethical claims in official versus citizen roles is also obvious.

For this study, managers were asked to compare and rank the code with six other potential claims or influences. While the categories of influences selected for comparative purposes included some of the ethical claims mentioned above, the focus was on sources of ethical support that might enable a manager to evaluate and/or resist multiple ethical claims more effectively. These sources were (1) laws and regulations related to ethics, (2) local community culture and/or local organizations that support ethics in government, (3) norms and values within municipal government supportive of ethics, (4) external professional peers such as other municipal managers, (5) personal values, and (6) university and college training. Specifically, managers were asked to rank the top four in order of importance.

Table 3 lists these sources of ethical guidance in the order in which they were ranked. Personal values is clearly first, with 64 percent ranking it first and only 7 percent failing to rank it in the top four. The ICMA code is a strong second, with more first-, second-, or third-place rankings than any other remaining sources of influence and with only 11 percent failing to rank it within the top four. The third most important influence indicated by the managers is law and regulations related to ethics, with more first-, second-, and third-place rankings than any of the remaining sources of influence and with only 23 percent failing to rank it among the top four.

Following this, there is a sharp drop to the fourth, or next most important source of ethical guidance: norms and values within municipal government supportive of ethics, with 49 per-

Table 3. *Manager rankings of ethical influences, including the ICMA Code of Ethics and Guidelines (n = 315).*

	Rankings				
Categories of influence	First No. (%)	Second No. (%)	Third No. (%)	Fourth No. (%)	Not in top four No. (%)
Personal values	203 (64)	48 (15)	30 (10)	13 (4)	21 (7)
ICMA Code of Ethics and Guidelines	50 (16)	121 (38)	79 (25)	31 (10)	34 (11)
Laws and regulations related to ethics	44 (14)	74 (23)	65 (21)	59 (19)	73 (23)
Norms and values within governments supportive of ethics	14 (4)	22 (7)	52 (16)	74 (24)	153 (49)
Local community culture and/or organizations supportive of ethics in government	10 (3)	17 (6)	39 (12)	48 (15)	201 (64)
External professional peers	6 (2)	22 (7)	39 (12)	59 (19)	189 (60)
University and college training	6 (2)	16 (5)	15 (5)	17 (5)	261 (83)

cent failing to rank it in the top four. Then there is another sharp drop to the fifth, sixth, and seventh most important sources: respectively, local community culture, external professional peers, and organizations supportive of ethics in government. In all three cases, fewer than half of the managers—only 40 percent for external peers and 36 percent for both local community culture and organizations supportive of ethics in government—ranked these sources among the top four. A clear last as a source of ethical guidance is university and college training, with 83 percent of managers failing to rank it in the top four sources of ethical guidance. Other sources of ethical guidance mentioned by managers but not in these categories include the Bible and religious values, the family, and military training.

These rankings suggest that the ICMA code is indeed an important source of ethical guidance for managers. It is not surprising, of course, that personal values ranked first, but the strong second ranking of the code—above laws and regulations relating to ethics—would appear to give the code an important role in the professional life of a municipal manager. The somewhat medium-level ranking of norms and values related to ethics in municipal governments suggests that such governments may generate internal ethical norms but that these norms are not particularly strong. The comparatively low ranking of the influence of managerial peers is puzzling because most peers are likely to be ICMA members. Perhaps the fact that peers may be available only occasionally in a group setting makes them less useful as sources of guidance for immediate and work-related ethical issues. The even lower ranking of the local culture and/or local organizations supportive of governmental ethics may suggest simply an absence or decline of "good government" or "reform" organizations that can serve as watchdogs on government. The very low ranking of university and college training as a source of ethical guidance suggests an absence of such courses in graduate public administration programs or, if present, their minimal impact.

Importance of individual tenets of the ICMA code

The ICMA Code of Ethics consists of twelve tenets that presumably reflect the core professional values of the local government management profession. That the individual tenets are taken seriously is evidenced by the fact that they have been revised several times since the initial adoption of the code in 1924. For example, Stillman (1974) states that the original code was designed to reflect the ideal of professionalism, a revision in 1938 reflected a commitment to scientific management, a 1952 change represented an attempt to find an ideological consensus on the policy and community leadership role of professional managers, and a change in 1969 reflected a move away from a commitment to the council-manager form and instead emphasized the dedication by managers to "effective and democratic local government." Then in 1976 the code was revised to make it gender neutral by dropping references to "he" and "himself" (ICMA 1988). Other revisions that have been made from 1986 through 1995 undoubtedly reflect ICMA's efforts to keep pace with changing professional philosophies and political environments. A question explored in this study was how managers viewed the individual tenets at this time.

Accordingly, managers were asked to indicate the importance of the twelve tenets of the code. Their responses indicated strong overall support. The results as presented in Table 4 show that from 79 percent to 97 percent of the managers indicated that each individual tenet of the code was either very important or important. Only a small percentage of managers viewed any of the tenets as being only somewhat important or less important.

However, if one uses the "very important" responses as comparative indicators of strong support for individual tenets, a rough ranking of importance of the tenets can be developed, as also shown in Table 4.[3] The range of strong support for individual tenets is from 30 percent to 86 percent. Two of the tenets, 5 and 9, are tied.

Table 4. *Manager perceptions of the importance of the tenets of the ICMA Code of Ethics and Guidelines^a (n = 315).*

Tenet	Very important No. (%)		Important No. (%)		Somewhat important No. (%)		Less important No. (%)		Ranking of tenets[b]
1. Be dedicated to the concepts of effective and democratic local government by responsible elected officials and believe that professional general management is essential to the achievement of this objective.	182	(58)	104	(33)	24	(8)	5	(2)	6
2. Affirm the dignity and worth of the services rendered by government and maintain a constructive, creative, and practical attitude toward local government affairs and a deep sense of social responsibility as a trusted public servant.	165	(52)	124	(39)	23	(7)	3	(1)	7
3. Be dedicated to the highest ideals of honor and integrity in all public and personal relationships in order that the member may merit the respect and confidence of the elected officials, of other officials and employees, and of the public.	265	(84)	40	(13)	9	(3)	1	(<1)	2
4. Recognize that the chief function of local government at all times is to serve the best interests of all the people.	185	(59)	102	(32)	26	(8)	2	(1)	5
5. Submit policy proposals to elected officials; provide them with facts and advice on matters of policy as a basis for making decisions and setting community goals; and uphold and implement local government policies adopted by elected officials.	162	(51)	122	(39)	27	(9)	4	(1)	8[c]
6. Recognize that elected representatives of the people are entitled to the credit for the establishment of local government policies; responsibility for policy execution rests with the members.	137	(43)	136	(43)	37	(12)	5	(2)	11

Tenet					Ranking[b]
7. Refrain from all political activities which undermine public confidence in professional administrators. Refrain from participation in the election of the members of the employing legislative body.	248 (79)	46 (15)	13 (4)	8 (2)	3
8. Make it a duty continually to improve the member's professional ability and to develop the competence of associates in the use of management techniques.[d]	95 (30)	153 (49)	53 (17)	13 (4)	12
9. Keep the community informed on local government affairs; encourage communication between the citizens and all local government officers; emphasize friendly and courteous service to the public; and seek to improve the quality and image of public service.	161 (51)	117 (37)	33 (10)	4 (1)	8[c]
10. Resist any encroachment on professional responsibilities, believing the member should be free to carry out official policies without interference, and handle each problem without discrimination on the basis of principle and justice.	138 (44)	132 (42)	37 (12)	8 (2)	10
11. Handle all matters of personnel on the basis of merit so that fairness and impartiality govern a member's decisions pertaining to appointments, pay adjustments, promotions, and discipline.	202 (64)	93 (30)	17 (5)	3 (1)	4
12. Seek no favor; believe that personal aggrandizement or profit secured by confidential information or by misuse of public time is dishonest.	271 (86)	36 (11)	5 (2)	3 (1)	1

Note. Percentages may not add to 100 percent because of rounding.
[a]Reproduced by permission of ICMA. See *Who's Who in Local Government Management* (Washington, D.C.: ICMA, 1993–94), 4–5.
[b]Ranking is based on the percentage of responses in the "very important" category.
[c]Tie ranking.
[d]For this tenet only, the base was 314 rather than 315.

Interpreting the results of such a ranking is difficult because several of the tenets appear to encompass more than one value or principle. In other words, what specifically were the managers evaluating? For example, tenet 2 may have three principles: (1) "affirm the dignity and worth of the services rendered by government"; (2) "maintain a constructive, creative, and practical attitude toward local government affairs"; and (3) "maintain . . . a deep sense of social responsibility as a trusted public servant." Tenet 9 would also appear to have at least four principles: (1) "keep the community informed on local government affairs," (2) encourage communication between the citizens and all local government officers," (3) "emphasize friendly and courteous service to the public," and (4) "seek to improve the quality and image of public service." A reading of tenets 1, 5, 6, 8, and 10 suggests that these also have more than one value or principle.

Nevertheless, for the purpose of interpreting the rankings, the tenets were placed in categories that seemed to suggest primary values or principles. The categories and the respective tenets and their rankings are as follows:

1. Professional integrity
   - Tenet 12, which admonishes members to seek no favor (rank 1)
   - Tenet 3, which emphasizes honor and integrity (rank 2)
2. Restrictions on political role
   - Tenet 7, which discourages nonparticipation in elections of the legislative body and in partisan activities, which would impair professional performance (rank 3)
3. The merit principle
   - Tenet 11, which urges that personnel decisions be based on merit (rank 4)
4. Dedication to democracy, the public interest, and government service
   - Tenet 4, which indicates that the function of government is to serve the best interests of the people (rank 5)
   - Tenet 1, which urges dedication to effective and democratic local government (rank 6)
   - Tenet 2, which affirms the dignity and worth of government services (rank 7)
5. Managerial role
   - Tenet 5, which instructs members to submit policy proposals to elected officials and to implement their policies (rank 8, tied)
   - Tenet 9, which instructs members to keep the community informed and to improve the quality and image of the public service (rank 8, tied)

- Tenet 10, which urges resistance to encroachment on professional responsibilities (rank 10)
6. Primacy of the legislative body
   - Tenet 6, which states that elected representatives of the people are entitled to the credit for local government policies (rank 11)
7. Professional development
   - Tenet 8, which urges continuous development of members and their associates (rank 12)

If such categories generally capture the values or principles underlying the respective tenets, one can argue that the ranking represents a rough ordering of professional values or principles of managers as represented in the ICMA code. Quite clearly, professional integrity is first. Perhaps this is the starting point for the role of the professional manager. Second in importance are restrictions on the manager's political role. Some managers may chafe under this restriction, but for most this clearly remains an important and perhaps essential operating value for the profession.

Third is the premise of merit in personnel decisions—a centerpiece ideal of governmental reform since the last century and one that managers appear to support strongly. Dedication to democracy, the public interest, and government service is fourth. While the tenets associated with this category might be regarded as the most fundamental in the code, managers may believe that professional integrity, restrictions on their political role, and the merit principle are more salient in their daily operating activities.

Managerial role, as defined by tenets that prescribe what managers are expected to do on an ongoing basis, is fifth. For some, this comparatively low ranking of managerial duties may seem surprising for professional managers. However, the ranking suggests that managers may regard these duties, while important, as the means rather than the ends or purposes of their governmental roles.

Sixth is the primacy of the legislative body. This ranking may also be surprising, given the formal subordination of managers to their legislative bodies and their commitment to democracy. It may be that tenet 6 simply does not indicate this as forcefully as it might; that is, commitment to democracy and giving credit for municipal policies are not the same thing.

The seventh and last-place ranking of the value of professional development may represent the ambiguity that some managers see when considering tenet 8 as an ethical idea in the same sense as other tenets of the code. While managers clearly support professional development, they may consider it to be out-side the purview of ethics.

Impact of the ICMA code

Managers were also asked to evaluate the overall impact of the code by assessing (1) its influence as either primarily *symbolic* in setting the tone for their professional roles or *substantive* in providing real direction for their behavior; and (2) its importance in defining their roles as professional municipal managers. The responses set forth in Table 5 indicate that 53 percent of manag-ers see the code as more substantive than symbolic; those in Table 6 indicate that a very large majority, 84 percent, see the code as very important in defining their roles as professional municipal managers.

Conclusions

The skepticism of scholars about codes of ethics seems not to be shared by ICMA members when they are assessing the impor-tance of their own code. The fact that 84 percent see the code as very important in defining their professional roles, that 87 per-cent report that it applies to most or to a high percentage of what they do, that it ranked below only personal values (and higher than laws and regulations related to ethics) as a source of ethical guidance, and that 53 percent see it as more substan-tive than symbolic is ample evidence of this. Clearly, ICMA mem-bers support the code and believe it is important in their professional roles.

A determination of the code's operational impact, however, requires additional empirical study. This is particularly the case for the policy and moral leadership roles of professional local government managers. For example, a recent study of the Inter-national Institute of Municipal Clerks indicated that 70 percent of those surveyed agree that their professional code of ethics is helpful when tough decisions have to be made (Bruce 1996). Stud-ies could be made to determine the impact of the ICMA code on such "tough" policy decisions by city managers. Another study focusing on the comparative ethics policies and practices in cit-ies and private corporations indicated that cities are less likely to codify ethical values and standards of conduct but more likely to implement such goals through training. The same study re-ported that the ethics management of cities is "(a) based on moral examples and leadership by senior managers which is comple-mented by (b) rules and regulations regarding specific problems such as financial disclosure and the protection of whistle blow-ing" (Berman, West, and Cava 1994, p. 198). If this is true, pro-fessional codes of ethics should be important as sources of values

Table 5. *Manager perceptions of the nature of the ICMA Code of Ethics and Guidelines (n = 312).*

	Mostly symbolic No. (%)	More symbolic than substantive No. (%)	About equally symbolic and substantive No. (%)	More substantive than symbolic No. (%)	Mostly substantive No. (%)
Extent to which the code is perceived as primarily symbolic in setting the tone of one's professional role or substantive in providing real direction for behavior	13 (4)	34 (11)	98 (31)	122 (39)	45 (14)

Note. Percentages do not add to 100 percent because of rounding.

Table 6 *Manager perceptions of the importance of the ICMA Code of Ethics and Guidelines (n = 315).*

	Very important No. (%)	Important No. (%)	Somewhat important No. (%)	Of limited importance No. (%)	Not important No. (%)
Extent of importance of the code, whether symbolic, substantive, or both, in defining the professional role of the local government manager	265 (84)	40 (13)	9 (3)	1 (<1)	– (–)

and standards for cities in general and for city managers in their role as moral leaders in particular. Studies could be undertaken to test this as well.

Policy studies could also be undertaken to determine how city managers assess the impact of individual tenets of the code in their decision making. How, for example, does a city manager operationalize the admonitions of tenet 2 to "maintain . . . a deep sense of social responsibility as a trusted public servant" when proposing a new policy for his or her community? Specifically, what do city managers believe this requires of them in policy deliberations? The same question could be raised in the case of tenet 4, which indicates that "the chief function of local government at all times is to serve the best interests of all the people." The guidelines that accompany the tenets generally deal with behavioral matters, such as length of service, restrictions on political activity, receipt of gifts, and private employment (ICMA 1993). Thus, case studies of policy development, policy negotiations, and policy implementation might be useful to determine how the code is involved in policy issues.

Another potential area for empirical study flows from the results of the managers' assessments of individual tenets. While the managers consider all the tenets important, some tenets appear to be more important than others. The rough ordering of the tenets reported here may have no practical implications for most day-to-day decisions, but the broad language of some of the tenets—for example, to "serve the best interests of all the people"—suggests a broad social responsibility that could involve a conflict with other tenets that may restrict behavior, such as that of the manager in the political arena. Lewis's (1991) conceptualization of multiple roles with competing ethical obligations may be relevant here. Additional studies that confirm a ranking of the tenets would lead to a greater understanding of tensions that the code might create for managers.

Finally, studies might be undertaken to determine why there appear to be so few sources of ethical guidance and support for city managers beyond their personal values, the ICMA Code of Ethics, and related laws. Why, for example, are there not support groups related to ethics within the community? What about other professionals within local governments, such as lawyers, engineers, finance officers, etc.? Why do city managers not rank peers more highly in providing guidance for ethics? Given the large range of potential ethical claims on a city manager (Cooper 1990, Lewis 1991, Waldo 1980), how does the code really provide guidance for the managers in their professional roles? These and other questions need to be explored if we are to better understand the role of the code and the ethical climate in which city managers operate.

Overall, the results of this survey suggest that the ICMA Code of Ethics and Guidelines as well as other codes warrant additional study. Only through studies designed to identify the impact of such codes can a determination be made whether the skepticism of the academic community or the perceptions of the city managers about the importance of their codes best reflect the realities of the individual code in question.

Notes

1. Several people provided valuable assistance for this study. These were (1) longtime ICMA members and municipal and county managers Eric Anderson, Des Moines, IA; Thomas DeGiulio, Munster, IN; Barry Evans, Escambria County, FL; Albert Ilg, Windsor, CT; and John Weichsel, Southington, CT; (2) Robert Andree, Indiana University Northwest; (3) Margaret Wheeler, formerly of Indiana University Northwest; and (4) Mary Grover, former ethics advisor for ICMA, and Catherine Tuck Parrish, current ICMA ethics advisor.

2. See Earl Babbie, *Survey Research Methods,* 2nd ed. (Belmont, CA: Wadsworth Publishing Company, 1990), for a discussion of sample sizes and confidence levels.

3. A combination of the "very important" and "important" rankings produces nearly the same result except that tenets 3 and 12 are tied for first; tenets 7 and 11 are tied for third; tenets 1, 2, and 4 are tied for fifth; and tenets 6 and 10 are tied for tenth.

References

Berman, E., West, J., and Cava, A. (1994). "Ethics Management in Municipal Governments and Large Firms: Explaining Similarities and Differences." *Administration and Society* 26:185–203.

Bowman, J.S. (1990). "Ethics in Government: A National Survey of Public Administration." *Public Administration Review* 50:345–353.

Bruce, W. (1996). "Codes of Ethics and Codes of Conduct: Perceived Contribution to the Practice of Ethics in Local Government." In J. Bowman (ed.), *Public Integrity Annual* (pp. 23–30). Lexington, KY: Council of State Governments.

Chandler, R.C. (1989). "A Guide to Ethics for Public Servants." In J.L. Perry (ed.), *Handbook of Public Administration* (pp. 602–618). San Francisco: Jossey-Bass.

Cooper, T. (1990). *The Responsible Administrator.* San Francisco: Jossey-Bass.

Denhardt, K.G. (1988). *The Ethics of the Public Service.* New York: Greenwood Press.

Gortner, H. (1991). *Ethics for Public Managers.* New York: Praeger Publishers.

Gulick, L. (1937). "Notes on the Theory of Organization." In L. Gulick and L. Urwick (eds.), *Papers on the Science of Administration.* New York: Institute of Public Administration.

International City/County Management Association (ICMA) (1988). File notes chronicling revisions in the Code of Ethics from 1924 to 1976, based on a conversation with Mary Grover, former ethics advisor for ICMA. Washington, DC: Author.

_____. (1993). *Who's Who in Local Government Management 1993–94.* Washington, DC: Author.

Lewis, C. (1991). *The Ethics Challenge in Public Service.* San Francisco: Jossey-Bass.

Plant, J. (1994). "Codes of Ethics." In T. Cooper (ed.), *Handbook of Administrative Ethics* (pp. 221–241). New York: Marcel Dekker.

Pugh, D. (1991). "The Origins of Ethical Frameworks in Public Administration." In J.S. Bowman (ed.), *Ethical Frontiers in Public Management* (pp. 9–33). San Francisco: Jossey-Bass.

Rohr, J.A. (1978). *Ethics for Bureaucrats*. New York: Marcel Dekker.

_____. (1990). "Ethics in Public Administration: A State of the Discipline Report." In N.B. Lynn and A. Wildavsky (eds.), *Public Administration: The State of the Discipline* (pp. 97–123). Chatham, NJ: Chatham House.

Starling, G. (1993). *Managing the Public Sector*, 4th ed. Belmont, CA: Wadsworth.

Stillman, R.J. (1974). *The Rise of the City Manager*. Albuquerque: University of New Mexico Press.

Svara, J.B. (1985). "Dichotomy and Duality: Reconceptionalizing the Relationship between Policy and Administration in Council-Manager Cities." *Public Administration Review* 45:221–232.

Waldo, D. (1980). *The Enterprise of Public Administration: A Summary View*. Novato, CA: Chandler and Sharp.

Enforcing Administrative Ethics

—————— Mark W. Huddleston and Joseph C. Sands

Until quite recently, most academic work on administrative ethics has been rather densely scholastic, marked, as John Rohr has noted, by sweeping philosophical speculation and abstract moral reasoning.[1] Practitioners brave enough—or desperate enough—to seek to penetrate the debate have needed either special dictionaries close at hand or a serious background in philosophy to decipher multitudinous references to deontology, consequentialism, act-utilitarianism, and similar ideas. More to the point, having decoded the language, a public manager will have found the corpus of work on ethics long on general analysis and short on specific remedies. In one sense, this is not surprising. Scholarly articles explaining in clear terms how to run an ethical organization have been scarce for much the same reason that we are not overrun with credible pieces on, say, preventing war or ensuring ethnic harmony: we simply do not know the answers. In fact, we are not even sure of the questions. Is unethical behavior a matter of character? A product of the organization? A reflection of the general culture? We have been contesting these points at least since the time of Plato.

Having said this, our world requires action, even in the face of incomplete information. Wars are to be avoided, communal harmony sought, and organizational morality pursued. The aim in this article is to contribute in a small way toward the last of these ventures by providing a catalogue of methods that public sector organizations have used to enforce ethical behavior by their employees.

From *The Annals of the American Academy of Political and Social Science (AAPSS* 537 (January 1995):139–149. Copyright © 1995 by Sage Publications, Inc. Reprinted with permission of Sage Publications, Inc.

Before we begin, however, several important caveats need to be set out. First, we make no claim that enforcement mechanisms that worked, or seemed to work, in one context will work in another—or, alternatively, that mechanisms that failed in one setting will necessarily fail in all. Any such claims would constitute, in effect, a theory of ethics enforcement, which, given the state of development of this field, would be premature at best. Our aim, rather, is simply to report and catalogue: What are the varieties of enforcement mechanisms that have been used? What effects were they seen to have had in their particular circumstances? At best, answers to these questions will provide grounds for hypotheses that can be explored further.

Second, we sidestep the often passionate arguments about the ultimate causes—and thus cures—of unethical behavior by taking a decidedly catholic approach. Some of the remedies we survey are rooted in the belief that morality is a function of individual integrity. Others emphasize the role of organization or society at large. Although this debate is certainly interesting— and it may even contain important guides for policy should it ever be resolved—to enter into it here, so long and involved is it, would mean never getting on to the main point.

Finally, and relatedly, our definition of ethics is fairly narrow, though reasonably casual. Public service ethics, for us, are primarily a matter of rectitude: an ethical public servant is an honest public servant, someone who does not abuse his or her office by seeking private gain at public expense. Our focus, that is to say, is mainly on mechanisms that guard against behavior that deviates from the law or agency procedures, not on attempts to hold administrators to transcendent standards of morality or social justice. Does this mean that we endorse the sort of stereotypical rule-abiding behavior that allows an official to ignore (or even to inflict) human suffering as long as his or her action (or inaction) is legal? Of course not. It is to say, though, that such behavior is not the problem with which we are primarily concerned in this piece. The cost of our approach is a tacit acceptance of the legitimacy of existing institutions. The benefit is saying something of immediate potential use to public officials and to the public.

We discuss three principal categories of enforcement mechanisms: first, codes of ethics, including laws, professional rules, and whistle-blower statutes; second, ethics police, or agencies or officials with specific responsibilities to oversee ethical standards; and, third, cultural strategies, efforts to forge organizational climates conducive to ethical behavior. Although we treat each category discretely, they are in practice often intertwined. Organizations or jurisdictions subject to whistle-blower laws, for instance, likely will have an ethics board or an inspector general somewhere in the environment.

Codes of ethics

Codes of ethics—statements of prohibited behavior and injunctions to employees to uphold high moral standards—are probably the most widely used enforcement mechanism, a fact that reflects their relatively low cost, at least when used alone. Virtually all units of government have enacted some sort of code, either on a jurisdiction-wide basis or organization by organization. Similarly, all of the leading professional organizations of public administrators—including the American Society for Public Administration (ASPA), the International City/County Management Association (ICMA), and the International Association of Chiefs of Police—have published codes of ethics.

Not surprisingly, such popularity entails considerable diversity. Codes vary tremendously, in fact, along three main dimensions: systematization, generality, and enforceability. Some codes are highly systematic. They draw together in one place all statutes, regulations, and statements that bear on bribery, conflict of interest, nepotism, competitive bidding, and so forth. Other jurisdictions that profess to have codes have a jumble of discrete legal and administrative instruments, with little if any overarching structure that relates one to another.[2]

Similarly, some codes are framed in very general terms. ASPA's principles, for instance, state that "conflict of interest, bribes, gifts, or favors which subordinate public positions to private gains are unacceptable."[3] By the same token, ICMA's code provides some fairly specific guidelines for members seeking to negotiate the shoals of conflict-of-interest dilemmas. Managers are advised, for example, that while they may not endorse products by allowing their photographs or quotations to be used in commercial advertising, they may lend their name, without compensation, to noncommercial endeavors, such as books or educational services, undertaken by nonprofit groups.[4]

Finally, codes of ethics vary with respect to the nature of the sanctions that violations carry. At one extreme are codes backed by serious civil or criminal penalties; these obviously are limited to governmental entities, though not all the codes of such entities by any means carry such serious penalties. At the other end of the spectrum are codes that are simply exhortations to be good.

While it is difficult to generalize about codes of ethics given this diversity, some observations can be hazarded. First, we know that codes have become increasingly popular in the past 25 years or so. Lewis notes that only 4 state codes predate 1973, while 19 were adopted in the period 1973–79, and 5 more from 1980 to

1988.[5] In 1989 alone there were more than sixty legislative and judicial actions bearing on ethics in 31 states.[6] The mid-1970s and beyond were particularly fecund years for ethics activities because of heightened sensitivity to these issues in the wake of the Watergate scandal.[7]

A second set of observations has to do with the content of these codes. Most codes focus predominantly on conflict of interest and financial disclosure. This is as true at the federal level as it is for state and local government. This tendency presumably reflects the wide social consensus that stealing and other forms of outright dishonesty are wrong, whereas there is less agreement about more esoteric ethical questions, such as the role of conscience, injunctions to promote the public interest, and so forth. Moreover, many codes maintain an "appearance of impropriety" standard, though it is not clear that this is a legally enforceable standard.[8] Codes also include provisions concerning outside incomes and restrictions on postemployment opportunities. By 1990, 23 states possessed such restrictions.[9] Another standard practice among the states—and now for certain federal officials—is the prohibition against lobbying former agencies on matters in which the official or employee was involved. Other common provisions place permanent bans on disclosure of "privileged information" and control the use of state resources for private purposes.[10]

It is interesting and important to note as a third point that ethics codes have grown in popularity despite widespread doubts about their efficacy. In his survey of 750 randomly selected ASPA members, for instance, James Bowman found that almost no one agreed with the assertion that "there is no real need for codes of ethics in work organizations." At the same time, he found that only 40 percent of those surveyed believed that the performance of agencies with codes differed from those without codes.[11]

What is the reason for this disjuncture? Why do codes of ethics so often meet "cynicism and derision," as John Rohr has put it, even while they are being adopted at a brisk pace?[12] To begin with, codes are drafted by legislators who feel pressed, often by still-fresh newspaper headlines, to do something, quickly, about ethics in government. The newly minted standards are then delivered to agencies for enforcement with little, if any, prior input, or consideration for enforceability. Indeed, the codes are often viewed by those they are meant to affect as punitive and unnecessarily restrictive, betraying a lack of trust and respect for public administrators.[13] This is particularly the case in the area of financial disclosure, where the public's right to know conflicts with the individual's right to privacy. Disclosure breaks down barriers between personal and public interests. Family and friendships become subject to public scrutiny.[14] An open invitation is given to media attention. Financial disclosure is seldom seen in a positive light by those who are required to comply.

Cynicism seems also to flow from codes that are clearly unenforceable, either because the standards are stated so vaguely or because no enforcement mechanism other than the code itself is in place. Codes backed by independent boards or commissions seem to take an active role in enforcement, and those clearly embraced by top agency management and embedded in an ethical organizational culture are more likely to win respect.[15] Indeed, continual reinforcement by management is essential if written codes are to contribute to ethical decision making, a point we explore below.[16] Codes that address specific standards of behavior for a particular agency are also more helpful. Agencies should "identify idiosyncratic practices and situations which require specialized ethical standards."[17] This is particularly true with respect to compliance and enforcement procedures. Codes may be more easily appropriated when they move beyond lists of dos and don'ts, and take on a positive tone of affirming ethical values.

Ethics police: Inspectors, boards, and ombudsmen

As we noted above, many agencies and jurisdictions support their codes of ethics with officers and organizations given the specific assignment of enforcing ethical guidelines. As with the codes themselves, organizational patterns and task assignments vary. In some cases, the enforcement agencies are weak and are given little to do other than collect and collate disclosure forms. At the other extreme are organizations with serious investigative powers and the ability to levy sanctions and initiate civil and criminal proceedings in court.[18]

Inspectors general (IGs) are independent officers attached to federal agencies. Their responsibilities include supervising audits, promoting economy and efficiency, rooting out fraud and abuse, and regularly informing Congress and the agency head of their activities.[19] Currently, there are some 27 presidential IGs—appointed by the president and confirmed by the Senate. They are assigned to all cabinet departments and other large agencies, including the Central Intelligence Agency, the General Services Administration, the Environmental Protection Agency, the Small Business Administration, the National Aeronautics and Space Administration, and the Community Services Administration. More than 30 additional nonpresidential IGs—appointed by the agency head and not subject to Senate confirmation—are assigned to smaller agencies.[20] The largest number of presidentially appointed IGs were products of the 1978 Inspector General Act, although the first IG position had been created for the Department of Health, Education and Welfare two years earlier, in 1976; the nonpresidential IGs were established pursuant to Public Law 100-504 in 1988.

Paul Light's analysis, particularly his review of the IG's role in the Department of Housing and Urban Development scandals during the mid-1980s, suggests that while the IG system is basically sound, it needs some adjustment. As matters now stand, says Light, IGs are too dependent on senior department chiefs to act on their recommendations. Either the "strong-right-arm-of-the-Secretary" model adopted in 1978, whereby the IG is construed, in effect, as a central part of the department's management team, needs to be modified to make the IG more of a "lone wolf," or better lines of direct communication need to be established between the IGs, on the one hand, and Congress and the Office of Management and Budget, on the other. Neither of these solutions, of course, will appeal to departmental administrators, though Light suggests that perhaps they should. In an age when the numbers of political appointees are growing just as their average tenure is shrinking, an independent, long-serving IG could represent a valuable reservoir of institutional memory and expertise upon which a secretary could draw.[21]

In addition to IGs at the federal level, over 36 states have boards, commissions, or offices dedicated to overseeing ethics regulations.[22] Lewis found that most of these were able to conduct investigations at their own instigation; most, too, were responsible for issuing advisory opinions, rulings, and clarifying statements.[23] How effective any of them have been, though, is difficult to judge. We know, for instance, that 10 times as many state, city, and county officials are convicted on federal corruption charges today as were convicted twenty years ago.[24] But what does this mean? Have we as a society become increasingly corrupt? Or are we just doing a better job, thanks to the new enforcement machinery, at catching the few who are? The answers are not apparent.

The office of ombudsman may also, in some circumstances, act as an enforcer of administrative ethics. Many such offices were created in the 1960s and 1970s in the hope that what had been a helpful experience in Scandinavian countries could be translated into practice in the United States.[25] The ombudsman is meant to facilitate complaints against government. The existence of this office is "an acknowledgement of the practical barriers to direct, individual participation in the complaint-resolution aspect of the administrative process."[26] Most ombudsmen perform the role of impartial investigator of complaints filed by those who are traditionally underrepresented. In this respect, the office exists as "a symbol of government's concern for citizens."[27]

In the United States, then, this office not only acts as a bureaucratic watchdog, but it also tries to represent individual citizens and make bureaucracy more approachable. This characteristic is also a political obstacle to creating more such offices and maintaining those that already exist. As Jonathan West points out, "Most legislators feel that they are already performing the ombudsman function and fear the loss of electoral benefits if they should give it up."[28]

In addition to usurping an existing role in U.S. politics, the office of ombudsman also faces other criticisms. Many offices are little known and underutilized. They deal with minor concerns, within fragmented or limited jurisdictions, and exert too little influence. They also share the risk of becoming too bureaucratic and of overlapping with other existing grievance mechanisms.[29] The office has had to struggle, sometimes unsuccessfully, to survive the threats against it due to shrinking government budgets.

At the same time, it may be premature to give up on the usefulness of the ombudsman. As bureaucracies grow larger and stronger, the potential for ethics violations—abuse of citizens in particular—grows as well. The ombudsman offers an additional external check to accompany and buttress routine organizational controls, thus enhancing accountability and safeguarding citizen rights.[30]

Like ombudsmen, special investigating commissions are designed to achieve their effects by working outside established organizational routines, though they are not usually intended to be permanent features of the administrative landscape. A recent example is the Mollen Commission, appointed by former New York City mayor David Dinkins in 1992 to investigate corruption in the New York Police Department, an organization that seems to suffer from a "cyclical epidemic . . . every twenty years."[31] The investigation of misdeeds by individual officers led this time to a focus not on systematic corruption but on the department's management practices. Although the investigation disclosed tales of "an underworld where police officers beat the innocent, traffic in drugs, and protect the criminal,"[32] the public hearings directed the spotlight on a "police culture that deters officers from reporting dishonest or abusive acts by colleagues."[33]

Why was there so much "institutional resistance" to pursuing allegations against suspected officers?[34] One officer stressed the lack of attention given to "integrity training" at the Police Academy.[35] He learned on the job that a "good cop" was one who did not "rat" on another.[36] Another "testified that desk officers and supervisors typically harassed people who filed civilian complaints for [police] misconduct and often tore up their reports after those complaining left the station house."[37]

The middle-level managers feel like scapegoats. In past corruption scandals, the top officials at police headquarters were never implicated, while dozens of supervisors were transferred or demoted. It was hoped that "in the future supervisors would ferret out and eliminate corruption at the first hint of trouble, if only out of fear for their jobs."[38] Unfortunately, the threat of punishment seems to have backfired. It made many supervisors so fearful "that they became loathe to unearth corruption in the first place."[39] The prevailing attitude among them encouraged minimizing any signs of corruption that might unfavorably affect their careers.

Before the public hearings concluded, the police commissioner announced the formation of a "committee on police culture to develop programs to discourage corruption and improve integrity education."[40] Seeking further controls, the Mollen Commission's final report recommended the establishment of an independent commission "to investigate corruption and to insure office accountability in corruption cases."[41] The architects of this approach argue that in order for corruption to be controlled, two "unpalatable truths" must be admitted: the police cannot by themselves successfully fight corruption over an extended period of time; and no external agency can reduce police corruption unless both police management and culture are made to conform. The anticipated external agency would control corruption by fostering a "department wide focus on values, culture, systems, and operations."[42] Reliance upon outside support and accountability will, it is maintained, encourage police officers, at all levels, to overcome the "blue wall of reluctance."[43]

It is difficult to judge the efficacy of these various external enforcement mechanisms. In some ways, their strengths are also their weaknesses. To the extent that they are strong, independent, and given clear sets of rules to follow, they may, while deterring egregious forms of unethical behavior, create an "us-versus-them" mentality that shifts attention away from the need for building ethical organizational climates from within. At worst, such mechanisms can create an atmosphere of fear and anxiety counterproductive to achieving agency goals. In the final analysis, however, ethics police of one sort or another may be unavoidable given the apparent failure of internal processes alone to curb ethical abuses.

Organizational culture

The most desirable method of maintaining high ethical standards, most observers would agree, is to foster an organizational environment in which individuals choose to behave morally as a matter of course, without having to make conscious reference to codes, laws, inspectors general, and so forth. The ideal is to prevent ethical transgressions from ever occurring, rather than to punish them after the fact. Because administrative choices are made in a world of extraordinary complexity—Herbert Simon's "buzzing, blooming confusion"—"no code of conduct can foresee all the conflicts people will encounter."[44] Consequently, training for ethical awareness and action needs to be proactive. People need to be encouraged to think for themselves, developing in the organization a collective level of ethical awareness that complements any external controls over behavior.

Staff development, case study, and the deliberate use of supervisors as ethical mentors may all help to raise moral consciousness and provide guidance through the conflict of everyday decision making.[45] As Judith Truelson puts it, "Training packages [can] stimulate the moral imagination, promoting recognition of ethical issues, developing analytical skills, eliciting a sense of moral responsibility, and fostering ethical action."[46] High-reliability management, for example, depends explicitly upon managers "who set the decisional stage," thereby giving employees a common frame of reference in which to exercise individual judgment and responsibility.[47]

While it may not be easy, owing to the structure of modern organizations, to encourage administrators to accept moral responsibility for their actions, it is not, according to Dennis Thompson, theoretically impossible, as some have averred. "Neither an ethic of neutrality that would suppress independent moral judgment, nor an ethic of structure that would ignore individual moral agency in organization," the two most frequently cited reasons for the purported inconceivability of administrative ethics, bears close scrutiny.[48] The real problem, as David Rosenbloom reminds us, is more practical: what is ethical may not be efficient.[49] While we may well be able to create organizational environments in which administrators are inclined to ponder the moral dimensions of the choices that confront them, we cannot do so without cost to an agency's mission, narrowly construed. Once the ethics consultants have gone and the role-playing exercises have faded in memory, the work of the office has to proceed. Efficiency once again challenges the priority of ethics. How can organizational incentives be structured to accommodate ethics in the long term?

Various conventional management practices themselves reinforce and solidify conditions that thwart such long-term ethical considerations. Gerald Gabris agrees that for typical administrators, overcoming organizational obstacles can indeed be quite formidable. He looks to the organizational development paradigm with its stress on trust, human dignity, and excellence so as to find a more stable foundation upon which to build credible ethics.[50] Even though excellence is as elusive as it is abstract, Gabris points to the high success rates of organizational development in the public sector.

Conclusion

Myriad enforcement mechanisms—ranging from codes and laws, through external monitoring agencies, to organizational climates—have been devised to enforce ethical behavior in public administration. All of them have proved useful in some respects, even if only symbolically. None can be considered fully satisfactory, however, at least not in the sense that it alone can be expected to ensure organizational morality. Adherence to norms of administrative ethics, like adherence to society's norms more generally, is a product of many influences: fear, individual inclination, social pressure, and so on. Until we find the key to utopia, a vigilant constabulary will be as necessary to social order as individual conscience and a clear statement of the law. Thus it is with the good order of the organization. Codes of ethics need to work hand in hand with proactive managerial strategies, which in turn need to be bolstered by external checks on behavior.

The analogy between administrative ethics and society's laws in general is instructive in another respect as well. In neither case will adherence to the rules be complete, no matter the lengths to which we are willing to go. Organizations and human beings are, by nature, imperfect. Attempts to make them what they are not—attempts, that is, to create a perfectly moral organization—are bound to be frustrated and frustrating. Such efforts are likely to be counterproductive to boot, for they will inevitably call forth increasingly draconian measures of control that will both interfere with the functioning of the organization and undermine the notion of volition from which the concept of ethics derives its meaning.

Notes

1. John A. Rohr, "Foreword," in *Ethics and Public Administration,* ed. H. George Frederickson (Armonk, NY: M.E. Sharpe, 1993).
2. See Carol W. Lewis, "Ethics Codes and Ethics Agencies: Current Practices and Emerging Trends," in *Ethics and Public Administration,* ed. Frederickson, 136–157.
3. Number Six of the "Principles for the American Society for Public Ad-

ministration," reprinted in *Applying Professional Standards & Ethics in the Eighties: A Workbook and Study Guide for Public Administrators,* ed. Herman Mertins Jr. and Patrick J. Hennigan (Washington, DC: American Society for Public Administration, 1982).
4. "ICMA Code of Ethics with Guidelines," reprinted in *Essentials of Government Ethics,* ed. Peter

Madsen and Jay M. Shafritz (New York: Meridian 1992), 388.
5. Lewis, "Ethics Codes," 139.
6. Ibid.
7. See Frederick C. Mosher et al., *Watergate: Implications for Responsible Government* (Washington, DC: National Academy of Public Administration, 1974).
8. Lewis, "Ethics Codes," 141.
9. Ibid.
10. Ibid. See also Steven W. Hays and Richard R. Gleissner, "Codes of Ethics in State Government," *Public Personnel Management* 10 (1981).
11. James S. Bowman, "Ethics in Government: A National Survey of Public Administrators," *Public Administration Review* 50 (May/June 1990):345–353.
12. John Rohr, "The Problem of Professional Ethics," *Bureaucrat* (Summer 1982):47.
13. J. Patrick Dobel, "The Realpolitik of Ethics Codes: An Implementation Approach to Public Ethics," in *Ethics and Public Administration,* ed. Frederickson, 160.
14. Philip H. Jos, Mark E. Tompkins, and Steven W. Hays, "In Praise of Difficult People: A Portrait of the Committed Whistleblower," *Public Administration Review,* 49 (November/December 1989):554.
15. See Bowman, "Ethics in Government."
16. M. Cash Matthews, *Strategic Intervention in Organizations* (Beverly Hills, CA: Sage, 1988), 135.
17. Hays and Gleissner, "Codes of Ethics in State Government," 52.
18. For instance, the ethics legislation enacted by the city of Los Angeles, considered among the strongest and most comprehensive in the country, provides that the ethics commission can require the appointment of a special prosecutor in cases where it determines that the city attorney has a conflict of interest. See Lewis, "Ethics Codes," 151.
19. This section is based primarily on Paul C. Light, "Federal Ethics Controls: The Role of Inspectors General," in *Ethics and Public Administration,* ed. Frederickson, 100–120.
20. For a complete list of all IGs and their agencies, see ibid., 104.
21. History, alas, suggests that political executives seldom see the wisdom of relying on the independent advice of career executives until it is too late in their tenure to have full effect. See Mark W. Huddleston and William W. Boyer, *Federal Career Executives: The Quest for a Higher Civil Service* (Pittsburgh: University of Pittsburgh Press, forthcoming).
22. Lewis, "Ethics Codes," 138.
23. Ibid., 139.
24. Elder Witt, "Is Government Full of Crooks or Are We Just Better at Finding Them," *Governing* (September 1989):33.
25. See Jonathan P. West, "The Role of the Ombudsman in Resolving Conflicts," in *Ethics, Government and Public Policy,* ed. James S. Bowman and Frederick A. Elliston (Westport, CT: Greenwood Press, 1988), 171–172.
26. Larry B. Hill, "The Citizen Participation-Representation Roles of American Ombudsmen," *Administration and Society* 1 (February 1982):427.
27. Ibid., 428–429.
28. West, "Role of the Ombudsman," 177.
29. Ibid., 179–180.
30. Ibid., 193.
31. Selwyn Raab, "Police Corruption Panel Goes Public This Week," *New York Times,* 26 September 1993.
32. Alison Mitchell, "Police Hearings' Effects Defy the Usual Wisdom," *New York Times,* 3 October 1993.
33. Selwyn Raab, "Similarities in Inquiries into Crimes by Officers," *New York Times,* 3 October 1993.
34. Unidentified Mollen Commission staff member, quoted in Selwyn Raab, "Ex-Rogue Officer Tells Panel of Police Graft in New York," *New York Times,* 28 September 1993.
35. Raab, "Ex-Rogue Officer."
36. Michael Dowd, quoted in Raab, "Ex-Rogue Officer."
37. Selwyn Raab, "Detailing Burglars in Blue: Violent Search for Booty,"

New York Times, 30 September 1993.

38. Craig Wolff, "Fighting Corruption," *New York Times,* 4 October 1993.

39. Ibid.

40. Selwyn Raab, "Head of New York Police Offers Compromise on Outside Monitor," *New York Times,* 7 October 1993.

41. Clifford Krauss, "2-Year Corruption Inquiry Finds a 'Willful Blindness' in New York's Police Dept.," *New York Times,* 7 July 1994.

42. Mark H. Moore and David M. Kennedy, "N.Y.P.D. Clean," *New York Times,* 25 January 1994.

43. James Dowd, quoted in Steven Lee Myers, "Officers Describe Police Watchdog as Ineffectual," *New York Times,* 2 October 1993.

44. Mary E. Guy, "Using High Reliability Management to Promote Ethical Decision Making," in *Ethical Frontiers in Public Management,* ed. James S. Bowman (San Francisco: Jossey-Bass, 1991), 201.

45. See Thomas R. Piper, Mary C. Gentle, and Sharon Daloz Parks, *Can Ethics Be Taught?* (Boston: Harvard Business School, 1993).

46. Judith A. Truelson, "New Strategies for Institutional Controls," in *Ethical Frontiers,* ed. Bowman, 233.

47. Guy, "High Reliability Management," 185–204.

48. Dennis F. Thompson, "The Possibility of Administrative Ethics," *Public Administration Review* 45 (September/October 1985):561.

49. David H. Rosenbloom, "The Constitution as a Basis for Public Administrative Ethics," in *Essentials of Government Ethics,* ed. Madsen and Shafritz, 48–64.

50. Gerald T. Gabris, "Beyond Conventional Management Practices: Shifting Organizational Values," in *Ethical Frontiers,* ed. Bowman, 205–224.

PART 3

The Ethical Frontiers

The Professional Edge

———————————————— James S. Bowman

Ever since George Washington required "fitness of character" for appointment to federal service, competence in public employment has been regarded as requiring more than mere technical skill. Instead, complete competence has been defined to include personal integrity. As symbolized by the oath of office, this "professional edge"—excellence in ethical bearing as well as in technical ability—has been a hallmark of American government.

Yet this noble ideal has been eroded in the last quarter century. This article first briefly considers why this erosion has occurred and how ethical concern has nonetheless experienced something of a renaissance. It next examines why that rediscovery has not come to full flower and how it might be made to flourish. The analysis closes with a call for a renewal of the proud heritage of American public service as the new millennium approaches.

Merit, morality, and modernity

The passage of the 1883 Pendleton Act (which abolished the spoils system and established the merit system), the embrace of Woodrow Wilson's "politics/administration dichotomy," and the subsequent adoption of scientific management firmly established a nonpartisan civil service based on merit. Public servants were responsible for the execution of policy and were not expected to exercise discretion in decision making; ethics was a product of rules and regulations, not necessarily of professional judgment. Although World War II, Vietnam, and Watergate all called this view into question, the neutrality of the civil service remained a powerful force in government. Ethical concerns, while important, could be regarded as an administrative matter as virtuous conduct was to be achieved by procedural reforms in the merit system.

However, in the last generation, a time of rapid change, ethics has become a highly salient topic. There are at least four reasons for this development: the search for certainty, the sports mania, the democratic "guilt reflex," and the indispensability of quality.[1]

First, the "nervous nineties" have idealized the Eisenhower era, a period of social obligation, stable families, company loyalty, pride in work, and economic prosperity. In the face of substantial social flux, a return to a time of such certainty is alluring. For those less certain about the fundamental values of the 1950s, the same desire to identify "the good life" has led many to the realm of ethics.

Similarly, the wild popularity of sports is based on its easily observed, measured, and calculated achievements. In an environment of instant gratification, a spillover into everyday life is inevitable. Ethics, precisely because it seldom yields carefree answers, becomes an easy target for reform—and oversimplification. Thus, there are calls for public officials (referees) to establish a "level playing field" (clear boundaries and rules), hold hearings (replays and NCAA-style investigations), and pass laws (final scores) as if ethics in real life were as simple as athletic entertainment.

A third explanation for the current interest in ethics is the guilt reflex in democracy. The hypocrisy of a self-governing people denouncing their own government and seeking scapegoats for its problems is obvious. When their complicity and guilt are realized, citizens seem motivated to renew the foundations of trust in democracy—or to establish a regulatory framework that makes it unnecessary.

Finally, many leaders are beginning to understand the importance of managing ethical values as an essential part of organizational quality, productivity, and vitality. In an era of competitive public and private enterprises, an institution's capacity must be optimized. This can be accomplished through an empowered workforce that continually improves processes to better serve the customer. This is impossible, however, without a foundation of mutual trust and cooperation between leaders and followers. A quality organization is, perforce, an ethical one as the open communication, access to information, and data-based problem solving so necessary to customer service, process improvement, and employee teamwork make unethical behavior undesirable and unnecessary.

The right stuff

These four pressures—the quest for certainty, the sports craze, the guilt reflex, and the quality imperative—have, in turn, led to a number of attempts to address ethical issues. These attempts include a stress on basic decency, conflict-of-interest legislation, and efforts to learn from scandals.[2] Yet while each of these reactions may well be necessary, they are hardly sufficient if real progress is to be made.

First of all, facile appeals to do the "right thing" are of limited help in confronting genuine dilemmas when a decision must be made between two (or more) equally deserving choices or competing obligations. Second, conflict-of-interest legislation and employee conduct codes may also have some value but are often hopelessly legalistic, negative, and largely irrelevant to daily management. Third, although contemporary interest in ethics may be the result of exposés, a focus on drawing lessons from them has important drawbacks. Not only is it like driving a car by looking in the rearview mirror, but it also tends to reduce ethics to staying out of trouble. Further, it ignores the fact that scandals are often not a problem of the career civil service; indeed, Hitler's SS, Nixon's "plumbers," and Reagan's Iran-contra enterprise were created precisely because the bureaucracy could not be trusted by elected officials to do what it was told.

All three of these approaches to dealing with ethics reveal an incomplete understanding of professionalism. As noted at the outset, the classic definition of a professional emphasizes both technical and moral proficiency. Yet ethical competence is simply assumed by basic decency, seen as unnecessary in official regulations and regarded as irrelevant in titillating scandals. It is exactly their public acceptance of responsibility, however, that provides professionals with an edge that makes them distinctive from other workers and gives them the "right stuff." Thus, ethics is key to the identity and legitimacy of public service.[3] Like medicine, consummate professional competence is defined as much more than knowing specialized skills; rather, it requires the responsible exercise of discretion.

The centrality of ethics is undeniable as managerial decisions often test one's values when they affect people's lives, distribute resources, and require judgment in so doing. Such discretion demands decisions that are both technically and morally sound. Professional practice, therefore, requires that moral criteria be integrated into decision making, given that conflicts are inherent in decision making and there is no "one best way" to deal with ethical quandaries. Managers need not only the technical ability to analyze problems but also the capacity to grasp those problems in a manner consistent with professional principles of role responsibility and personal integrity. Ethics comes with the territory.

Public service magnifies these considerations in two ways. First, many government problems are not "tame" or technical ones that have straightforward solutions (e.g., how to build a highway); rather, they are "wicked" or political ones that have only imperfect, temporary solutions (e.g., where to build a highway).[4] The challenge is that officials must attempt to "correct" wicked problems in order to make them manageable. Second, whatever decisions are made come to be seen as "moral and absolute," as they publicly represent both the symbolic and real authoritative allocation of values in a society.

Stated differently, a concern for the "bottom line" of technical ability must be complemented, if not superseded, by the "top line" of ethical responsibility—the essence of the professional edge. The worst form of incompetence, then, isn't not knowing *how* to do something, but not knowing *why* it is to be done; an irresponsible manager is at least as dangerous as technically deficient one.

Conclusion

Few people would accept poor financial performance from an executive who explained that the corporation is a big place with a lot of people and that he really could not be expected to know what everyone was doing. It is precisely that kind of explanation, though, that is routinely accepted for poor ethical performance. Unless or until ethical responsibility is taken as seriously as financial responsibility, such claims will likely continue to be accepted as an administrative excuse instead of an admission of failure.

It is in government, however, that ethical standards are found to a degree unknown in most other professions. Achieving these standards—capitalizing on the professional edge—is both complex and simple in public management. It is hard because there is no agreed-upon way to detect and address the multitude of challenges that confront government, and yet it is easy because most public servants want to be ethical, to work in virtuous organizations, and to serve the greater good. Even those who are not so inclined still pay tribute to virtue as they invariably attempt to cast their actions in ethical terms.

In either case, how someone handles a moral dilemma is likely to be the only thing that anyone remembers about that person. Indeed, the only real credibility a public administrator has today is his or her integrity, given that management sticks are hard to use, carrots are trivial, and loyalty is denigrated by downsizing. As Socrates reminds us, "the greatest way to live is to be what we pretend to be." Even though it is invisible to the eye, it is easy to spot such a commitment—and even easier to spot its absence.

Notes

1. Adapted, in part, from Simon Longstaff, "What Is Ethics Education and Training?" in *Ethics for the Public Sector,* ed. Noel Preston (Sydney, Australia: Federation Press, 1994), 139–140. See also Michiko Kakutani, "The Sporting Life," *New York Times Sunday Magazine,* 31 August 1997, 24.

2. John Rohr, *Ethics for Bureaucrats* (New York: Marcel Dekker, 1989).

3. See James S. Bowman, "The Lost World of Public Administration Education: Rediscovering the Meaningful Professionalism," *Journal of Public Administration Education* (in press).

4. Michael M. Harmon and Richard T. Mayer, *Organization Theory for Public Administration* (Boston: Little, Brown, 1986).

Is Public Entrepreneurship Ethical?

Steven Cohen and William Eimicke

The Orange County, California, financial debacle captured the imagination of public administration theorists and practitioners at nearly the same level of interest as the reinventing government revolution. Indeed, reinvention and Orange County have become very much connected. H. George Frederickson (1995) has used the county's plight to illustrate that one of reinvention's principles—enterprising government: earning rather than spending—is seldom appropriate behavior for public officials and is often unethical.

While we share Frederickson's concern, we believe that public entrepreneurship is appropriate, is increasingly necessary and can be ethical. However, it requires a large measure of care, caution and competence if the mistakes of Orange County are not to be repeated. To examine this premise, three recent entrepreneurial projects are reviewed—the Orange County bankruptcy, the Visalia, California, hotel project and the Indianapolis wastewater treatment plants. Taken together, the three provide a useful list of "do's" and "don't's" for fledgling public entrepreneurship as well as contribute to the formulation of a more generic code of ethics for public administration.

What is public entrepreneurship?

How can those concerned with public sector management ensure that government benefits from the advantages of small-scale organizations, and modern communication and transportation technology? All over the United States, public management has become a visible and widely discussed political issue. In the name of reinventing government, the issue of management innovation has entered the everyday language of politics. The public debate has reached this point after more than two decades of attacks on government. The current political environment, in part because of its antigovernment tenor, may allow and even encourage large-scale public sector management reform. Resources are being reduced, expectations are rising and many public officials are desperately searching for a way out of the crisis they face. This may be a moment of great receptivity to the promise and potential of management innovation and creativity.

A little more than a decade ago, the best-selling private management book *In Search of Excellence* began to describe a quiet revolution in management technique that was beginning in a number of successful firms. Reduced hierarchies, a focus on quality, customers and team work, and creative entrepreneurship were lauded in Peters and Waterman's (1982) landmark volume. Public management scholars, journalists and practitioners began to discuss the need to apply these ideas to public management. These ideas were synthesized and popularized by David Osborne and Ted Gaebler's *Reinventing Government* (1993). The core reinvention concept was to rethink how government delivered, managed and paid for public programs. Reinvention was an effort to "save" the public sector and the idea of promoting collective welfare, by admitting that government sometimes did a poor job but proposing a series of creative methods to improve its performance.

Osborne and Gaebler's seldom-quoted full title is *Reinventing Government: How the Entrepreneurial Spirit Is Transforming the Public Sector.* What do they mean by "entrepreneurial government"? The authors looked to the French economist J.B. Say who, in the early 19th century, developed the concept of shifting resources out of an area of lower productivity and into an area of higher productivity and greater yield (Osborne and Gaebler, 1993, p. xix). Accordingly, the entrepreneurial public manager habitually acts in this manner, always working to use resources in new ways to increase efficiency and effectiveness.

But what of the risk-taking associated with entrepreneurship? Osborne and Gaebler explicitly recognize that most citizens do not want to see government bureaucrats taking risks with their precious tax dollars. Entrepreneurs are not risk-takers; they are opportunity-seekers, claim the authors (Osborne and Gaebler, 1993, p. xx). To strengthen their case, they embrace Drucker's characterization of a successful entrepreneur as one who defines risk and then confines it, pinpoints opportunity and then exploits it. Drucker goes on to argue that an organization can be structured to encourage or deter entrepreneurial behavior and that government organizations are inherently anti-entrepreneurial (Osborne and Gaebler, 1993, p. xxi).

Osborne and Gaebler's emphasis on entrepreneurship is frequently attacked by public administration scholars for its avoidance of issues of constitutional law and representational democracy (Moe and Gilmour, 1995; Schachter, 1995). Three issues are most frequently raised: What gives this unelected bureaucrat the right to take risks with the public's money? What is the role of elected officials in authorizing these creative programs? How can these programs be held accountable and overseen by elected officials?

Despite the reservation of scholars, public administration practitioners have jumped on the reinvention bandwagon with great enthusiasm. Bill Clinton and Al Gore campaigned on reinvention in 1992. Mayors such as Stephen Goldsmith from Indianapolis, Ed Rendell from Philadelphia and Rudolph Guiliani from New York pride themselves on being reinvention mayors (Cohen and Eimicke, 1995). Perhaps the most extensive and sustained reinvention effort to date has been at the federal level, beginning in early 1993 when President Clinton gave Vice President Gore the assignment of applying reinvention concepts to the federal government. The administration asked David Osborne to help lead the effort that became known as the National Performance Review (NPR).

While much has been written about and against the NPR experience (Kettl and Dilulio, 1995), far less has been written about the impact of reinvention on the local level. At this level, officials exercise direct authority over the public's money and are potentially likely to cross the line of ethical conduct in their zeal to be entrepreneurial. To expand the debate on the appropriateness and advisability of entrepreneurship in local government, we have examined the recent experiences of Orange County, California, Visalia, California, and Indianapolis, Indiana, from the perspective of the ethics of entrepreneurial behavior in the public sector.

The financial collapse of Orange County

On December 5, 1994, Robert L. Citron resigned as the county treasurer for Orange County, California. His resignation came in the face of mounting pressure from state and local officials after disclosure that his aggressive strategy in managing a public investment pool could result in losses of $1.5 billion for the $7.8 billion pool of 170 government agencies. In an unusually risky approach for a government fund manager, Citron (who held the position for more than 24 years) borrowed heavily to leverage the municipal pool into an investment portfolio valued at $20 billion.

Citron had been a sophisticated, aggressive and successful investor who had been a hero to local elected officials, who he enabled to do more with less, to increase services without increasing taxes. According to *The New York Times,* he was "a legend in financial circles nationwide" (Margolick, 1994, p. 1). He was known to buy discount clothes, travel infrequently and never take free tickets or favors. He would always pick up his own check. He was a Democrat in a Republican county who survived and prospered by being very effective, honest and quiet.

For more than a decade, Citron generated annual returns of about 10 percent by investing in derivatives, among other volatile instruments, whose returns are linked to bonds, currencies and other securities. In this case, they were dependent on falling interest rates. The problem with Citron's strategy was not the use of derivatives per se but that he was using borrowed money and betting heavily that interest rates would continue to fall. When interest rates started to rise, the fund's earnings started to drop and Citron was required to put up more cash as collateral to cover borrowings, leading to the liquidity problem that prompted the resignation of the elected treasurer-tax collector.

The resignation was brought on, at least in part, by someone who had been a major supporter of the county treasurer's aggressive investment strategies, Peer Swan, president of the Irvine Ranch Water District Board and a local government participant in the pool managed by Citron.

In late October 1994, Swan asked the county to begin to return his $400 million investment in the fund in $50 million weekly chunks. According to Swan, Citron told him in October he had more than $1.3 billion in cash when the actual cash balance was closer to $400 million. Citron provided the investor jurisdictions with monthly reports on the asset value and interest earnings of the fund, but not details on the fund's liquidity, the amount of assets tied to interest rates, the interest it was paying on its holdings and the adequacy of its collateral.

On December 6, 1994, Orange County, California, one of the wealthiest local governments in the country, filed for bankruptcy protection to keep investors from draining its investment fund and thereby worsening its problems. The bankruptcy was the largest in U.S. history involving a unit of government and the first involving a large county government. Bankruptcy became necessary when Wall Street brokerage firms refused to renew the $1.2 billion in short-term loans that came due on December 6th. The funds were part of the more than $12 billion Citron borrowed to leverage a pool of slightly less than $8 billion into a $20 billion portfolio. The county had about $400 million of cash in the fund, another $400 million in investments payable within a year and $450 million in property taxes due before the end of 1994, but it could not have met its obligations if all of its lenders did not roll over their repurchase agreements.

How did Citron lose $1.5 billion of the Orange County taxpayers' money? While many in the press point to derivatives, the answer is really more complicated and yet more simple than that. In an attempt to be "entrepreneurial" and maximize the earnings for the agencies participating in the pool he managed (thereby holding down taxes and fees and maximizing the amount of public services provided), Citron borrowed approximately two dollars for every dollar he had in the fund. The fund had to pay interest on the funds it borrowed, and when interest rates rose faster than the return on the fixed rate instruments the loans were used to purchase, the fund was in trouble. Returns actually declined on some of the more exotic instruments purchased, including derivatives. While those investments may return to face value in future years, they did not produce sufficient income to pay off the loans Citron made to purchase them. Citron was in many instances investing long term and borrowing short term and he guessed wrong on the path of interest rate fluctuation.

The bankruptcy of Orange County shook the nation's municipal bond market, making it more difficult and more expensive for many localities to borrow money and costing many municipal investment firms millions of dollars. While a recent survey of more than 1,300 local finance officials in the U.S. and Canada indicated that they had followed a conservative investment strategy before the Orange County bankruptcy, almost a third of the respondents indicated that they had reviewed or revised their policies since the Orange County problems came to light (Ganos, 1995, p. 11). And while most jurisdictions had written investment policies before the bankruptcy, more than 20 percent of the respondents have yet to promulgate such a document.

Robert Citron's impressive track record of earning more than three times the average money market rate for short-term investments was the envy of his peers and other jurisdictions for nearly a decade. His downfall came in large part due to a serious error in judgment for a government financial officer—placing yield first and virtually ignoring the risk involved.

Visalia: Trouble in public entrepreneurial paradise

The most entrepreneurial of reinvention's 10 commandments—enterprising government—was "invented" by Ted Gaebler as city manager of Visalia, California, in the late 1970s and early 1980s.

Indeed, if there is a Mecca of reinvention, it might well be Visalia. *Reinventing Government*'s index includes 25 citations for Visalia, hailing its innovations in everything from budgeting to personnel policies to energy efficiency. But the city's claim to fame (and its recently reported dissatisfaction with reinvention) centers on its history of success and subsequent problems in running government like a business.

Visalia is a small, conservative city of safe, clean streets in California's agricultural San Joaquin Valley. Its commitment to enterprising government was in large part created by the financial constraints placed on local governments in California by the now famous Proposition 13, which cut Visalia's property tax base by 25 percent.

The city's first significant, successful experience with acting like a business involved the acquisition of an Olympic-size pool at half the market price by a "third-level parks and recreation employee" (Osborne and Gaebler, 1993, p. 3). The acquisition was possible because City Manager Ted Gaebler instituted a creative and flexible program budget system that permitted departments to keep some of the money they did not spend in one year and invest it creatively in a subsequent year to achieve the agreed-upon mission of the department. Thereby, a parks employee, encouraged to act in an entrepreneurial fashion, was able to acquire a pool that the community wanted from a Los Angeles surplus sale and install it for half of what the city would have paid through normal procedures.

With Gaebler's encouragement the Police Department used a creative lease-purchase arrangement to acquire patrol cars, the sanitation department experimented with the proper intervals for street cleaning and grass-cutting, mechanics reduced energy consumption in their shop, bonuses were given for successful innovations, and joint ventures with private entities were developed to bring in desirable cultural events and build affordable housing. To encourage innovation and risk-taking, Gaebler explicitly gave his people latitude to fail and continue, just as Tom Peters and Robert Waterman, and notably Bill Gates, had been doing in the private sector since the early 1980s. Gaebler even invented an award—the Nugmeyer Award (named for the city employees who came up with the idea)—for the year's most spectacular failure. To make sure the message was totally clear, Gaebler gave himself the award one year (Osborne and Gaebler, 1993, p. 136).

Gaebler had worked for and learned from "new town" developer James Rouse, known for his development of Boston's Quincy Market, Baltimore's Inner Harbor and the new town of Columbia, Maryland. It was from Rouse that Gaebler learned the potential of the profit motive in government. It was a lesson that he applied often and well in Visalia. Gaebler engineered a land swap that provided Visalia with the site and funds it needed to build a new school. He recruited sponsors and a concessionaire to replace city subsidies for its softball league with private financing, more amenities and a share of the profits for the government. And when the major league baseball New York Mets dropped its affiliation with Visalia's minor league franchise, the city bought the club, made money for six years and then sold the team to private interests for a profit. And then came the Radisson Hotel project.

There was wide support for a downtown hotel in the city to spur economic development and help create the image of the city as the preeminent municipality in the region. A site was assembled and several administrations, including Gaebler's, sought to move the project forward, without success. In 1988, Gaebler's successor, Don Duckworth, struck a deal with San Francisco developer William Courtney to lease the land from the city and put up a hotel.

The deal did not go smoothly and in order to keep the project moving, the city's commitment escalated from providing the land to loaning the developer money and providing loan guarantees, in return for a share of the project's revenues. By 1991, continuing problems forced the city to buy the hotel and assume its debts, raising the city's obligation/risk for the project to $20 million. The city council and the public, who had generally supported the project all along, became vocal in their opposition and ultimately, less than a year after the hotel opened, Duckworth resigned (Gurwitt, 1994, p. 38).

What went wrong? It proved to be much more difficult to attract a qualified developer to the deal than the city originally anticipated. The developer selected was not sufficiently investigated and subsequently proved to be unable to secure the required private sector financing *after* the city signed its lease agreement. As the city kept moving forward with him, the errors compounded. The developer never was able to meet his obligations and the city was faced with bailing out his project or leaving an empty lot. So they bought the hotel and assumed its debts.

Today, the hotel is generally regarded as a success but Visalia is "a more sober place than it was in the heyday of entrepreneurism" (Gurwitt, 1994, p. 40). And while entrepreneurship in the city is not dead, there is now a much stronger city council and a greater emphasis on limits and accountability, primarily in response to the Radisson project.

Reinventing Indianapolis: Injecting and managing competition

Indianapolis has prospered under an effective and popular city government for more than 25 years. Under then-Mayor Richard Lugar, Indianapolis merged 20 city and county departments and incorporated 16 towns to create a metropolitan government, putting most important local services under direct city control.

William Hudnut followed Lugar into the mayor's chair and succeeded in his economic development agenda, in large part by making Indianapolis "the amateur sports capital of the world." As a result of two decades of strong, popular and effective leadership, Indianapolis avoided most of the fiscal and social ills that plagued other cities, consistently receiving triple A bond ratings, incurring only small deficits and keeping its unemployment and crime rates well below the national average.

During his 1991 campaign for mayor, candidate Stephen Goldsmith emphasized the fragile nature of the city's success and stressed the need for privatization to keep the costs of government low. He argued that if the city did not shrink the size and thereby the costs of government, it was in danger of losing jobs and the middle class to the suburbs. The result would be fewer and poorer services for those who could not afford to leave. Goldsmith's original vision was a reinvented government that was much smaller, contracting out many of its responsibilities to private and nonprofit neighborhood-based vendors. He articulated his vision for the city as "a competitive city with safe streets, strong neighborhoods and a thriving economy" (Cohen and Eimicke, 1995, p. 5).

As one of his first acts as mayor, Goldsmith created the Service, Efficiency and Lower Taxes for Indianapolis Commission (SELTIC). Comprised of the city's top private sector leaders and entrepreneurs, SELTIC is encouraged to examine virtually every activity of the city government to determine whether or not the city should continue to be involved in providing that service or product. If the answer is no, privatization plans are developed. If the answer is yes, methods to open that service to competition and/or decentralization are recommended.

To date, more than 40 city services have been opened to competition or privatized, saving an estimated $100 million; the city budget is smaller than when Goldsmith took office four years ago and is balanced for the first time in a decade. In addition, 13,000 new jobs have been created in the city's private sector. The most significant single project to be subjected to competition is the city's wastewater treatment plants.

Although the city's plants were considered among the nation's most efficient, Goldsmith fought for and was selected by the federal government as one of three national pilot sites for contracting out management. After commissioning a consulting firm to undertake a six-month study of the plant operation, Indianapolis accepted statements of qualifications from seven firms.

One of the finalists, Advanced Water Treatment (AWT), was formed by city employees of the treatment plant. AWT proposed cutting costs by $12 million over five years, while keeping all of its employees, except those lost through attrition. The White River Environmental Partnership (WREP), a firm based in France and 51 percent owned by the local Indianapolis Water Company, proposed reducing costs by $65 million over the same time period. WREP was able to run the plants less expensively because it has superior technology and resources. WREP's proposal included the dismissal of 122 of the 138 city workers employed at the facility, regardless of seniority.

Goldsmith had the authority to choose a new operator independent of the City-County Council since no additional spending was involved. He chose instead to create an eight-member evaluation committee that included three council members. In the end, the council unanimously awarded the contract to WREP.

The union problem remained. Stephan Fantauzzo, executive director of the American Federation of State, County and Municipal Workers, decided not to fight the WREP decision but instead to take the city to court in an effort to save the jobs. It proved to be an effective strategy, as the mayor agreed out of court to settle the case by finding jobs at comparable pay in other city agencies for the displaced workers. Within eight months, the reassignment effort was completed successfully.

Two years later, the city has a cleaner, cheaper water system, all those city employees seeking to remain in city service have been able to do so and labor-management relations are better than ever. Mayor Goldsmith, who came in committed to privatization, now speaks eloquently of the evils of monopoly, public or private. His philosophy of governing has evolved into one of managed competition, where public, private and nonprofit organizations compete to provide government-funded services of the highest quality for the best price.

The results have been impressive—lower cost of government, improved public services and less red tape. From the union side, a joint city-union career advancement program has actually resulted in moving services such as vehicle maintenance, electrical, HVAC (heating, ventilation, air-conditioning), landscaping and custodial care out of the private sector and back into government, increasing quality while lowering costs. City union officials and members have become confident that on a level playing field, they can win more than their fair share of city contracts.

What are the lessons?

Over the past two years, we have used Orange County, Visalia, and Indianapolis as case studies in graduate seminars as examples of the risks and rewards of innovative management in the public sector and as illustrations of the complexity of ethical behavior when a public official is pulled in multiple directions (with the advocates of each of the competing strategies touting the ethical importance of their option). The responses of students have been reasonably consistent.

They generally find Robert Citron guilty of unethical behavior and incompetence. They argue that he took inappropriate risks with the public's money, that he falsified reports on the status of his investments and that he failed to establish a set of clear, prudent investment guidelines to prevent such problems in the first place. They grudgingly concede that he was pushed hard to stretch the envelope of prudence by his investor governments and their citizenry, who wanted more and better public services and lower taxes. They also observe that he was "competent" for many years. The old adage of hindsight being 20/20 applies, at least to a degree. The clearest example of unethical behavior took place when Citron lied about his cash reserves.

In the case of Visalia, our students are far less clear about the ethical lessons, if any, from this case. Most agree with H. George Frederickson's (1995) rather strong conclusion (based on Orange County) that government really should not try to act like a business; its primary responsibility is to act like a government. They generally think that Visalia's successful entrepreneurial efforts prior to the Radisson project were very good indeed. Some argue that the city got too caught up in its own success and could not admit that the Radisson project was at least ill-timed, if not a bad idea altogether. If there are ethical questions for the students, they have been limited to the propriety of financing public relations for the developer and the "sin" of pride, not being able to admit that one of their entrepreneurial pet projects was going very wrong.

The Indianapolis case routinely gets rave reviews as innovative, successful, consensus-building and compassionate. Those who side strongly with the Frederickson conclusion on Orange County have no problems supporting Goldsmith's managed competition strategy, even when it results in privatization, as it did in the wastewater case. The bottom line for most of the students on Goldsmith is that his entrepreneurial behavior continues to work and it has broad-based support, even from public employee unions.

From a teaching perspective, the cases are most valuable if they provide guidance that can be broadly applied—that is, that they contain decision rules that can help graduates keep their ethical compasses on course in the real world. Staying on a sound ethical course is particularly difficult in today's public sector— as the Orange County and Visalia cases illustrate—when the public and media relentlessly press for more and better services with fewer and lower taxes and fees and less government.

Searching for ethical guidance

In "Ethics and the Public Administrator" (Cohen and Eimicke, 1995), we look first and often to colleagues for ethical guidance. Walter Lippmann used the concept of the public interest as an ethical compass, characterizing it as "what men would choose if they saw clearly, thought rationally, acted disinterestedly and benevolently" (Lippmann, 1955, p. 42). More recently, ethicist Michael Josephson simplified and modernized the Lippmann doctrine thusly, "Do more than you're required to do and less than you're allowed to do." In his seminal work, A Moral Sense, James Q. Wilson (1993) sets out four values with which to set your ethical compass—sympathy, fairness, self-control and duty. The American Society for Public Administration (ASPA) provides five principles in its Code of Ethics: serve the public interest, respect the Constitution and the law, demonstrate personal integrity, promote ethical organizations and strive for professional excellence.

Now armed with these four ethical tool kits, could we handle the Orange County, Visalia, and Indianapolis situations more effectively than was described above? Using the Lippmann criteria, Citron, Duckworth and Goldsmith all appear to have acted as if they saw clearly, thought rationally and acted benevolently. The less than optimal results achieved by Citron and Duckworth may have improved had they acted a bit more disinterestedly and been less personally involved in the strategy as originally devised. It may well be that Goldsmith's better result came in part from the involvement and appearance of distance created by his evaluation committee.

Josephson's guidance provides similar assistance in that if Citron and Duckworth had voluntarily involved others in the evaluation process, their results would have probably been far better; but at a minimum, the fallout would not have been nearly as bad and neither would probably have been forced to resign. Wilson's value of self-control provides the same type of help.

As laudable as the ASPA Code of Ethics is in its essence, it does not provide a great deal of practical assistance for decision-makers in the three case studies under consideration. In fact, two of the three principals in the cases failed from an ethical standpoint and were forced to resign even though they both strove to serve the public interest, generally respected the Constitution and the law, promoted ethical organizations and strove for professional excellence. Both Citron and Duckworth also demonstrated personal integrity, although late in the game. Citron's handling of disclosure statements and Duckworth's surreptitious efforts to promote his troubled developer violated that principle.

Overall, Citron and Duckworth would have done better and may have even kept their jobs if they had Lippmann, Josephson, Wilson and the ASPA Code of Ethics on their desk. Mayor Goldsmith acted as if he had those principles within easy reach, even if he never actually read any of the four doctrines. At the same time, it is equally clear that even taken together, the guidance of the four ethicists would not have prevented either Citron or Duckworth from heading down what many believe was an ethically problematic course of action from the very beginning.

Whether the policies of Citron and Gaebler/Duckworth are ethically questionable at their core is an important question. H. George Frederickson takes the issue head-on with respect to Orange County. His primary diagnosis is that the Orange County debacle was caused by applying the market model to government without reservation and without questioning whether government can and should be run like a business. His cure has five components: democratically adopted laws and regulations must be followed; making money is not one of the purposes of government; public funds should never be put at risk; citizens should not have to beware of their government; and the primary responsibility of public officials is to vouchsafe the legitimacy of democratic government in the eyes of citizens (Frederickson, 1995).

Frederickson's cure is surely specific and, if followed directly, would have prevented the problems that eventually developed in Orange County and Visalia and would not have precluded the Indianapolis wastewater success. At the same time, it would have precluded the years of successful investments by Citron prior to 1994 and even more problematic, most if not all of the reinvention efforts in Visalia prior to the Radisson project. Followed to its logical conclusion, virtually any contemporary money management method would be considered unethical under Frederickson's formulation. In fact, a significant number of the success stories profiled in *Reinventing Government* and now routinely described in *Governing* magazine would be ruled out by Frederickson's second and third principles.

Conclusion

We share Frederickson's view (1993, pp. 247–258) that government is not business and that as government becomes more businesslike, corruption is likely to increase. At the same time, reinvention is a proven strategy that has successfully used earning rather than spending and responsible risk-taking to truly do more with less in government, as citizens throughout the world are demanding.

What we learn from the Orange County, Visalia and Indianapolis cases is risk-taking and innovation are increasingly necessary in the public sector. However, we also conclude that even the most creative public officials are not fully equipped to determine the degree of risk and innovation that is ethical and responsible. Nor are they clear about the proper process to follow when seeking to make decisions regarding risk and innovation. In our view, Frederickson's limits are too severe. Where, then, can the ethical but innovative public decision-maker turn for help?

Carol Lewis's *Ethics Challenge* (1990) has been most helpful to us in our own public sector work and in trying to provide guidance to our students. Her 21 rules of thumb are specific enough to guide actual decisions but far-reaching enough to touch virtually every area of the public realm. For us, the 21 points can be reorganized around five core principles:

1. Obey and implement the law
2. Serve the public interest
3. Avoid doing harm
4. Take individual responsibility for the process and its consequences
5. Treat incompetence as an abuse of office.

Taken to heart and mind, and followed on a daily basis, these principles would have prevented the disaster in Orange County, the time of turbulence in Visalia and facilitated the success in Indianapolis. Ethics and entrepreneurism cannot only peacefully coexist, they can actually be mutually reinforcing. In particular, the last two principles are especially relevant to entrepreneurship. Public managers must be willing to be individually accountable for failed initiatives. There is also an ethical dimension to gross incompetence. Failure due to changed conditions or bad luck is one thing; failure due to lack of technical expertise and an appropriate level of skill to perform a task is a form of dereliction of duty. Exercising such incompetence at the public expense is a violation of public trust, an abuse of office and a breach of ethics.

References

American Society for Public Administration, National Council, 1993. "Code of Ethics and Implementation Guidelines," *P.A. Times* (May 1, supplement).

Bowman, James S., ed., 1991. *Ethical Frontiers in Public Management.* San Francisco: Jossey-Bass.

Cohen, Steven, and William Eimicke, 1995. *The New Effective Public Manager.* San Francisco: Jossey-Bass.

Cohen, Steven, and William Eimicke, 1995. "Ethics and the Public Administrator," *The Annals of the American Academy of Political and Social Science* 537 (January), pp. 96–108.

Cohen, Steven, and William Eimicke, 1995. "Reinventing Government: A Critical Analysis from Three Cities," presented at the Trinity Symposium on Public Management. San Antonio, Texas (July 23).

Denhardt, Kathryn G., 1988. *The Ethics of Public Service: Resolving Moral Dilemmas in Public Organizations.* Westport, Conn.: Greenwood.

Eimicke, William B., 1995. "The Financial Collapse of Orange County: An Ethical Lapse or Just Bad Judgment?" Columbia University MPA Case Study (August).

Finkel, Ed, 1995. "Cutting Waste(water)," *The Public Innovator* No. 40 (November 16), pp. 2–3.

Frederickson, H. George, ed., 1993. *Ethics and Public Administration.* Armonk, N.Y.: M.E. Sharpe.

Frederickson, H. George, 1995. "Misdiagnosing the Orange County Scandal," *Governing* (April), p. 9.

Ganos, Todd C., 1995. "Defining Risks for Government," *P.A. Times* (October), p. 14.

Gore, Al, 1993. *Creating Government That Works Better and Costs Less: Report of the National Performance Review.* Washington, D.C.: U.S. Government Printing Office.

Gurwitt, Rob, 1994. "Entrepreneurial Government: The Morning After," *Governing* (May), pp. 34–40.

Josephson, Michael, 1989. "Ethicist," in Bill Moyers, ed., *A World of Ideas.* New York: Doubleday, pp. 14–27.

Kettl, Donald F., and John J. Dilulio Jr., eds., 1995. *Inside the Reinvention Machine.* Washington, D.C.: Brookings.

Lemov, Penelope, 1995. "Managing Cash in a Post-Orange County," *Governing* (May), pp. 60–61.

Lewis, Carol, 1990. *The Ethics Challenge in Public Service.* San Francisco: Jossey-Bass.

Lippmann, Walter, 1955. *The Public Philosophy.* New York: The New American Library.

Margolick, David, 1994. "Ill-Fated Fund's Manager: Mr. Main St., Not Wall St.," *The New York Times* (December 11), pp. 1, 36.

Moe, Ronald C., and Robert S. Gilmour, 1995. "Rediscovering Principles of Public Administration: The Neglected Foundation of Public Law," *Public Administration Review* Vol. 55, No. 2 (March/April), pp. 135–146.

Osborne, David, and Ted Gaebler, 1993. *Reinventing Government.* Reading, Mass.: Addison-Wesley.

Peters, Thomas J., and Robert H. Waterman Jr., 1982. *In Search of Excellence.* New York: Warner Books (also New York: Plume Books, 1993).

Petersen, John E., 1995. "Misreading Investment Risk," *Governing* (August), p. 80.

Schachter, Hindy Lauer, 1995. "Reinventing Government or Reinventing Ourselves: Two Models of Improving Government Performance," *Public Administration Review* Vol. 55, No. 6 (November/December), pp. 530–537.

Wilson, James Q., 1993. *A Moral Sense.* New York: Free Press.

Privatization and Cozy Politics

———— Peter Kobrak

Over the last 25 years, privatization has enjoyed increasing popularity, thanks largely to some success at the local level when applied to such services as solid waste collection, fire protection and surface or air transportation (Savas, 1982, pp. 89–117). Privatization is also increasingly being proposed as an appropriate remedy for overgrown state and federal programs.

A review of the available literature and selected case studies suggests that if privatization is to fulfill its promise, then the conditions necessary for market competition must be in place; administrative means must not become entangled with programmatic goals; agencies, even as they shrink, must be able to monitor contracts effectively; and, most importantly, "cozy politics" must not be allowed to jeopardize agency goals or client needs. Achieving successful public/private partnerships thus requires a clear sense of the promise and pitfalls of privatization, a higher quality of politics and administration than often practiced, and the avoidance of "pseudo-privatization."

The purpose of this paper is to indicate under what conditions cozy politics, in the form of political corruption, is likely to supplant the intent of privatization, and thereby undermine public agency implementation. The following sections discuss privatization, cozy politics, contracting out and political corruption, and the U.S. Department of Housing and Urban Development (HUD) as a case study in pseudo-privatization.

Reprinted with permission from *Public Integrity Annual I.* Copyright 1996 by the Council of State Governments.

Privatization

The difficulty in understanding privatization begins with its definition. Savas views privatization as "the act of reducing the role of government, or increasing the role of the private sector, in an activity or in the ownership of assets" (Savas, 1987, p. 3). This definition, however, incorporates elements of three markedly different ideas, which often are confused in public dialogue over privatization.

The first meaning addresses a shift in the ownership of assets from the public to the private sector. Thus, privatization in much of the world, including Europe, China and Russia, has meant such a shift. This situation is rarely the scenario in the U.S., where historically most utilities, modes of transportation and other organizations have operated in the private sector.

The second element refers to the act of shrinking the size of government. In the hands of most academic advocates, emphasis is placed here on shifting the policy implementation role from the public bureaucracy to private and nonprofit administrative agencies. Governmental functions would thus continue to be carried out. In the popular debate carried on in the Contract with America, on talk shows and in newspaper accounts, though, privatization is seen largely as the act of reducing the government. The ends of government—its appropriate size and role—along with the means of policy implementation thus become entangled in a reductionist "privatization equals shrinking" equation.

The third strand in Savas' view refers to *how* we should deliver goods and services and *who* should do it, rather than *whether* the good or service should be delivered at all (Savas, 1987, pp. 58–92). This public/private choice, as Donahue (1989, p. 7) points out, then depends essentially on who will pay for the service and who will deliver it. Privatization is thus touted simultaneously as a remedy for solving state and national problems, as a vehicle for shrinking the size of government and as a means of policy implementation. As such, it must be evaluated not only as a public choice theory, but also as an administrative reform and a political movement.

The public management literature largely views competition as a handy stick for prodding recalcitrant public agencies to achieve administrative reform.[1] Conservatives like Savas differ in theory from neoliberals, like Osborne and Gaebler (1993), because conservatives want to make government smaller, while the neoliberals want to make it better. In practice it is sometimes difficult to distinguish the two. Vice President Gore's *Report on Reinventing Government,* for example, boasted that it would make the federal government better even while it removed 250,000 federal employees from the payroll (Gore, 1993, p. iii).

Conditions under which privatization is appropriate

The big payoff from privatization is clearly thought to be greater efficiency—more "bang for the buck." The benefits of competition can come from pitting public units against one another, but the big advantage will come through public/private partnerships to which the private sector can bring its technical know-how, vigor and commitment to the bottom line.

The question then boils down to those conditions under which privatization (usually achieved through "contracting out") can be successfully achieved. Ideally, the discipline of competition would be sufficient to produce prices in accord with supply and demand forces. Adherents and opponents of privatization have long agreed, though, that a relatively efficient market can function only where monopoly and other forces inimical to successful markets can be eliminated or at least neutralized. Kettl thus emphasizes that "Under these circumstances, the administrative agency must be a 'smart buyer.' In spite of imperfect competition and incomplete information, 'market imperfections' must be prevented from becoming 'market failures'" (Kettl, 1993, pp. 20–30).

In the public sector these limitations to contracting out are complicated by several unique problems. Donahue (1989, p. 45) thus highlights the problems of using privatization when the government agency's goals are uncertain; the product is difficult to monitor; switching from one contractor to another in midstream is difficult; and the government agency itself knows considerably more about the best means to accomplish the goal.[2]

State and federal agencies are particularly prone to difficulties in defining public goals. It is hard to draw up a contract with sufficient specificity when we know so little, for example, about how to rehabilitate prisoners, define "normality" in mental health or break the cycle of welfare dependency. Under these circumstances, the government must be heavily involved throughout the process of implementation. This involvement enables the agency and its staff to learn how to deal with these difficult issues and how to build that knowledge into reformulated goals and strategies through its policy formulation role.

There is also the festering problem of inadequate contract monitoring. Privatization proponents and critics agree in theory that more monitoring and evaluation are needed to gauge how well alternative strategies are dealing with these complex issues (Rehfuss, 1989, p. 47). It is, therefore, disappointing that, even as privatization arrangements have continued to grow, monitoring and evaluation activities have declined at the federal and state levels. For example, after studying implementation of the community health system, Milward, Provan and Else characterized the federal government as a "hollow state," lacking the personnel to perform its programmatic role. Its monitoring and evaluation capability were assessed as "very low, close to nonexistent" (Milward, Provan and Else, 1993, p. 319).[3]

Cozy politics

There is also a political dimension to privatization that has received comparatively less attention from scholars. Public/private partnerships are basically collaborative arrangements between a number of business leaders and some conservative and neoliberal politicians and political executives. These groups seek to "avoid political interference" even as they draw on private sector know-how and funds to tackle complex economic and social problems. Politics in this sense has negative connotations for these actors. It refers primarily to the power of public employees, government monopolies and career-conscious politicians seeking to develop programs at the expense of the taxpayer, as well as to the machinations of bureaucrats and bureaucracies able to manipulate the rules and an agency's mission for their own, rather than the public, interest (Savas, 1982, pp. 17–24). Privatization, seen in this light, becomes a healthy antidote to big government. Political interference should not be allowed to hinder the adoption of the contracting out mechanism.[4]

The coming of "cozy politics"   Distaste for the "politics of politics" does not prevent some actors in the public and private sectors from turning privatization to their own political purposes. What might be termed "cozy politics" comes into play when goal displacement occurs. Cozy political arrangements enable companies or nonprofit agencies to win public agency contracts through political influence rather than technical core competence. The result is that those designated to provide the goods and services, along with their legislative and political executive allies, benefit at the expense of the intended program beneficiaries. On occasion, the public agency itself may become involved in such contracting out agreements.

For the comparatively weak public agency, the point of distorting its policy is to bring greater political power to the aid of its cause. Seeking such power becomes particularly necessary, Hargrove and Glidewell (1990, pp. 5–8) point out, when the agency has an "impossible job." Such jobs involve attempting to achieve programmatic gains with a difficult clientele, where legitimacy with the public is low and the professions constituting the heart of the agency possess relatively low status.[5] The number of large, complex agencies with such impossible jobs is considerable; it includes agencies concerned with social welfare, mental health, public safety and corrections. Cozy politics has also manifested itself in the 1980s and 1990s, when an agency was under pressure to produce quickly or when the political burden of proof was on the agency to perform in a manner acceptable to a jaded citizenry.

Private and nonprofit sector partners, with their greater power and status in the society as a whole and increasingly in both political parties, become valuable allies in achieving an agency's ends as well as determining its means. Thanks to the prevalence of contracting out among agencies, privatization is frequently already on the scene when the opportunity for cozy politics knocks. Where public agencies are working under pressure, such an alliance offers private or nonprofit organizations a particularly welcome opportunity to provide valuable political support when these contractors cannot meet all of the implementation conditions.

Contracting out without competition   Large, private and nonprofit organizations prefer to avoid the price discipline of the competitive prescription. While competition is good for the economy as a whole, individual companies understandably seek to insulate themselves from it. To the extent that they succeed, reality becomes distinctly at odds with orthodoxy. The discipline of the corporate "bottom line," after all, provides much of the justification for privatization's potency as a reform movement. It is in two senses here that reality departs from theory. First, numerous conditions are necessary, as shown above, to achieve even reasonable, much less perfect, competition. On the basis of case studies of contracting out in large, complex organizations, even limited competition seems all too rare. Second, the problem becomes more convoluted in this era of privatization and political action committees (PACs). Like their public sector allies, these private actors in the political process are often well positioned either to influence the terms of the competitive bidding process or to arrange later for more profitable adjustments to the contract. Neither companies nor nonprofit organizations have been bashful in taking advantage of such access.

While empirical studies of privatization in complex public organizations generally identify some advantages to contracting out, saving money is rarely one of them. DeHoog (1984, p. 127) concluded that contracting out did not result in significant cost reduction in her two state agencies even though they used outside experts as monitors. She did find that contracting out led to greater political activity, particularly by those suppliers "dependent upon government contracts for their very survival" (1984, p. 26). The politicians drawn into this "politics of co-optation" often proved successful, since "contracting decisions and results are often not produced in a vacuum—they are the outcome of political and administrative pressures" (1984, p. 11).

Like DeHoog, Smith and Lipsky found that the resulting contracts often led to beneficial client services; indeed, they found that contracting out led to a more robust state service sector. But claims of cost saving could not be substantiated—largely because "the problem of producing human services of high quality on a sustained basis is so different from the problem of producing standardized products at a fixed price" (Smith and Lipsky, 1993, p. 193). Nonprofit firms might enter into mutually beneficial relationships with the state, but their financial future rested with these contracts. Hence, they too emerged, as Smith and Lipsky put it, as "players in a political process" rather than as "sellers of services" (1993, p. 171). Cozy politics has thus resulted from such contracting out arrangements, playing into the hands of state legislatures that are notorious for their attempts to make themselves indispensable to companies, nonprofit agencies and interest groups.[6]

These public/private partnerships are often long-term, mutually beneficial and somewhat productive, even if they do not reduce costs. Often there is no alternative to such partnerships. Historically, government has turned to contracting out not because of public choice, but because of the absence of any other choice. There is little justification for the duplication of existing private or nonprofit organizations when implementing public policies. The boundary line, however, between such close relationships and cozy politics is a fuzzy one.

Contracting out and political corruption

Corruption does indeed exist in a number of contractual relationships. It seems to stem as much or more from the actions of politicians and political executives than from those of civil servants. Privatization is involved because the corruption would not be possible without the cooperation of both partners and because privatization as a political movement has weakened public bureaucracies. Rourke (1992, pp. 226–229) argues that Americans are "exceptional" in the extent of their antagonism toward government, and "third party government" is one of the forces that has exploited this view. Bureaucratic expertise is now largely replaced by advice to policy makers from other actors, and political perspectives permeate more bureaucratic layers even

while private and nonprofit agencies are increasingly responsible for policy implementation. Furthermore, adherents of the
privatization movement do not evince a belief in any version of
the public interest. Goal distortion of an agency and even political corruption thus seem less reprehensible and certainly less
shocking.

As more systematic treatments of the federal government
scandals in the 1980s have emerged, it is remarkable how many
involved public/private partnerships. Meier argues that where
privatization occurs, evidence of corruption is pervasive. He points
to the exploitation by the Wedtech Corporation of the Small Business Administration's minority business program and to "privately owned vocational schools (that) sometimes appear to be
no more than fronts to collect student loan money" (Meier, 1993,
p. 221). Sympathetic critic John Rehfuss regards "lubrication
politics" as the price for obtaining contracts in the case of pork-
barrel projects:

As long as money, geographical choices, and votes are at stake, political
decisions will continue to be made about who gets contracts, for how
long a period, and in which location. When the contract or project is
large enough, pork-barrel politics will rule, to the detriment of program
efficiency and effectiveness (Rehfuss, 1989, p. 189).

But not all these cases are comparatively small pork-barrel
projects. The savings and loan (S&L) debacle began in the 1980s,
when interest rates rose to a point where a number of S&Ls could
no longer reinvest their funds into higher-yielding assets (normally residential mortgage loans). When the S&Ls could not
maintain a sufficient spread between the return on their assets
and the interest payments, they were obligated to pay their depositors. At that point the solution would have been to close the
weak thrifts. Instead, as Kane (1989, p. 4) has expressed it, bankers and government regulators were equally reluctant to acknowledge the problem. They allowed these "zombie thrifts" to continue,
and, thanks to deregulation, to assume even greater risks with
depositors' money to balance their books. Bank creditors were
content with this arrangement since they were protected "by the
black magic of federal guarantees." As one bank official who unsuccessfully sought help from the Office of Budget and Management (OMB) put it, "The administration was so ideologically
blinded that it couldn't understand the difference between thrift
deregulation and airline deregulation" (deLeon, 1993, p. 156).

Meanwhile, new S&L executives, such as Charles Keating,
emerged who were willing to assume high risks and seek political assistance when even these weak regulations became a hurdle.
Developers were not to be outdone. Mayer found an observer

aware of the developers' mind set: "You give a builder a chance to build with insured deposits he can raise with a phone call whenever he needs the money, and he'll cover the earth with housing" (Mayer, 1990, p. 97). Judge Stanley Sporkin, when ruling on one of the S&L cases, seemed to capture this "brittle environment" (as deLeon put it) in stating that it "demonstrates the excesses of a misconceived and misapplied regulatory program along with a group of individuals . . . bent on exploiting these excesses" (deLeon, 1993, p. 217).

Academic proponents intend that supply and demand requisites of competition be met before privatization can be justified. When hooked to cozy politics, however, two of its other meanings can be exploited for money. Even when the goals of greater economy and efficiency are not met, its adherents can advocate privatization for personal and corporate gain and as a relentless quest for smaller government.

Politically motivated privatization

The result under these circumstances is what might be called *pseudo-privatization,* the pretense of drawing on the efficiency and effectiveness of the private sector when in actuality, the rationale of privatization serves merely as ideological camouflage for dramatic cases of pervasive corruption. These cases stand out for three reasons. First, they involve actors from both the public and private sectors. Second, these actors share a political approach to privatization that fiercely condemns public bureaucracy as of such limited social utility that weakening its rule-making capacity structure, or organizational culture, is fair game. Third, the corruption is systemic in nature, and places in question the agency's integrity and purpose.

We have already looked briefly at the S&L debacle that provides one such example. Haynes Johnson (1991, p. 169) counted 20 federal administrative agencies where scandals occurred during the Reagan administration, including the Agriculture Department, Synthetic Fuels Corporation and the Consumer Product Safety Commission. Let us now look at another case study that reflects these problems—the Department of Housing and Urban Development (HUD). True, this agency is an extreme case, but it does demonstrate something of the problem's dimensions.

HUD: A case study in pseudo-privatization

While it received its greatest notoriety during the Reagan years, HUD's fall from grace has occurred over 25 years. While this description is limited to the Reagan administration, Eugene Meehan has condemned what he called a "programmed failure in public housing" that occurred for similar reasons during Democratic administrations in the 1960s and 1970s. He bitterly criticizes the multiple goals of the policy formulators who framed "a stimulus to the construction industry, a way of assisting the cities to clear slums and a source of needed low-income housing" (Meehan, 1979, p. 195). As for the policy implementation stage, Meehan found the resulting public/private partnership thoroughly wanting. He characterized the HUD bureaucracy over the 35-year period as "blundering, incompetent, insensitive, expensive, and unable or unwilling to learn and improve" (1979, p. 194). But, he observes, "local housing authorities did not design or construct apartments; those activities were carried out by architects and construction firms in the private sector, hence the mistakes and inadequacies that characterized that dimension of the program should be charged to the private sector account" (1979, p. 206).

When Ronald Reagan assumed the presidency, Office of Management and Budget Director David Stockman made clear that they intended to control and dramatically reduce the size of HUD (McAllister and Spolar, 1989, p. A-10). These goals would be achieved by shifting agency control to the new Republican political appointees. This message was conveyed early, according to accounts years later by Secretary Sam Pierce, when he held a meeting of his top political appointees and civil servants. "This is the board of directors," he said pointing to the political appointees. "We make all the policy decisions." Nodding at the career workers, he continued, "You are to carry out those orders. And not ask questions" (1989, A-1). The civil servants were not to be allowed to assist their superiors, drawn almost exclusively from the private sector, in learning the formidable thicket of HUD regulations.

These new appointees were unusually young and inexperienced. The powerful position of executive assistant to the passive Sam Pierce fell to 28-year-old Deborah Gore Dean. Her prior experience consisted of tending bar, while spending eight years obtaining her college degree, and working in a minor position in Reagan's presidential campaign. More significant, speculated columnist Haynes Johnson (1991, p. 182), was her wealthy family's connection to former Attorney General John Mitchell. Together she and the other political appointees became known as the "Brat Pack" or "Kiddie Corps," as they centralized power, ignored advice from housing experts, and pursued their own agenda (McAllister and Spolar, 1989, p. A-1).

Over the six years (before the scandal dwarfed budget-cutting efforts), HUD's budget was reduced by 57 percent and the number of employees fell from 16,323 to 11,470 in 1986 (1989, p. A-1). Whole divisions of HUD were eliminated, including the

Office of Organization Management and Information responsible for surveying the effectiveness of HUD field offices (1989, p. A-10). In its place, HUD sent out people, in the view of a longtime HUD observer, "who did not know what they were doing," but the attitude became "don't rock the boat, don't criticize the staff" (1989, p. A-10). This combination of circumstances weakened the resolve of HUD civil servants to try to curb the corruption. "You could hear it all over the place," said one senior executive. "Why worry? I may not have a job next week" (1989, p. A-10).

There were others with more direct, institutional responsibility for monitoring and oversight who failed to carry out their duty. Congress has little incentive to conduct hearings under normal conditions, since there are more productive ways for a congressman or senator to invest his or her time politically. Key committee chairs later admitted that they were unaware of the problems. This ignorance need not have been the case, since General Accounting Office reports strongly criticized HUD during this period. HUD's own inspector general also took HUD's management to task, but did not criticize HUD's top echelon. Furthermore, even when several different inspectors general did warn of breakdowns in the system, they did so in hushed tones or, as conservative columnist James Kilpatrick wryly observed, in "pianissimo" (Kilpatrick, 1989, p. A-25).

Oversight failed in part because of the absence both of internal and external pressure. The Democratically controlled Congress could have acted, but it was under little pressure from the mayors, home builders, mortgage bankers and housing advocates who, as the "HUD lobby," had traditionally fought for the agency, because "the money (had) dried up" (McAllister and Spolar, 1989, p. A-10). The Office of Management and Budget could have acted, but, as one of Reagan's budget directors later admitted, "OMB was preoccupied with trying to terminate some of the programs at HUD rather than trying to police it" (1989, p. A-10).

Oversight would have proved particularly useful because HUD's executives early in the game, by their own subsequent accounts, abandoned the agency's mission (as well as any ethical compunctions). Instead, they turned to using the agency's money to reward developers who contributed funds to the president's campaign, to powerful Republicans in the administration and in Congress, and, last but not least, to themselves. In the mind of Sam Pierce's administrative assistant, Debbie Dean, HUD at this point "was set up and *designed to be a political program*" (italics added), and "I would have to say that we ran it in a political manner" (Pound and Bacon, 1989, p. A-1). A former consultant to the Reagan White House put it more colorfully. "The Administration was pursuing a deliberate 'antipolicy' with regard to housing. That created a feeding frenzy in which some HUD officials believed it was OK to take the crumbs" (Steinbach, 1989, p. 2,260).

This was aided and abetted by the newly centralized nature of HUD's bureaucracy and by the abandonment of the key regulations that underlay the traditional decision-making process. HUD's secretary, a man of some stature at least before coming to Washington, could have provided some guidance for his administrative assistant, but, with some notable exceptions, apparently took little interest in daily activities. In his absence, Debbie Dean "was the ward heeler . . . the political expediter" (McAllister and Spolar, 1989, p. A-10), a role made easier since she apparently had access to Pierce's autopen whenever she chose to use it. According to accounts compiled by investigative reporters Bill McAllister and Chris Spolar, she attended meetings with what her aides called "Debbie's list," consisting of about 30 projects on a clipboard. "As Dean would announce what projects were to be funded, the aides would leaf through the notebooks, hoping to find an application from the community involved. If no letter could be found, the aides would call the communities the following day and urge them to submit an application" (p. A-10).

The "Scandal Scorecard," as one observer termed it, was long and deep, but a few examples give the idea. New York Senator Alfonse D'Amato received significant campaign contributions from Puerto Rican developers, and, recalled a HUD political appointee, "took a very real interest in housing programs in Puerto Rico." Indeed, within HUD, Mr. D'Amato was known as "the senator from Puerto Rico" (Pound and Bacon, 1989, p. A-1). Frederick Bush, deputy finance chairman for President George Bush's Election Committee, worked with two partners in a consulting firm formed to win subsidies for apartment construction. The partners brazenly submitted a typed description of the firm to HUD, indicating that it had succeeded in developing "an extensive network throughout the White House and most federal agencies" as well as with Congress. The firm stressed that its "unique assets" included its "access to government officials" (1989, p. A-12).

More resourceful than most, the firm stood ready to deal with Democratic as well as Republican administrations since one of its officials maintained close relations with the Kennedy family. Indeed, perhaps that partner had already swung into action before Reagan even appeared on the scene. According to the *Boston Globe,* "70 percent of the money [President Jimmy] Carter raised in Massachusetts in 1979 came from HUD contractors, each of whom received a new project in return" (Steinbach, 1989, p. 2,262). Included among the other Reagan influence peddlers, each of whom was paid $75,000 or more literally to make a few telephone calls, were former Department of Interior secretary James Watt, President Gerald Ford's housing secretary Carla Hills, former Republican senator Edward Brooke, and even band leader Lionel Hampton (*The New York Times,* 1989, p. E-3).

Particularly because of the loss of public trust and confidence in Washington's leadership, the price paid as a result of these revelations was high. Even higher, however, was the price paid in total programs crippled by the revelations. By the end of this period, HUD officials admitted that "at least 28 of the department's 48 programs and activities had 'significant problems' attributable to fraud, mismanagement, and (political) favoritism" (1989, p. E-3).[7]

Conclusion

Such pervasive corruption over an extended period underscores how difficult it is to insure that privatization does, indeed, meet its objectives even while protecting the public sector from the dangers of cozy politics. "The bureaucracy," as well as the involved elected officials and civil servants, suffer substantial damage from a scandal of this magnitude (though the private sector interestingly does not seem to suffer comparable public condemnation for its role). There are several conclusions relating to privatization that are relevant here.

First, for better or worse, the political push for privatization will continue at least for the remainder of this decade. Meanwhile, as a result of deficit reduction and downsizing, the federal government will decrease in size and power. In attempting to "do more with less," the federal and state governments will enter into even more public/private partnerships. It thus becomes imperative that governments at all levels maintain their monitoring and evaluation capability even while they downsize.

Such positions may be perceived as "staff overhead," and thus as prime candidates for elimination. This attitude must be countered. These are the line officials responsible for contract enforcement and for monitoring the competitive environment in the contract state. As deLeon has pointed out, "in the Wedtech, HUD and, most notably, S&L corruptions, government auditors were not only insufficient, but were subjected to cutbacks mandated by OMB at the very moment when their programs were most vulnerable" (deLeon, 1993, p. 227). When agencies support their auditors, however, they can make a significant difference. Riccucci (1995, pp. 160–161) describes how the Small Business Administration eventually backed its Office of Inspector General in pressing the Wedtech investigation, and subsequently supported legislative reforms that led to greater competition among qualified firms for large SBA contracts.

Second, the danger of privatization excesses can be alleviated only by bolstering government before more extensive privatization occurs. The conditions necessary for the success of privatization require a more widespread appreciation among the governing and governed alike of the need not necessarily for "big" but definitely for strong government. A vacuum in the capacity to govern produces cozy politics whether the villains be Clinton Democratic devotees of Whitewater real estate or Reagan Republican cabinet devotees of HUD housing projects. Lip service to "steering," while bashing public bureaucracies, is not sufficient. Those favoring a reduction in the size of government must accept public accountability as a precondition to effective privatization. Other conditions likely to foster success in implementing privatization must also be nurtured. Presidential and agency leadership from the top, necessary to cope with political pressure and to lend backbone to an agency's culture, enable it to implement contracts in accord with its mission. Kettl has described how the Carter and Reagan administrations made serious efforts to put teeth into the contracting out provisions of the A-76 program. While these reforms were not sufficient, the program was able to achieve "some unquestioned cost savings" (Kettl, 1993, pp. 41–63).

Third, the federal government has largely limited its concern with ethics to individual acts that violate conflict of interest statutes. Governments at all levels must transcend these limited, though important, concerns, and devote more attention to the institutional rot that leads to cozy politics. James Kilpatrick captured HUD's institutional and moral climate well when he described such influence peddlers as "cats that came for the cream" who "lapped up" fat consultancy fees "in exchange for a wink, a nod, a nudge and a couple of phone calls. Nothing illegal. Nothing even unethical. It was the 'system'" (Kilpatrick, 1989, p. A-25). High-echelon line executives from every agency involved in public/private partnerships must sponsor, and themselves participate in, training sessions to increase the likelihood that these *institutional* ethical concerns will become part of the administrative agency's culture. Thompson seems on the right track in arguing for new standards of ethics where we would "see more concern about the mixing of private profit and public service, more attention to the merits of constituents' claims and more worry about the effects of practices of individual representatives on the broader process of democratic representation" (Thompson, 1993, p. 377).

Fourth, the danger of privatization run amok, and related corruption stemming from interest group and PAC demands underscore that the public administration profession has an urgent stake in some type of campaign reform. The candidates' need to feed the media every two, four or six years has created innumerable opportunities for developers, corporations and interest groups to influence policy through the medium of campaign funds. While some politicians are scrupulous in defining under what conditions they will accept such contributions, these scruples are under increasing pressure every year as the price per TV minute rises. Chester Newland has emphasized that "today's public and private providers of public services need to join with others to clean up their acts and the systems of political financing and high level spoils which are entangled with them" (Newland, 1987, p. 55). The American Society for Public Administration and other organizations representing civil servants have a vested interest in preventing an instant replay of the HUD disgrace elsewhere by advocating alternative ways of financing elections.

Finally, advocates of privatization, civil servants, political executives working in the administrative agency, and private and nonprofit contractors must recognize that they have an obligation to the agency's clientele. HUD's vulnerability to criticism, brought on partially by this debacle, has left its unorganized, relatively worse-off clients utterly defenseless politically. No longer does the political debate center around reducing agency funding; now it is over whether the agency should be abolished. For those earning too little to qualify for unsubsidized apartments built by the private sector and unable to obtain public housing, the result will be more inadequate, unregulated dwellings. Perhaps the next time, instead of being required to pay light fines or take brief sabbaticals to white collar prisons, those caught engaging in cozy politics should be sentenced to live under the same conditions as the clients they defrauded.

Notes

1. As Kettl has observed, neoliberals like Osborne and Gaebler want to "reinvent government" by infusing it with a new entrepreneurial spirit driven by the engine of competition. Such competition among service providers "empowers citizens—now rechristened customers—by giving them the power of choice and creating inescapable incentives for government workers" (Kettl, 1993, p. 2).

2. Paul Starr thus seems on the mark in arguing that "given the American experience with defense production, construction projects and health care—all mostly produced privately with public dollars—it is remark-

able that anyone could see a path toward budgetary salvation simply by shifting the locus of service production from the public sector to the private sector. Advocates of privatization show an undue tenderness toward private contractors and an undue hostility toward public employees" (Starr, 1987, p. 128).

3. In noting the absence of sufficient contract monitoring in Michigan state agencies, DeHoog criticized those officials responsible for the "watchdog role" who at least "should have tried to maintain the impression, if not the reality, that these factors were critical to contractors'

future funding" (DeHoog, 1984, p. 112). Kettl, after a particularly systematic review of contracting out in several federal administrative agencies, concluded that "practice has galloped madly ahead of theory. The government's reliance upon the private sector has grown faster than its ability to manage it" (Kettl, 1993, pp. 4–20).

4. Privatization advocates acknowledge that fraud may be a danger in public/private arrangements and that effective implementation requires a balance of power between the two sectors. Savas thus agrees that fraud can result from privatization arrangements, but points out that such behavior occurs in government service as well (Savas, 1987, p. 99). For their part, Osborne and Gaebler caution that private firms may "at times develop enough political power to stifle competition" (Osborne and Gaebler, 1992, p. 106). In neither case, however, is there any hint that the problem may be systemic in nature.

5. Hargrove and Glidewell (1990) do not link their discussion of impossible jobs to privatization, but it is often agencies with such missions and roles that appear vulnerable to cozy politics.

6. Smith and Lipsky thus conclude that nonprofit "private organizations are politically organized and have influence and strength to voice their positions to government leaders. But they are linked to the decision-making structures of the state and, in the case of contracting, are financially dependent" (1993, p. 187).

7. For example, one of the lower-income assistance programs provided rent subsidies and tax credits to developers who would rehabilitate low-income housing. These subsidies were supposed to go to projects on the basis of competition, but most of the big consultant fees were paid to win these project bids. Four programs, including this one, were suspended until procedures could be changed" (*The New York Times,* 1989, p. E-3).

References

DeHoog, Ruth Hoogland, 1984. *Contracting Out for Human Services.* Albany, N.Y.: SUNY Press.

deLeon, Peter, 1993. *Thinking about Political Corruption.* Armonk, New York: M.E. Sharpe.

Donahue, John D., 1989. *The Privatization Decision.* New York: Basic Books.

Gore, Al, 1993. *The Gore Report on Reinventing Government.* New York: Times Books.

Hargrove, Erwin C., and John C. Glidewell, 1990. *Impossible Jobs in Public Management.* Lawrence, Kan.: University Press of Kansas.

Johnson, Haynes, 1991. *Sleepwalking through History.* New York: Anchor Books.

Kane, Edward J., 1989. *The S&L Insurance Mess. How Did It Happen?* Washington, D.C.: Urban Institute Press.

Kettl, Donald F., 1993. *Sharing Power.* Washington, D.C.: Brookings.

Kilpatrick, James J., 1989. "It's Reagan's Mess at HUD," *Washington Post* (August 11), p. A-25.

"The Many Paths of the H.U.D. Investigation." 1989. *The New York Times* (August 13), p. E-3.

Mayer, Martin, 1990. *The Greatest-Ever Little Bank Robbery.* New York: Charles Scribner's Sons.

McAllister, Bill, and Chris Spolar, 1989. "The Transformation of HUD: 'Brat Pack' Filled Vacuum at Agency," *Washington Post* (August 6), pp. A-1 and A-10.

Meehan, Eugene J., 1979. *The Quality of Federal Policymaking: Programmed Failure in Public Housing.* Columbia, Mo.: University of Missouri Press.

Meier, Kenneth J., 1993. *Politics and the Bureaucracy.* 3rd ed. Pacific Grove, Calif.: Brooks/Cole.

Milward, H. Brinton, Keith G. Provan, and Barbara A. Else, 1991. "What Does the 'Hollow State' Look Like?"

in Barry Bozeman, ed., *Public Management*. San Francisco: Jossey-Bass, pp. 309–322.

Newland, Chester A. 1987. "Public Executives: Imperium, Sacerdotium, Collegium? Bicentennial Leadership Challenges," *Public Administration Review*, Vol. 47, No. 1 (January/February), pp. 45–56.

Osborne, David, and Ted Gaebler, 1992. *Reinventing Government*. Reading, Mass.: Addison-Wesley.

Pound, Edward T., and Kenneth H. Bacon, 1989. "Housing Subsidy Plan for the Poor Helped Contributors to GOP," *Wall Street Journal* (May 25), pp. A-1 and A-12.

Rehfuss, John, 1989. *The Job of the Public Manager*. Chicago: Dorsey Press.

Riccucci, Norma A., 1995. *Unsung Heroes: Federal Execucrats Making a Difference*. Washington, D.C.: Georgetown University Press.

Rourke, Francis E., 1992. "American Exceptionalism: Government without Bureaucracy," in Larry B. Hill, ed., *The State of Public Bureau-cracy*. Armonk, N.Y.: M.E. Sharpe, pp. 223–229.

Savas, E.S., 1982. *Privatizing the Public Sector*. Chatham, N.J.: Chatham House Publishers.

Savas, E.S., 1987. *Privatization: The Key to Better Government*. Chatham, N.J.: Chatham House Publishers.

Sclar, Elliott D., 1994. "Public-Service Privatization: Ideology or Economics?" *Dissent*, Vol. 41 (Summer), pp. 329–336.

Smith, Steven Rathgeb, and Michael Lipsky, 1993. *Nonprofits for Hire*. Cambridge: Harvard University Press.

Starr, Paul, 1987. "The Limits of Privatization," in Steve H. Hanke, ed., *Prospects for Privatization*. Proceedings of the Academy of Political Science, Vol. 36, No. 1, pp. 124–137.

Steinbach, Carol, 1989. "Programmed for Plunder," *National Journal* (September 16), pp. 2,259–2,262.

Thompson, Dennis F., 1993. "Mediated Corruption: The Case of the Keating Five," *American Political Science Review*, Vol. 87, No. 2 (June), pp. 369–381.

Ethics Management in the Cyber-Workplace

Donald C. Menzel

Cyber-managers and cyber-workers are now populating a rapidly growing workforce in private and public sectors worldwide. The Information Age is upon us, and with it are the fast-forward buttons of the Internet, the World Wide Web, electronic mail, direct television beamed from orbiting satellites, and other breathtaking and powerful communication technologies. The future, so it seems, is here; it is now. It may be a virtual now, but it is very real. Elected officials and public managers, like their private sector counterparts, must not only understand and harness information technology within their organizations, but also be able to understand and manage the ever-changing human-technical-organizational dynamics that information technology brings to the workplace.

The knowledge explosion wrought by the electronic age of personal computers and high-speed communication has truly transformed the world, giving meaning to the global village and citizen in ways unimaginable just a decade ago. The globalization of economies, communication, education, commerce, and even peace and warfare are redefining the nation-state and presenting innumerable challenges to public officials in the United States and abroad. Public agencies, like private profit-making firms, must add value to their products and services to withstand the pressures of worldwide competition. Responsive, high-performing organizations are a necessity, not a luxury. Governments are not immune to these pressures, and political executives and career public managers know this. They also know that the forces of globalization can tempt governments to devalue the ethical overhead that is part and parcel of getting things done. Getting things done and staying competitive can be—but are not necessarily—compatible with the promotion of high ethical standards in government.

According to tracking statistics compiled by Prof. Chris C. Demchak of the School of Public Administration and Policy at the University of Arizona, governments worldwide are going on-line at a very rapid rate. The U.S. government leads all countries. In 1997, 160 U.S. government agencies had established World Wide Web sites, and agencies had been coming on-line over the previous two years at an average rate of 7.5 agencies per month. Canada, with 150 agencies on-line, and Australia, with 122 agencies on-line, were close behind. In Europe, the French national government had 89 agencies on-line (http ://w3.arizona.edu/~CyPRG/webhome.htm), as reported in January 1997.

At the subnational level in the United States, Professor Demchak's tracking study shows that more than 2,500 state agencies had established Web sites, with Texas leading all states with 134 agencies on-line. At the local level, a 1997 technology survey conducted by the International City/County Management Association (ICMA) found that 39.5 percent (n=1,377) of the 3,487 cities reported Web sites (Moulder and Huffman 1996). In short, there has been enormous movement by public agencies at all levels of government in the United States and throughout the world to climb onto the information superhighway.

These statistics document the rapid diffusion of a new information technology that many believe is having a profound, perhaps revolutionary impact on society. "We are moving rapidly," writes Vartan Gregorian (1997, p. 597), "to the dawn of an information revolution that may well parallel the Industrial Revolution in its impact and far-reaching consequences." Transformations in education, commerce, industry, entertainment, politics, government, and even church and family are taking place. But while the magnitude of change in these many sectors is substantial, we have only rudimentary knowledge of the consequences.

This article speculates about the nature and effect of the changes taking place in the workplaces of public organizations in the United States that are going on-line, with specific attention focused on ethics management issues and challenges. Three specific topics are examined: Internet use and abuse, the nature of group life in the cyber-workplace, and the democratizing influence of cyber-technologies in the workplace.

Internet use and abuse

One set of ethics management challenges facing public managers whose organizations are either on-line or about to go on-line is defining, implementing, and monitoring acceptable usage practices and behaviors for the Internet. Consider the following behaviors: surfing the Web for entertainment; downloading or viewing obscene or sexually oriented material; advertising or soliciting for personal financial gain; making political statements or promoting candidates for public office; posting or downloading derogatory racial, ethnic, or religious material; waging, betting, or selling chances; and using pseudo or pen names when transmitting electronic messages. This short list of "don't do" behaviors points to the need for public organizations to put into place policies that deter or prevent such behaviors.

At the same time, many public managers recognize that access to the Internet can stimulate and empower employees, which, in turn, can produce a more innovative and responsive government. Thus, there is a substantial incentive to support employees' access to and experimentation with the vast storehouse of data and information on the World Wide Web, electronic bulletin boards, listservs, and the Wide Area Information Server.

Still, finding the balance between Internet use and abuse is likely to be a major challenge for public managers. Yet that challenge must be met, and many on-line governments are attempting to do so. Not all acknowledge the potential for abuse, however; some government officials believe that once the novelty of the Internet diminishes, there will be little to worry about. After all, one might argue, the Internet is really like any other new information technology such as the telephone, FAX machine, and the copy machine, and in time it will be treated like a routine part of the workplace. How many workers do we see making a photocopy of their foreheads these days?

Survey of state-local government Web sites   To obtain information on what public organizations are doing to manage Internet practices and behaviors, I surveyed state and local government agencies that have established Web sites. The Demchak tracking study cited earlier reports the electronic mail addresses of the Webmasters at many state sites. Thus I was able to contact a number of agencies and retrieve their Internet Acceptable Use (IAU) policies. I was also able to surf the Web to locate government sites and, in many instances, communicate directly with the Webmaster. Altogether, I retrieved policies from 1 special district, 14 cities, 11 counties, and 34 agencies in 31 states. Although these 60 policies do not constitute a random sample, I believe they provide useful, first-cut information about cyber-management policies and practices in the public sector.

What do these policies emphasize? How comprehensive are they? And what kind of guidance do they give? Before these questions are addressed, it may be helpful to sketch out the kinds of Internet usage that an employee might pursue. There are four primary categories of Internet usage: sending and receiving electronic mail (known as e-mail), accessing and posting hypertext documents on the World Wide Web, sending and retrieving computer files (known as File Transfer Protocol, or FTP), and joining electronic discussion groups (such as news groups, listservs, and Internet Relay Chat groups). E-mail is the most widely used Internet service, although substantial numbers of Internet users are active in all categories.

Internet acceptable use policies A review of the 60 IAU policies noted above indicates that the vast majority place some type of restriction on who can access the Internet. This is usually couched in terms of "need" or job relevance. Accounts and passwords must be requested by a user and justified to and approved by a higher authority. Open access, meaning that nearly anyone in the organization can obtain an account, is uncommon; the village of Downers Grove, Illinois, is an exception. Its two-page IAU policy offers employees trial subscriptions to the Internet. Employees may use the account for three months at no cost but are required to contribute three dollars per pay period once the trial subscription period expires.

It is also uncommon for public organizations to allow employees to use Internet accounts for personal purposes. The vast majority of public organizations among those surveyed limit Internet use to official business. There are, however, some exceptions. Washington County, Minnesota, for example, allows its employees to use computers, networks, and e-mail for "incidental and occasional personal business use," provided that such use is (1) done on the employee's personal time, (2) does not interfere with the employee's or other employees' job activities, and (3) does not result in incremental expense for the county. The state of Oregon has a similar policy, which states that "limited personal uses are allowed." Such use must be "at virtually no cost to the state" and "trivial compared to use for assigned work." The state of Washington also permits employees limited personal use of state resources (e.g., local telephone calls and Internet messages) so long as it does not result in additional costs to the state. Another state agency, the New York State Office of Real Property Services, has deliberately refrained from prohibiting personal use of the Internet because "we want to get folks thinking about how they can use it to do their jobs better" (message posted on the GOVPUB listserv by Fran Pinto, Internet coordinator, 6 September 1996).

Nearly every IAU policy contains a statement of purpose, although most use generic language, such as "to advance the mission" of the city, county, or state or "for conducting official state business" (Missouri). The New Jersey policy document asserts that the state's public presence on the Internet presents opportunities to (1) improve communications, (2) improve public service, (3) extend government service hours, and (4) enhance the government's image. But perhaps the most thoughtful statement of purpose among the IAU policies reviewed for this article is contained in the IAU policy of Fort Collins, Colorado. The dissemination of information over the Internet, according to Fort Collins's policy document, is expected to (1) contribute to the economic development of the city by providing favorable information via the World Wide Web to current and potential visitors and residents; (2) aid in policy development and decision making by enabling employees with immediate access to research material, technical, and professional information; (3) conserve resources otherwise consumed by the use of paper and fossil fuels and the gathering of information electronically rather than by conference attendance; (4) foster participatory democracy by encouraging citizen involvement in and understanding of local issues; and (5) improve service delivery by promoting and facilitating efficiency and innovation.

Cyber-management approaches   Regarding the use and abuse of the Internet, the policy documents reviewed here generally reflect one of three cyber-management approaches. The *generic* approach is to remind the user that the Internet is no different from any other information technology (telephone, fax machine, copying machine, etc.) and that the user is subject to the same ethical and legal do's and don'ts. There may also be a brief enumeration of unacceptable behaviors, such as "don't harass or threaten" others. Some agencies cite the relevant city or county ordinances or state statutes regarding the illegal uses of communication technologies.

A second approach is to develop a much more detailed statement of acceptable and unacceptable behaviors that users are expected to follow. This approach might be labeled *formalistic*. The California Housing Finance Agency (CHFA), for example, lists the following as acceptable activities:

- General communications with state, federal, or local government personnel, vendors, contractors, consultants, or other business partners on bona fide CHFA business matters
- Electronic mail exchange with business associates outside the agency on matters that directly relate to the user's state job duties

- World Wide Web access for bona fide agency-related and specific job-related reasons.

Unacceptable activities—those that do not conform to the purpose, goals, and mission of CHFA—include

- Private or personal for-profit activities, such as consulting for pay and selling goods or services such as Avon, Amway, or income tax preparation
- Use for personal gain in any form
- Access to the Internet World Wide Web or FTP, or other Web sites that have no direct relevance to CHFA business (e.g., sports scores, games, hobbies, etc.)
- Use for any illegal purpose
- Transmission of threatening, obscene, or harassing messages or use of inappropriate language for which CHFA could be held liable
- Access to or downloading of obscene, sexually explicit, or tasteless and offensive materials in any form, including multimedia photos, video, or audio sounds
- Downloading of software or data without authorization
- Excessive use of e-mail for personal or nonbusiness-related communication
- Intentional search for unauthorized information about, receipt of copies of, or modification of data or passwords belonging to others, unless expressly authorized in writing
- Interference with or disruption of operations, including the distribution of unsolicited advertising, propagation of computer viruses, or use of the network to gain unauthorized entry to another computer
- Divulgence of passwords, phone numbers, or other network access information to any unauthorized persons.

This cyber-management approach typically includes a requirement that the user sign a statement that he or she read, understands, and agrees to abide by the agency's IAU policy. Failure to abide by the policy can result in disciplinary action including, but not limited to, termination of access privileges or, in serious cases, termination of employment.

A third approach might be labeled a *guidelines* approach. This type of IAU policy is long on guidelines, brief on do's and don'ts, and nonpunitive in nature. For example, the Greene County, Ohio, library's IAU policy requires that the Internet be used in a responsible, efficient, ethical, and legal manner. It then proceeds to identify four guidelines, one of which describes acceptable uses and another of which describes unacceptable uses. Finally, two pages are devoted to describing on-line etiquette.

Given the nonrepresentative nature of the study sites and policies, any observed similarities or differences between city, county, and state IAU policies are suggestive at best. One possible difference did emerge, however. State agencies appear to be more inclined than city or county agencies to take a formalistic cyber-management approach. That is, they are likely to set forth in some detail those behaviors regarded as acceptable and unacceptable for Internet users; to closely restrict who has Internet access, with need being a key criterion; to require users to sign written statements of their willingness to abide by the IAU policy; to provide a mechanism (managerial or technological) for monitoring Internet use; and even to install access restricting software to block out inappropriate Web sites. One might speculate that this difference between state and local agencies simply reflects the greater bureaucratization of state agencies. At the same time, it may be due to size differences. Further study might show that larger city and county governments are just as likely as state agencies to adopt a formalistic cyber-management approach.

Perhaps the more important issue associated with this preliminary investigation of cyber-management policies is the (positive or negative) consequences that a more or less restrictive, formalistic approach taken by public managers to deal with Internet use may have for the organization, including group life in the workplace.

Group life in the cyber-workplace

The technical aspects of accessing the Internet, while challenging, may pale alongside the challenge faced by managers to understand and abate the possibly undesirable and sometimes unethical consequences that the use of this technology may have on social or group life in public agencies. For example, a study by M.L. Markus (1994, p. 119) of the negative effects of e-mail on social life in the corporate workplace found that such effects (e.g., making the workplace less personal) were a product of two factors: the technology itself (e.g., the depersonalization of social relations due to the absence of face-to-face interaction), and the intentional choices by users or employees "to avoid unwanted social interactions." In other words, e-mail technology itself is not singularly responsible for negative social effects in the workplace. Employees can and do make intentional choices in deciding who they do and do not want to communicate with.

A similar lesson is suggested by Wanda Orlikowski's study of the introduction of groupware (Lotus Notes) in the office of a large consulting firm. She was interested in learning about "how the use of a collaborative tool changes the nature of work and the pattern of social interactions in the office, and with what intended and unintended consequences" (Orlikowski 1997, p. 174). After conducting more than 90 interviews with organizational members at all levels, she concluded that the sharing of information, which is essential for groupware technology to be effective, is likely to be resisted by members of the organization who "feel little incentive to share their ideas for fear that they may lose status, power, and distinctive competence" (Orlikowski 1997, p. 184). This is especially likely to occur in organizations that reinforce individual effort and ability. In other words, the lesson here is that information technology behaviors such as those reported above for e-mail are adjusted in ways that take into account the prevailing organizational ethos and value system.

IAU policies and their consequences   Given the earlier discussion of IAU policies, one might speculate or hypothesize that those policies that foster liberal access to the Internet are more likely to promote a participatory workplace which, in turn, will have a "democratizing" influence. Conversely, those IAU policies that are more restrictive and formalistic are likely to have a "chilling" influence on organizational innovation and employee creativity.

How these influences might interact with the predominant culture of an organization is also of importance and in need of study as part of the larger matter of introducing a new technology or innovation into an organization. Such an introduction is typically received with mixed reactions and sometimes with considerable resistance. Doing things differently often results in a disruption of work routines and is therefore a destabilizing influence. At the same time, once the new technology or innovation permeates the organization (i.e., has been routinized or absorbed into the organizational culture), some mutual adaptation has most likely taken place between worker attitudes and behavior and the norms or culture of the workplace.

Consequences for the ethical environment   The often-acclaimed revolutionary aspects of information technology, including the World Wide Web and e-mail, also have the potential for influencing the ethical environment of the workplace. One fear is that such change could diminish that environment. The "frontier" character of the Web, which stresses individualism, along with the depersonalization of relationships, could encourage employees to engage each other and the public they serve in a manner that devalues human dignity and respect for others. Alternatively, either there will be a "hold harmless" effect or the values that define the ethical environment will be reinforced, not changed. Kenneth Kraemer and James Danziger's (1984) research on how the introduction of computer technology in an organization shapes power relationships is suggestive in this regard: their findings indicate that the introduction of new computer technology does not change the prevailing power structure but rather reinforces it. By implication, it might be suggested that if the prevailing values of an organization's ethical environment are weak, Web access and usage will merely reinforce, not change, that environment. A similar outcome would be expected for an organization with a strong ethical environment; the ethical environment would continue to be strong.

Democratizing the workplace

Both the idea and ideal of a democratic workplace is the self-managed workplace (Cheney 1995). Participative management, M. Sashkin (1984) argues, is an ethical imperative because it is consistent with democratic principles, satisfies the basic needs of individuals in the workplace, and promotes organizational performance. We should consider once again the Internet and its potential for fostering worker self-management (i.e., a more democratic workplace) and perhaps a more ethical workplace. As Richard Sclove maintains in *Democracy and Technology*, "personal computers and telecommunications harbor the potential for allowing more democratic, decentralized, and debureaucratized social coordination, but much remains to be learned about effective strategies for realizing that potential" (1995, p. 232).

Organizational posture   Other ethical and perhaps legal challenges go beyond employee access and use of the Internet and have to do with the posture of government itself. Presumably in a democracy, on-line governments and their leaders should posture themselves so as to maximize and promote practices such as easier and greater citizen access to public information, while at the same time protecting or preventing the disclosure of sensitive information stored in government databases. It is one thing to post information about neighborhood crime rates or AIDS statistics and another to allow public access to names or addresses of victims. Likewise, the question might be asked whether a public service is being provided when a county's property appraiser's office creates a searchable database containing the names, addresses, and property values of residential and commercial real estate. Or is this merely making it easier for scam artists, thieves, and other criminals to use the same technology to target potential victims?

This brings up the next challenge for a governmentally assembled database—namely, how to prevent it from being used for inappropriate commercial or even criminal purposes. Consider the case of driver's license and automobile registration in Texas. This has been public information for some time and has been drawn upon by insurance companies, private investigators, and even family members looking for missing relatives. Recently, a private firm in Dallas placed driver's license and automobile registration information in a searchable database on the Internet (http://www.publiclink.com/). This site enables anyone who has a Texas driver's license, owns a personal computer, and has an Internet connection to look up any other Texan and any Texas license plate number. The site developers inform visitors that the database will be expanded in the future. Is it likely that an expanded database might include information about arrest and conviction records, marriage records, and voter registration?[1]

Many governments are facing tight budgets and could be motivated to sell advertising space on their official home page and perhaps even endorse a product as the official product of the city or county. Would such a practice be ethical? Legal? Would such use of a Web site be any different than the placement of commercial ads on municipally owned buses or city subways? The commercialization of the Internet is, of course, well under way. But how far should we go in commercializing government?

Finally, there is the matter of electronic communication between and among public officials (elected and appointed) and citizens. Few residents would object to e-mail replacing FAX messages between citizens and public officials, but it may be an entirely different matter when the communication path is between officeholders or between public employees and their elected bosses. While some small communities such as Downers Grove, Illinois, encourage employees that hold Internet accounts to "communicate information to elected officials, as needed," this is more likely to be the exception than the rule. Direct electronic communication between elected officials in the same city, county, or state government may be of even more concern, given the public's preference for government in the sunshine. Will the information (r)age, especially in its electronic form, cast a cloud over government in the sunshine? Or will public officials exercise due care, diligence, and caution before jumping on the keyboard and sending an important message to elected peers or top managers in their government?

And there is another important question: is the ethical environment of a public organization strengthened or weakened when it goes on-line? It might be hypothesized that the ethical environment will be strengthened because as organizational members use the Internet, trust and respect for fellow employees and superiors will grow. This will occur because information as a scarce resource will become less scarce and therefore act as an organizational equalizer of status and differences among employees and between superiors and subordinates. Flattening the status or authority structure will require workers and managers to treat each other with greater respect and will engender trust.

The democratization of information and communication is likely to promote a more democratic workplace, one in which employees feel a sense of participation, ownership, empowerment, and self-management. There is some, albeit limited, evidence supporting this proposition. In a study of municipal employees' use of e-mail, it was found that greater e-mail use resulted in employees becoming more committed to their employers and developing a stronger bond with their city government (Huff, Sproull, and Kiesler 1989). This finding is especially suggestive because the study compared computer communication with more traditional forms of communication—telephone exchanges and written memos—and in so doing, found no relationship between employee commitment to the organization and the extent to which the employee communicated with others via telephone or written memorandum.

Conclusion

Ethical government is not an oxymoron, and ethical workplaces can be found in many public organizations. While there is no "one size fits all" organizations, managers might think about the size of the ethical workplace they desire by noting the advice of John F. Kennedy nearly 40 years ago, when he stated that "the ultimate answer to ethical problems in government is honest people in a good ethical environment." Honest people can contribute to an ethical workplace. But notice that a good ethical environment is needed as well. Part of a good ethical environment includes the community as well as those who assume the public trust by virtue of their employment in government.

But where does one get a good ethical environment? Certainly not from the manager's everyday bookshelf, as helpful as that might be. Rather, a good ethical environment is built and maintained the same way a new home owner builds and maintains a house: stick by stick, nail by nail, day by day. Ethical public organizations require the same kind of care, competence, and daily attentiveness to build and maintain. There is no magic elixir to ingest or wand to be waved that will produce them. And without a strong infusion of ethics in public organizations, it is not likely that we will find ethical government. Public managers can—indeed, must—do all within their power to promote ethical workplaces in their organizations.

Note

1. Information gathered from a message posted on the GOVPUB listserv by Mike Wegner, 4 June 1997.

References

Cheney, George. "Democracy in the Workplace: Theory and Practice from the Perspective of Communication." *Journal of Applied Communication Research* 23 (August 1995):167–200.

Gregorian, Vartan. "Technology, Scholarship, and the Humanities: The Implications of Electronic Information." In *Computerization and Controversy,* ed. Rob Kling. San Diego: Academic Press, 1997.

Huff, C., L. Sproull, and S. Kiesler. "Computer Communications and Organizational Commitment: Tracing the Relationship in a City Government." *Journal of Applied Social Psychology* 19 (1989):1371–1391.

Kling, Rob, ed. *Computerization and Controversy.* San Diego: Academic Press, 1997.

Kraemer, Kenneth L., and James N. Danziger. "Computers and Control in the Work Environment." *Public Administration Review* 44 (January/February 1984):32–42.

Markus, M.L. "Finding a Happy Medium: Explaining the Negative Effects of Electronic Communication on Social Life at Work." *ACM Transactions on Information Systems* 12 (April 1994):119–149.

Moulder, Evelina R., and Lisa A. Huffman. "Connecting to the Future: Local Governments On Line." In *The Municipal Year Book 1996.* Washington, D.C.: International City/County Management Association, 1996.

Orlikowski, Wanda J. "Learning from Notes: Organizational Issues in Groupware Implementation." In *Computerization and Controversy,* ed. Rob Kling. San Diego: Academic Press, 1997.

Sashkin, M. "Participative Management Is an Ethical Imperative." *Organizational Dynamics* (Spring 1984):5–22.

Sclove, Richard E. *Democracy and Technology.* New York: Guilford Press, 1995.

Public Cynicism: Manifestations and Responses

———————————————— Evan M. Berman

Widespread concern exists about public cynicism toward government.[1] Manifestations of this cynicism include pervasive beliefs that government policies and public officials are corrupt, inept, or out to take advantage of citizens. Such disillusionment causes alienation and disengagement and is therefore of key interest to public administration and processes of democratic governance. Yet little is written about the role of public administrators in shaping public attitudes, and much of what *is* written focuses on administrative processes for managing citizen involvement.[2]

This article provides a theory of citizen cynicism that is relevant to public administration. It also reports the results of a national survey among city managers and chief administrative officers (CAOs) about perceptions of public trust in local government and the efficacy of municipal efforts to increase it.

A theory of cynicism

Cynicism is discussed, in general terms, in the literatures of trust and social capital. Many authors argue that all human relations and exchanges (economic, political, and social) require the trust that promises will be honored and that individuals will not be taken advantage of.[3] Trust is seen as purposive—a lubricant of relations—and also as serving the emotional needs of individuals to belong. Cynicism is defined as low trust—specifically, as a pervasive "disbelief in the possibility of good" in dealing with others. Cynicism increases social distance and diminishes the public spirit.[4]

Adapted with permission from "Dealing with Citizens' Cynicism," *Public Administration Review* 57 (March/April 1997):105–112.

Cynical attitudes regarding government often concern the integrity, purpose, and effectiveness of government and its officials.[5] Ardently cynical beliefs are usually linked to ideological views that are highly critical of government—for example, "government is always out to get the ordinary citizen." Facts are used selectively to justify claims that "nothing ever changes" and that authorities use "smoke and mirrors" to appease and mislead the masses. Milder expressions of cynicism are often characterized by beliefs that are less harsh about government (e.g., "government tries its best, but it just doesn't have the resources") or that give greater weight to facts (e.g., "government doesn't deliver on its promises: the roads are still not fixed"). Because of the greater role of facts, the latter form of cynicism may be more open to persuasion by reason.

Theories of human motivation and behavior suggest that citizens question their relationship with government and feel disenfranchised when they (1) believe that local government is using its power against them (or otherwise not helping them), (2) do not feel part of local government (e.g., they feel misunderstood or ignored), and (3) perceive local government services and policies to be ineffective. When these perceptions and feelings are mild (e.g., when citizens believe that "things aren't done because government doesn't care much about us"), mild forms of cynicism may develop. When these perceptions and feelings are strong (e.g., when citizens believe that government is plotting to exploit and brainwash them), citizens become ardently cynical and withdraw from government.

Analysis suggests that many people develop slightly *negative* orientations about their local governments. They regularly experience government using its power to tax them, charge fees and fines, and cater to special interests. Although citizens often do have positive encounters with agencies, such experiences are incidental and discounted as they do not reflect the full range of citizen contacts that shape public opinions about government power.[6] Thus, because citizens are often less informed about how government helps them through environmental programs, quality education, economic development planning, and so on, negative experiences of government power outweigh positive ones. Citizens also do not normally experience a sense of belonging to government; indeed, many seldom even think of it[7] and usually become aware of local government services only after they fail. Although many services do work, traffic congestion, overcrowded public schools, and a lack of public safety are often cited as evidence of government failure and incompetence. Widespread ideologies favoring privatization also suggest that government is an ineffective service producer. Moreover, citizens frequently discount positive outcomes that are viewed as legal entitlements or as being "due" them in exchange for payment of taxes. Thus, the psychology of citizen satisfaction is stacked against positive public attitudes.

This theory of cynicism suggests three sets of public administration strategies to reduce public cynicism.[8] The goal of the first set of strategies is to show that government uses its power to help citizens rather than to harm them. The above analysis suggests that many citizens are not aware of local government activities and of how these activities help further their own aims. The lack of such awareness reduces trust and suggests a need to reach out to citizens to explain what government does and how it serves the interests of "average" citizens—for example, via communication strategies that involve persistent, diverse, and consistent information campaigns such as mailings.

The second set of strategies aims to incorporate citizen input into public decision making. Traditional public hearings often fail to attract much citizen participation except in unusual, crisis-laden situations. Citizen surveys and panels are two alternative participation strategies.[9] Use of these strategies suggests that frequency and breadth of participation are important conditions, as are the communication and implementation of results and recommendations.

A third set of strategies aims to enhance the reputation of local government as being competent and efficient. Communication is necessary because citizens may be unable to evaluate the cost and quality of government services unless they are provided with information. In this regard, reputational strategies are not a panacea for poor performance; rather, good performance is the foundation of public communication.[10]

Findings

Current levels of cynicism   A survey was conducted among city managers and CAOs to assess current levels of citizen cynicism.[11] The results in Table 1 show that, according to city managers, most citizens "agree" or "strongly agree" that services meet their needs (69.7 percent), that local government treats citizens fairly (63.0 percent), and that local government does not take advantage of citizens (59.8 percent). However, according to city managers, fewer citizens believe that local government is competent (56.1 percent), honest (46.3 percent), fulfills its promises (43.0 percent), understands citizen needs (41.6 percent), and can be trusted (41.5 percent). This latter rating reflects negative assessments across different concerns and is therefore lower than specific ratings.[12]

Table 1. *Perceptions of citizen trust in local government.*

	Percentage of cities responding
Citizens agree or strongly agree[a] that	
Government services meet citizen needs	69.7
Government treats citizens fairly	63.0
Government does not take advantage of citizens	59.8
Government is competent	56.1
Government officials are honest	46.3
Government fulfills its promises	43.0
Government understands citizen needs	41.6
Government can be trusted	41.5
Analysis[b]	
Mean response of "somewhat agree" or less	33.6
(Sub): Mean response of "somewhat disagree" or less	(8.3)
Mean response of between "somewhat agree" and "agree"	43.0
Mean response of "agree" or more	23.4
(Sub): Mean response of three or more "strongly agree" responses	(9.0)
Total	100.0

[a]Responses are based on a seven-point Likert scale, ranging from "strongly agree" to "strongly disagree."
[b]Analysis excludes the general item "government can be trusted." See text for discussion.

One-third of respondents (33.6 percent) have mean responses that fall within the range of "disagree" to "somewhat agree." Their cities are classified in this study as having "cynical" citizen attitudes. The low ratings imply problems of trust because, for example, a city that only "somewhat" meets citizen needs (or less) cannot be viewed as an effective partner in helping citizens to achieve their goals. About one-quarter of cynical cities (or 8.3 percent of all respondents) have average ratings of "somewhat disagree" or less. Citizen attitudes in these cities are considered ardently cynical. Interviews with respondents in ardently cynical cities corroborated the presence of dark attitudes. Specific concerns included the use of government power (e.g., a lack of consideration for minorities), a lack of openness in decision-making processes, a catering to special interests, and the ineffectiveness of local government to solve important community problems such as traffic congestion and crime.

Municipal strategies   Cities use a variety of strategies that affect citizen trust (Table 2). Although information strategies are

Table 2. Municipal strategies in dealing with citizens.

	Use (%)	Association with cynicism[a]
All strategies	61.2	Yes
Two or more strategies from each group	68.9	Yes
Information		
Informing citizens of changes in rules and programs	82.3	No
Using mailings to explain what government does	72.5	Yes
Informing citizens about service performance	63.9	Yes
Using mailings to explain how government meets citizen needs	57.1	No
Using mailings to explain the purposes, benefits, and results of taxes	55.1	No
Using mailings to explain how government fairly balances different interests	34.8	Yes
Group mean	60.4	Yes
Participation		
Conducting public hearings	97.5	No
Adopting open meeting policies	94.7	No
Using citizen panels for controversial issues	73.4	Yes
Using surveys to elicit citizen preferences	57.8	No
Using voter referenda or ballots	50.0	Yes
Group mean	74.4	Yes
Reputation		
Seeking awards of national or regional distinction	76.3	No
Making positive statements	70.5	No
Using campaigns to portray a positive image	50.4	Yes
Responding to negative comments in the media	39.2	No
Demonstrating commitment to ethics through sanctions	32.2	No
Informing citizens regularly of high ethical standards in city	25.7	No
Group mean	49.0	No

[a]All associations are negative and significant at better than the 10 percent level. The associations of "all strategies" and "two or more strategies" with cynicism are significant at the 1 percent level.

widely used (group mean = 60.4 percent), the nature of information provided through these strategies varies. Only half of the cities explain how government meets citizen needs (57.1 percent) and the purpose, benefits, and results of taxes (55.1 percent). Even fewer explain how government fairly balances different community interests (34.8 percent). Cities also use a range of reputation strategies (group mean = 49.0 percent). Seeking awards of distinction (76.3 percent) and encouraging managers to make positive statements about the city (70.5 percent) are common. Half of the cities use media campaigns (50.4 percent), although follow-up interviews suggest that many of these campaigns are targeted toward businesses rather than citizens. Few cities respond to negative comments in the media (39.2 percent), and even fewer inform citizens of high ethical standards in municipal government (25.7 percent). Participation strategies are also widely used (group mean = 74.4 percent). Citizen participation through public hearings and open meeting policies is widespread (respectively, 97.5 percent and 94.7 percent), which reflects that such participation is often mandated by law. Other strategies are the use of citizen panels (73.4 percent), which some cities (e.g., Seattle, Washington) use as a principal strategy for engaging citizens at both city and neighborhood levels; citizen surveys (57.8 percent), which many cities (e.g., Memphis, Tennessee; Dallas, Texas; Palo Alto, California) now use to identify citizen preferences, some reporting these poll results and accomplishments through mailings; and voter referenda (50.0 percent).

Public attitudes are shaped by many factors, and it is no surprise that diverse and consistent efforts are needed. Indeed, individual strategies alone are not always associated with lower cynicism. It should be further noted that efforts to reduce cynicism are more effective in cities in which cynicism is high than in those in which high levels of public trust are already present. Thus, as recorded on Table 2, it is important for local governments to use a *range of strategies*. Interviews with respondents in cities with low levels of trust identify the use of public hearings, public-access broadcasts of council meetings, a few citizen advisory panels, annual reports, and sporadic surveys of citizen attitudes as important cynicism-reduction initiatives. By contrast, interviews and survey comments by respondents in "high-trust" cities identify the use of a much broader range of strategies; in addition to the "standard" strategies noted above, these cities use dozens of citizen tasks forces and focus groups, have strategies to respond immediately to citizen queries and complaints, use surveys to identify citizen preferences (in addition to attitudes), meet regularly with neighborhood activists, prepare bimonthly newsletters, and consistently explain what government does and how it meets citizen needs. Some cities use more than 300 citizen panels and advisory boards, many of which arise from neighborhood activism, and these venues increase the dialogue between city hall and community leaders. In Arvada, Colorado, city officials schedule meetings with residents at their homes. These high-trust cities also often use various reputational strategies. Some have "pride" programs through which local governments increase community awareness among neighborhoods or targeted groups such as children. These and related efforts also help to balance the negative media coverage of local events.

Although performance awards have received much attention in recent years, respondents give mixed assessments regarding their value. In cities such as Phoenix, Glendale, and Scottsdale in Arizona, national and state awards for service excellence are seen as very positive. As one respondent noted, "Before, people did not even acknowledge that we did things like pick up trash until something went wrong. Now, the press gives the city more respect, the neighborhood associations know they are dealing with a competent entity . . . and people take pride that the city is moving in a positive direction." Respondents in other cities that have also won awards state that "awards are a nice pat on the back, but they have little effect on citizen attitudes. . . . It is an ongoing helpful attitude from city hall that the citizens value." Another respondent stated that "the thing of importance is having many citizen and neighborhood groups, openness, low crime, and pleasant parks, good services, etc." This ambivalent assessment is consistent with data in Table 2, which show that this strategy of touting awards is not significantly associated with decreasing public cynicism.[13]

Finally, this study also finds that the level of perceived cynicism is greatly affected by economic and social conditions. Well-educated populations and cities with above-average economic growth rates are less cynical toward government; conversely, cities with large poor populations are more cynical. Cities with low crime rates have less public cynicism, as do cities in which citizens take pride and have a historically strong interest in municipal affairs, and in which community groups cooperate well together. Cities where council persons and the media are cynical experience greater levels of public cynicism. These results, such as the association of low crime rates with increased trust, are robust even when controlling for the level of economic growth. Further analysis shows that the efficacy of using a broad range of strategies is also robust even when controlling for these social and economic conditions.

Discussion

Democracy requires a degree of trust that we often take for granted.[14] In this regard, the continuing slide of citizen trust suggests that new approaches are needed to restore public confidence. To this end, manifestations of cynicism should be understood not only as poll statistics, misplaced understandings, or the result of systemic or isolated ethical wrongdoing; rather, as this article suggests, cynicism and trust are deeply rooted in the management of government-citizen relations. That is, public administration matters. To restore trust, citizens must increase their commitment to the purpose of government. Specifically, they must believe that government serves their needs, that they can affect decision making, and that government is able to deliver. Public administration affects these outcomes: cities that use a number of information, participation, and reputation strategies experience less cynicism, even where there is a broad range of community conditions.

This study finds that cynicism is present in about one-third of all cities with populations above 50,000, and that about one-quarter of these cities have widespread ardently cynical attitudes. Thus, although cynicism about local government is not ubiquitous, it is common. Managers who seek to affect the level of trust might begin by considering how the communications that citizens receive about their agencies and jurisdictions affect their attitudes. In this regard, what do citizens know and believe about the performance and relevance of municipal services? Managers might then use the measures of cynicism reported in Table 1 as an instrument for assessing citizen attitudes in their own jurisdictions. Such surveys provide further evidence for administrators' perceptions, can be linked to local conditions, and identify citizen preferences for information and participation strategies. The strategies reported in Table 2 provide a benchmark of such efforts. Consideration of the latter will lead some jurisdictions to broaden and enhance their efforts, and to develop multifaceted and durable strategies.

This study advances cynicism as a phenomenon that is linked to unsatisfied citizen needs. However, much further research is needed on the subjects of trust and social capital in public administration. Specifically, careful case studies are needed of jurisdictions or agencies that have turned around negative public attitudes. Detailed attention must be paid to the strategies, contexts, and actors' abilities. For example, the role of culture is much understudied as a cause of cynicism, as a barrier to developing anticynicism strategies, and as a self-corrective mechanism against ardent cynicism. The efficacy of different strategies might also be examined in greater detail, focusing, for example, on the psychology of citizen perceptions and on the impact of strategies on the formation of social capital in communities in general. Finally, in public administration, it is often assumed that managers who seek to serve the public interest also develop the skills to ensure trust. It would be useful to know how public administrators perceive their tasks of increasing trust and dealing with cynicism. A role also exists in public administration education to ensure that students have adequate skills and perspectives in this area.

Undoubtedly, in many public settings, greater efforts must be made to combat cynicism. As this study suggests, ensuring the public trust is not a simple task: a broad range of strategies is needed. The time has come to ensure that agencies receive the public support that they deserve.

Notes

1. Gore, Al, 1994. "Cynicism or Faith," *Vital Speeches,* October 1995, 645–649; Dubnick, Mel, and David Rosenbloom, 1995. "Oklahoma City," *Public Administration Review* 55 (September/October):405–406; Greider, William, 1992. *Who Will Tell the People: The Betrayal of American Democracy.* New York, NY: Simon and Schuster; Lipset, Seymour M., and William Schneider, 1987. *The Confidence Gap: Business, Labor and Government in the Public Mind.* Baltimore, MD: The Johns Hopkins University Press; Cisneros, Henry G., and John Parr, 1990. "Reinvigorating Democratic Values: Challenge and Necessity," *National Civic Review* 79 (September/October):408–413.

2. Frederickson, H. George, 1991. "Toward a Theory of the Public for Public Administration," *Administration & Society* 22 (February):395–417; Luton, Larry S., 1993. "Citizen-Administrator Connections," *Administration & Society* 25 (May):114–134; Stivers, Camilla, 1994. "The Listening Bureaucrat: Responsiveness in Public Administration," *Public Administration Review* 54 (July-August):364–369; Box, Richard C., 1992. "The Administrator as Trustee of the Public Interest," *Ad-*

ministration & Society 24 (November):323–345.

3. Coleman, James S., 1990. *Foundations of Social Theory.* Cambridge, MA: The Belknap Press; Putnam, Robert D., 1993. *Making Democracy Work.* Princeton, NJ: Princeton University Press; Mansbridge, Jane J., ed., 1990. *Beyond Self-Interest.* Chicago, IL: University of Chicago Press.

4. Merton, Robert K., 1957. *Social Theory and Social Structure.* Glencoe, NY: Free Press; Barber, Benjamin, 1983. *The Logic and Limits of Trust.* New Brunswick, NJ: Rutgers University Press. The origin of the word *cynicism* is canine or dog. The Greek school of Cynicism believed that to find happiness, people must train their minds to want nothing and, hence, live like dogs. Cynics abandoned most earthly desires and social conventions. The present definition of *cynicism* shares the belief that the world is a bad place, but it does not adopt the ascetic lifestyle.

5. Starobin, Paul, 1995. "A Generation of Vipers: Journalists and the New Cynicism," *Columbia Journalism Review* 33 (March/April):25–33; Durant, Robert F., 1995. "The Democratic Deficit in America," paper presented at the 56th Annual

Research Conference of the American Society for Public Administration, San Antonio, July 22–26.

6. Goodsell, Charles, 1994. *The Case for Bureaucracy*, 3rd ed. Chatham, NJ: Chatham House Publishers.

7. Respondents illustrated this point in various ways. One city manager stated: "Well, there are always folks who don't know in what city they live, but most of the informed ones seem pleased." Another city manager noted: "Most people just aren't interested. After a hard day of work, most people just want to be entertained and many city issues just aren't that exciting. It is hard to compete with *NYPD Blue*."

8. By attempting to reduce the level of citizen cynicism, this study does not imply that cynicism is undesirable; for example, the notion of checks and balances is built around distrust. The present concern is that the level of cynicism is too high. It is unlikely that efforts to reduce cynicism will result in too little cynicism.

9. Giancoli, Donald, 1993. "Citizen Survey Use in Lauderhill, Florida," paper presented at the Southeastern Conference on Public Administration (SECOPA), Cocoa Beach, Florida, October; Glaser, Mark A., and James W. Bardo, 1994. "A Five Stage Approach for Improved Use of Citizen Surveys in Public Investment Decisions," *State and Local Government Review* 26 (Fall):161–172; Bacot, Hunter, Amy S. McCabe, Michael R. Fitzgerald, Terry Bowen, and David H. Folz, 1993. "Practicing the Politics of Inclusion: Citizen Surveys and the Design of Solid Waste Recycling Programs," *American Review*

of Public Administration 23 (no.1):29–41.

10. The position adopted here is that advertisement should be informative, not misleading or deceitful. Concerns about government marketing are usually allayed by solely reporting factual data.

11. The survey was sent to all 502 city managers and CAOs in cities with populations above 50,000. A total of 302 useable responses was received (response rate = 62%).

12. These results were compared against the results of other national polls of citizens and found to be consistent with the direct assessments of citizens (ABC/*Washington Post*, January 1990, poll of 1518 citizens; *Changing Public Attitudes on Government and Taxes*, 1993. Washington, DC: Advisory Commission on Intergovernmental Relations; National Opinion Research Center, 1987. *General Social Survey*. Storrs, CT: Roper; Gallup, 1995, monthly poll of citizen attitudes). Table 1 shows that more respondents meet citizen needs than understand citizen needs. This may suggest that although citizens perceive services to be effective, other needs are unaddressed. This analysis also shows the dangers of relying on broad measures of trust.

13. It should be noted, however, that the composite measure of reputation is not associated with cynicism. Two possible explanations are that these efforts are not yet fully developed and that they are targeted at a business audience.

14. Bellah, Robert N., Richard Madsen, William M. Sullivan, Ann Swidler, and Steven M. Tipton, 1991. *The Good Society*. New York, NY: Vintage Press.

The Ethics of Community Building

_____ Evan M. Berman and Stephen J. Bonczek

Community building is renewal from within that enhances a citizen's sense of ownership and concern with the long-term sustainability of the neighborhood. It involves government and citizens in mutually supportive relationships and commitment to the common good in such areas as economic development, environmental protection, social welfare, transportation, and education (Giles 1993; Heffernan and Ruiz 1996; Oliver 1995; Ostrom 1993). Thus, the importance of community building in defining relationships between government and citizens is critical for cities and counties in an era of declining group membership, public cynicism, and limited resources. For example, youth violence cannot be addressed effectively by increased policing or sentencing alone. Rather, it requires coordinated and committed actions among schools (e.g., after-school programs), parents, teen organizations, and businesses (malls, movie theaters, etc.) to minimize the opportunities and reasons for violence. The effectiveness of such efforts, as well as the personal and spiritual needs that bring people to community, creates optimism for increased citizen participation.

This increased need for citizen self-reliance—taking responsibility for one's own children, neighbors, and community—demonstrates the need to activate and engage community groups in self-governance. In this regard, community building acknowledges the limitations that exist when governments try to address vital social and economic issues by acting alone and imposing solutions on neighborhoods; instead, it emphasizes the need for coordination and many forms of direct, ongoing collaboration between citizens and the leaders of organizations that serve neighborhoods to "get the job done." Managers are increasingly aware of new ways in which they are partners in drawing other organizations into building stronger communities. Government leaders foster collaborative attitudes and efforts by supporting community-wide planning processes; providing resources to community organizations; and strengthening neighborhood organizations to become more effective, collaborative partners. For example, some cities work with local community banks that finance neighborhood improvements by residents and small business start-ups. Governments are also increasingly sensitive to the barriers to community building that are created through needless regulations and restrictions. Thus, its leaders focus their energies and resources on creating conditions that encourage citizens to be responsible for more aspects of their neighborhoods and lives (Carpenter 1989; Chrislip and Larson 1994; Gates 1991, 1997).

These efforts by government leaders to direct and facilitate community-building activities require not only *strategy* (e.g., knowledge of how to conduct community-based strategic planning, how to create successful local economic revitalization programs, etc.), but also *ethics* that inform and drive strategy and that must be considered to ensure that the public interest is consistently served. Ethics are important both because they help maintain strategic focus and direction and because government leaders must be viewed as credible, sincere, and competent by others in their community. Managers must also deal with myriad challenges that are ethical in nature. This article discusses the ethics of community building by focusing on four key values that greatly affect the success of community building. These values are *shared responsibility, inclusiveness, openness,* and *results orientation.* Although other values are important, such as being honest or caring and nurturing, we believe that these four values, which often contain other values and ethical considerations, are the most important. This article examines these values as well as various ethical challenges that arise in community building.

Shared responsibility

The notion of shared responsibility implies that organizations must contribute according to their distinctive strengths and capacities. Each organization must take responsibility for fulfilling its role as part of a larger, concerted effort. The strengths of local governments often involve funding, policy development, and service efforts that support other organizations and neighborhoods. The strength of many local organizations is their solid connection to their constituencies, which enables them to draw on volunteer efforts and expertise that reduce the cost of program implementation.

However, shared responsibility does not mean that organizations necessarily band together in jointly formulating, accepting, and executing new responsibilities. Priorities that are key to some organizations may be less critical or even prohibited by others. Local government power is constrained by law, regulation, and political processes. Thus, shared responsibility implies that organizations must acknowledge their different roles (Bryson and Crosby 1992).

Because of their different purposes, organizations and their leaders often must work toward establishing common ground. Community-based planning processes emphasize the development of a sense of shared history, commonalities of identity, the understanding of common challenges, and mutually supportive efforts in shaping the future. A useful tool in this regard is the identification of bioregions; this is done by dividing the community along naturally occurring divisions such as climate, watershed, mountains, and travel, thereby defining the natural neighborhood. The involvement of neighborhood groups in the process of identifying natural neighborhoods builds community (Bull Frog Films 1997).

Problems quickly arise, however, when organizations are not perceived to be effective or responsible partners in community building. Cities vary in their commitments to this effort, sometimes because they lack political will or resources. In other instances, community organizations fail to act with integrity. As an illustration, a community church received a city loan to renovate its property and establish a restaurant that would provide on-the-job training to disadvantaged youth. In the first two years of the project, which was economically unsuccessful, the church made only two payments on its loan of $20,000 while investing $25,000 of its own money in the renovation of its main building. When the church later approached the city for more money for counseling and outreach, it was turned down on the basis of past experience: it was not viewed as a reliable partner in community development. Organizations must work hard toward creating a mutual trust that assumed responsibilities will be honored in ways that show high levels of commitment to common purposes.

A similar problem occurs when community organizations ask government to do work that is tantamount to assuming their own responsibilities. For example, is it the job of the local humane society, government, or both to inform citizens of the functions of this organization? Issues arise when community organizations refuse—or lack the adequate capacity—to do what is perceived as their "fair share." For example, the local chamber of commerce may lack adequate resources and vision to develop a comprehensive strategy for local economic development. In these instances, local governments must decide whether they wish to support efforts to increase that capacity.

Local governments must delineate the areas of their responsibility. Specifically, cities must choose which issues they will support. Because local governments must balance the interests of constituencies, they give most issues less priority than is accorded by single-issue organizations (such as those dealing with homelessness, the environment, handicapped persons, etc.). Local governments may also lack the needed resources to assist the full range of organizations that seek support for their missions. These practical constraints require local officials to justify their support of some causes over others. The ethical bases for making these hard choices involve considerations about (1) the moral and legal legitimacy of municipal involvement, (2) the willingness and ability of organizations to assume responsibility as partners in addressing the problem, and (3) the effectiveness and fairness of proposed solutions. A further consideration is the political will to see municipal commitments through to completion.

Decisions about community priorities should not be made in isolation from concerned parties. Community-based decision-making processes help generate understanding and commitment to these decisions and avoid political suspicions of favoritism or discrimination that sometimes arise. For example, when a Latino community organization had its proposal rejected for a community development project shortly after a similar proposal from an African-American organization was rejected, suspicion arose that the council failed to support the Latino proposal to avoid the appearance of favoritism and the anger of African-American groups. In fact, both proposals were rejected for lack of adequate organization and financial capacity. Community-based planning processes foster positive interactions among community organizations, generate understanding, and provide an opportunity to infuse neighborhood efforts with proper, objective standards for funding and shared responsibility. In the above example, instead of encouraging separate submissions, the city might have done better to create a process of community-based decision making that would have resulted in concurrent and perhaps more suitable proposals.

Inclusiveness

The premise of community building requires the involvement of a broad range of organizations that are willing to participate and share their capabilities. When many organizations participate, resources increase and organizations find support and new connections with actors with whom they may be unfamiliar. For example, community-based efforts for local economic development often bring together key employers as well as area universities and community colleges. Leaders from these institutions seldom interact with each other because their spheres of activity are very different. When they do meet, however, they may find areas of common interest and develop new initiatives that were not foreseen by any strategic planning activity. For example, a community college decided to invest in new computer-aided design and manufacturing technology upon learning that area companies needed employees with these skills (National Civic League 1996; Wood and Gray 1991).

Thus, inclusiveness often improves decision making and broadens support. In another instance, a city had to address the safety of a bank's customers who often parked illegally on a heavily used, one-way thoroughfare while using the bank's automated teller machine. Whereas the city could have acted single-handedly and decided to hand out parking tickets, it opted instead to involve both the bank and the state Department of Transportation, which maintained the road, in the decision making. Inclusion of the state resulted in a study to install temporary parking on the thoroughfare; this study addressed many of the bank's concerns as well. Clearly, community building is enhanced by encouraging even unwilling stakeholders to share in the responsibility of problem resolution.

The pursuit of inclusion increases the acceptance of initiatives. A community involved in a significant downtown revitalization program established special task forces of community leaders and affected business people to help in the planning process. After numerous meetings, discussions, and analyses, the plan was completed and presented to the council at a public hearing. At this time, significant citizen concerns were voiced about the plan and its impact on the residential neighborhood. Because scant attention had been paid to the value of inclusiveness in this instance, the plan was not approved. After significant additional outreach, however, the plan was modified to ensure both political and community support for its implementation. Thus it can be seen that inclusiveness is enhanced when government supports, rather than displaces, community neighborhood networks.

A key to developing inclusiveness is identifying common values and interests that motivate organizations and leaders to join. These values and interests must be broad enough to accommodate diverse organizations. This is not merely an intellectual activity but also a political one. Local government leaders often encounter centrifugal forces that work against inclusion. Typically, when community organizations are rivals, they exert pressure on other organizations and public officials to limit citizen participation in their opposition and may pressure elected officials to exclude some organizations. Conversely, some elected officials may have animus against other community leaders and wish to see them excluded. For example, business leaders and elected officials may distrust certain community activists and thereby seek to limit the scope of the proposed community-based efforts. Local officials must guard against such exclusion efforts lest they be seen as biased, elitist, and self-interested.

It should be noted that the inclusion of organizations, leaders, and citizens also provides opportunities for those who are vocal critics. Within each community there usually are active citizen critics who thrive on dissension, division, and personal attacks on the credibility of public leaders. These individuals often seek out opportunities to express their concern with public initiatives. They sometimes complain that decision-making processes are rigged and that leaders have used "secret meetings" to make up their minds. They are rarely interested in solving problems as they seldom offer viable solutions. Their disruptive tactics are a challenge to the processes of collaborative decision making.

Clearly, people have the right to make up their own minds and not have the government think for them. The challenge is to accommodate these vocal critics in ethical and legal ways. An often-mentioned strategy for public officials to neutralize this opposition is to appoint these individuals to advisory boards, committees, or task forces. The intent is to have them become more involved in the structure of government operation in the hope that they will become "enlightened" and support the value of the government initiatives with which they were concerned. The risk, however, is that they will become more enlightened and find more things to attack from the more legitimized position of being part of the local government, even in an advisory capacity. In essence, the citizen complainer in this case gains the credibility of position to disrupt the board's ability to conduct business. For example, a very vocal local businessperson, upset with the establishment of an improvement district that imposed rules, regulations, and an additional tax burden, was incensed when he was not considered for appointment to the advisory board. Yet he had made it very clear that his sole purpose was to work toward the abolition of the improvement district and that he was not concerned with community-building efforts in the downtown area of the city. The challenge, then, is to acknowledge the concerns of such critics and nay-sayers while ensuring that disruptive tactics do not derail the work of the community.

Another example of the challenge of inclusion concerns a community social worker who, while under municipal contract to assist neighborhood organizations, organized a march against city hall by these organizations in order to "empower" them. Under such circumstances, the challenge is to respect the need for inclusion while keeping the primary goal in mind—namely, the creation of viable bases of shared community responsibilities toward common ends. From an ethical perspective, what is needed are individuals demonstrating political courage in addressing controversial yet important community issues in a nonadversarial and nonconfrontational way. While local leaders must often tolerate their critics, they should not fail to support and encourage those who work collaboratively toward common solutions.

Openness

Trust is key to the success of community-based efforts. Community organizations and their leaders, as well as citizens, must believe that other organizations honor their commitments and that these commitments are made primarily to resolve community problems rather than to serve the individual interests of participating organizations and individuals. Double dealing, hidden agendas, and private pursuits diminish trust and, ultimately, cooperation and contribution. The key to building trust is openness (sometimes called "transparency") of intentions and decision-making processes. Leaders must provide adequate information for others to judge that community-building efforts are what they appear to be: actions that address the welfare of communities and welcome the participation of all. Openness is especially critical in efforts to overcome the voices of skeptics and cynics. In this regard, a recent survey finds that community leaders have only moderate trust in local government officials to understand the needs of community organizations and fulfill their promises (Berman 1996). The failure to share pertinent information undermines trust and the democratic process while diminishing the value of openness in community building.

The legal requirements of "sunshine laws" are often insufficient to ensure adequate openness. While it is important that minutes of public meetings are available, the purpose of openness is to foster trust and a positive climate of cooperation. Since some participants are unknown to each other and others are skeptical, the good intentions of leaders must be communicated in a consistent and persistent way if they are to have impact. Further, openness should be shared as a value and reinforced by other members of community-building efforts. People do not change their opinions because someone else has said something to the contrary; they change their opinions because they see factual confirmation and because opinions are shared by others in strong and persuasive ways.

Openness is increasingly important in community building. A local government administration that supported community building by using federal funds to acquire and demolish houses in a transitional neighborhood became very controversial. Although the purpose of the project was to support programs of the Police Athletic League Association and institute a food bank in a local church, the controversy emanated from the fact that the houses were owned by an existing minority member of city council who was also a pastor at the church that was receiving funds for the food bank. To add to the controversy, the councilperson had recently complained at a public meeting about neighborhood plans to establish boundaries for community-building efforts that appeared to exclude his church. Therefore, powerful conflict-of-interest issues—both perceived and real—were involved in the use of federal funds to achieve community-building objectives through the acquisition of property and the provision of food bank services to an elected official. The perception of conflict was fueled by a sense that the assistance may have been recommended by the local government administration in response to the councilperson's criticism that the neighborhood plan lacked inclusiveness.

Both the administration and the councilperson who benefited from these initiatives failed to provide adequate information at public meetings discussing community development plans. Therefore, the rest of the council and the community became aware of the conflict-of-interest impact of the project after the fact, which created the appearance of an intentional withholding of information. Local government leaders must be open to providing essential information on controversial issues. With poor communication and a lack of sensitivity to the political and ethical impact of policy proposals, the result is a perception of deceit, which feeds a lack of trust in government. Successful communication efforts focus on how to do things right and ethically. A comprehensive communication policy that stresses responsiveness provides strategic support to the ethical value of openness (Thomas 1995).

A complicating ethical factor is that municipal officials have a strategic interest in controlling the amount of information that is provided, especially to disruptive critics. Although managers are often legally required to provide certain information, they still have much leeway in deciding what other information to present or withhold. Ethically, there needs to be an appreciation of what others need to make informed decisions on public policy related to community building. Openness is a means, not an end, and there is little reason to encourage those who work against common purposes. Managers need to consider their obligation to provide information while fostering trust and strong working relations.

Results orientation

Community building must be efficacious. Local government officials must search for "best practices" in community building and then design strategies to ensure that such efforts add value to the community. Concentrating on outcomes is necessary to help form productive relations among organizations and also to divert attention away from philosophical or political concerns. Local officials often search for efforts that have been successful elsewhere and can be used as models for their jurisdictions; this helps avoid unnecessary attempts to "reinvent the wheel." In this regard, various Web sites are now available that are replete with examples of community-building strategies; one might turn, for example, to the site of the National Center for Public Productivity (http://newark.rutgers.edu/~ncpp/), which has links to many other sites with award-winning best practices. The International City/County Management Association (ICMA) IQ Service and the Innovation Groups headquartered in Tampa, Florida, are also excellent resources for successful efforts of community-building initiatives (Roberts 1995).

Accountability is ethically necessary and helps focus implementation efforts. Responsibilities must be assigned, and as the saying goes, "what gets measured gets done." Thus, performance measurement must be integrated into community-based efforts. For example, economic development efforts often include standards for expected outcomes. Collection and distribution of such information adds to openness and may increase trust for future efforts. Some community-building efforts include client and citizen surveys. A fundamental questions is, "Have we improved your quality of life?" This allows leaders to measure success according to "citizen-defined values" and thus incorporate their views into decision making (Berman 1998).

Managers and public leaders have the ethical responsibility to identify and implement the best practices that create value in all service areas. Community building in itself reflects a best practice to establish new partnerships to solve community problems in innovative and more connective ways. Managers have an obligation to educate staff in this effort. There are healthy community coalitions across the country that bring citizens, business leaders, and community leaders together to strategically plan for the future of the region. This process is an excellent source of training for individuals or small groups who wish to become more involved in the important process of community building.

A manager pursuing the best practice of community building must be consistent with the values and direction of the governing body and the community, or the pursuit will be viewed as another effort to enhance his or her career, professional reputation, and résumé. It could even be perceived as the ethics of self-interest versus the use of best practices to serve the needs of the community. A critical question is, "Is career reward a primary driving force to use best practices for community building or a positive by-product of this effort?" The business of government is in building communities. Success depends on the mobilization of grass-roots efforts and the leveraging of resources from all areas to deal effectively with problems and issues. This requires consistency with council priorities.

In conclusion, the process of community building tapping into the creative energies of those who care creates a powerful blueprint for social change. Active citizenship is needed where individuals inform themselves on key issues confronting their communities, participate in civic improvement groups, struggle to find common ground with others, and become responsible for local governments and their communities. Ethics must guide specific community-building strategies. Public managers cannot always anticipate what situations will arise. As an essential component of community building, ethics are critical to the success of local governments as they engage the hearts and minds of the community.

References

Berman, E. *Productivity in Public and Nonprofit Organizations.* Thousand Oaks, CA: Sage, 1998.

Berman, E. "Restoring the Bridges of Trust: Attitudes of Community Leaders toward Local Government," *Public Integrity Annual* 1 (1996):31–39.

Bryson, J., and B. Crosby. *Leadership for the Common Good.* San Francisco, CA: Jossey-Bass, 1992.

Bull Frog Films. *Ways We Live, Exploring Community, Maps with Teeth.* Reading, PA: Author, 1997. Video.

Carpenter, S. "Solving Community Problems by Consensus." Washington, DC: International City/County Management Association, *MIS Report* 21 (October 1989).

Chrislip, D., and C. Larson. *Collaborative Leadership: How Citizens and Civic Leaders Can Make a Difference.* San Francisco, CA: Jossey-Bass, 1994.

Gates, C. "Making a Case for Collaborative Problem Solving," *National Civic Review* 80, no. 1 (1991):113–119.

Gates, C. "Notes from the President," *National Civic Review* 86, no. 1 (1997):1–2.

Giles, M. "The Atlanta Project: A Community-Based Approach to Solving Urban Problems," *National Civic Review* 82, no. 4 (1993):354–362.

Heffernan, T., and Ruiz, J. "Forming Partnerships with Neighborhoods."

Public Management 77 (October 1996):10–13.

National Center for Public Productivity. 1997. Web site: http://newark.rutgers.edu/~ncpp/

National Civic League. "Connecting Government and Neighborhoods," *Governing* 10, no. 1 (1996):48–54.

Oliver, M. "Building Healthy Communities," *Orlando Sentinel,* 1 October 1995, p. G1.

Ostrom, E. "A Communitarian Approach to Local Governance." *National Civic Review* 82, no. 3 (1993):226–232.

Roberts, D. "Delivering on Democracy: High Performance Government for Virginia," *University of Virginia Newsletter* 71, no. 6 (1995).

Thomas, J. *Public Participation in Public Decisions.* San Francisco, CA: Jossey-Bass, 1995.

Wheeland, C. "City-Wide Strategic Planning: An Evaluation of Rock Hill's Empowering the Vision." *Public Administration Review* 53 (1993):65–72.

Wood, D., and B. Gray. "Toward a Comprehensive Theory of Collaboration," *Journal of Applied Behavioral Science* 27 (1991):139–162.

Current Ethics Issues for Local Government Managers

Elizabeth K. Kellar

The ICMA code of ethics has guided the conduct of professional local government managers since 1924. Its twelve tenets address many topics that are common to other ethical codes, such as conflict of interest and acceptance of gifts, but it also provides guidance to nonpartisan professionals in local government on such sensitive matters as political activity and investments in real estate.

By joining the association, a member subscribes to the ICMA code of ethics. The code is enforced by the organization's executive board with the assistance of its Committee on Professional Conduct, which receives and investigates complaints, determines whether a violation has occurred, and levies sanctions.

On behalf of the board and the committee, designated ICMA staff respond to ethics inquiries, provide advice based on committee decisions, and carry out public censures. For educational purposes, situations that have resulted in private censures are disguised to protect the individuals involved and then published in the *ICMA Newsletter*. Advice on ethics questions raised by members is published in *Public Management* magazine.

Salient issues

Over the past two decades, ICMA's members have debated a number of ethical questions. What are appropriate and inappropriate investments for a manager whose job gives him or her influence over property values, code enforcement, and community services? What is a manager's responsibility if his or her spouse holds a job or position that may create a conflict of interest? What products or services, if any, can a manager properly endorse?

Political activity and employment agreement issues generated the most intense discussion among ICMA members in the late 1990s. This article examines these questions in detail and provides some additional thoughts on ICMA's enforcement and education efforts.

Political activity After some debate, the Committee on Professional Conduct issued a private censure to a manager who had become involved in political activities in her former community. As with other private censures, ICMA published a brief summary of the ethics violation in the *ICMA Newsletter*. A highly respected city manager wrote in response to suggest that the committee had erred:

As city managers, we may become so effectively neutral, that we are unable to convey the truth. To avoid being nonpartisan, a city sometimes suffers through months of harsh criticism. If we fail to respond, the profession can appear weak. I believe there must be the latitude to speak out to the community if certain mistruths are stated.

The city manager's concern was disconcerting because this particular case had so troubled some ICMA Executive Board members that the only real debate had been whether the conduct warranted a public rather than a private censure. The member had engaged in political endorsements for one of the candidates for the governing body that had once employed her. She had identified herself as the former city manager and extolled the virtues of the candidate in paid advertisements that aired throughout the region.

Another member was publicly censured for his continued political contacts with a faction of the city council that had once employed him. He argued that his lobbying was appropriate and necessary to protect his reputation after state auditors had criticized the city's financial management. The two city managers who followed him in the community disagreed. One manager pointed out that he had not only contacted the council faction without informing her, but also testified against the city staff and the findings of a state audit at council meetings. The ICMA Executive Board found that the member had violated tenet 2, which describes the importance of maintaining "a constructive, creative, and practical attitude toward local government affairs and a deep sense of social responsibility." It also includes a guideline requiring the member to inform the administrator of a community when the member advises or responds to inquiries from elected or appointed officials from that community.

While there is a consensus that ICMA members should stay out of political campaigns involving their present employers, there is less agreement that members should avoid political activities in their former communities. Clearly, members should not lobby or do favors for a candidate who promises to rehire them. But what about other political activities, such as participating in "good government" groups that might take stands on issues or endorse a candidate who agrees with that agenda?

Seven former members of the Committee on Professional Conduct provided feedback on the question of whether it is compatible with the ICMA code of ethics for a member to contribute to a political action committee (PAC) dedicated to local government issues. Three said such contributions would violate tenet 7 of the ICMA code, which requires members to "refrain from . . . all partisan political activities which would impair performance as a professional administrator." Four opined that they would permit such contributions so long as the individual members did not take personal action for or against any candidate or issue. Even among these four members, however, two said they would not make such contributions personally. Since some states require the names of individual PAC contributors to be reported, the publication of a member's name could be construed as a public endorsement of a candidate.

One manager explained his reasoning this way:

Tempting though it may be to wish to support candidates who are sympathetic to issues of local government management, candidates may have a wider manifesto. By supporting particular candidates, the member could be seen by the public to be endorsing publicly a candidate running in a series of campaigns of which local government management is only one. In my view, the safest course is to follow the guideline on elections to the letter and not be involved personally or with an organization which campaigns for candidates for the state legislature.

Yet another political activity that has troubled some in the profession is when the former city or county manager decides to run for elected office in the jurisdiction where he or she once served as a professional administrator. The current managers express concern that such decisions blur the image of the profession in the eyes of the public. If a former city manager runs for the city council, would the average citizen think a city manager is a politician after all? While acknowledging the potential confusion, the ICMA Executive Board has not found a way to discourage this practice and still recognize the right of a former appointed administrator to run for elected office.

When ICMA publishes news of ethics violations involving political activity, more members call with questions about which activities are permitted and which are prohibited. One city man-

ager asked for advice on dealing with the governor's proposal for
a highway bond project that would result in a tax increase. This
proposal would provide the city with about $300,000 a year in a
revenue turn-back program. The state municipal league had voted
to endorse the proposal and had prepared resolutions for adoption by local governments. The city council approved the supportive resolution by a vote of 6–1, and the chamber of commerce
wanted the city manager to speak out in support of it, too. After
reviewing the guideline on "Presentation of Issues," the city
manager was reassured that it was appropriate to participate in
radio programs and to respond to questions from newspaper reporters. He would make it clear that the proposal had been approved by the municipal league and the city council and that he
would provide factual information about it.

The city manager later reported that the ballot measure had
failed badly, and he wondered if he had inadvertently crossed
the line into political activity that might hurt his reputation as
a professional administrator. While a controversial bond issue
carries some risk for the manager who represents the city council's
position, it is appropriate and ethical for the manager to serve
as the city's spokesperson.

In another community, a disgruntled former employee running for the city council made waves in the city's usually genteel
municipal campaign practices. The city publishes and distrib-
utes candidate profiles, which have traditionally included noncontroversial information such as biographical data. The former
employee used his candidate profile to claim that the city owed a
substantial amount of money to a water fund. When the city
manager saw the statement, which was factually incorrect, he
distributed a memo to the city council to correct the record. At a
candidate's briefing the next morning, the challenging candidate
accused the member of interfering with the election. ICMA staff
advised the manager to keep a low profile for the rest of the
election, to continue to provide factual information to the elected
officials, and to urge them to take the lead on the budget issues.

Political activities in the context of two-career families present
some of the most challenging waters to navigate in the local government management profession. A spouse is not bound by the
ICMA code of ethics, yet his or her political activities can create
headaches. A typical problem is the spouse's desire to support a
candidate or get involved in a controversial community issue.
One member who called for advice had served on the school board
and as a selectman in another county before he became a town
administrator. He and his wife still lived in the county where he
had been an elected official, residing on a highly visible corner
lot. They wanted to put up yard signs for various individuals

and causes, and the town administrator wondered if that presented any ethics problems. This political activity probably would not create any problems for the town administrator since it involved local issues some forty miles away from his current place of employment. At the same time, there were certain risks involved, and the town administrator and his wife were advised to develop a mutually acceptable policy to express their political preferences in that community.

A more difficult two-career challenge that has occurred with greater frequency is when one spouse is an elected official or plans to campaign for elected office. An assistant city manager's wife, who before their marriage had served on the city council for several years, was running for the office of mayor in the same community that employed the assistant. The assistant city manager reports to the manager, and the mayor's primary responsibility is to serve as the city's chief lobbyist. The mayor has veto power but does not vote on hiring or firing the city manager. In some respects, the assistant believed that his wife's service as mayor would be less of a problem than her service as a council member. He agreed to have regular discussions with the city manager about what he could do to keep his home life and work life separate. Although it could be awkward at times, the couple decided to seek others who could act as confidants on work issues.

As the ICMA Executive Board has interpreted tenet 7 over the years, members have been found to have violated the ICMA code of ethics for engaging in the following political activities:

• Campaigning for a current or former elected official of the member's governing body
• Campaigning for a local elected official in the member's former community
• Endorsing candidates for state or national office
• Allowing the member's photograph or quotation to appear in a candidate's campaign materials
• Circulating petitions for a candidate
• Making financial contributions to a local candidate
• Attempting to influence employees to support particular candidates
• Running for office while serving as the local government manager
• Supporting or contributing to a recall effort involving members of the governing body.

Although members continue to debate the application of tenet 7, they are advised to avoid activities of this kind.

After nearly three years of discussion about tenet 7 and political activity, the ICMA Executive Board revised the guideline on elections and proposed that the membership approve new language for the tenet to clarify its meaning. The membership approved the new language for tenet 7 in May 1998, reversing the order of the tenet's two phrases so that the broad principle comes first, followed by the more focused one. The board recommended this change to make it clear that even political activities outside of the employing local government can be violations of the ICMA code of ethics. The new tenet 7 reads:

Refrain from all political activities which undermine public confidence in professional administrators. Refrain from participation in the election of the members of the employing legislative body.

In January 1998, the Executive Board revised the guideline on "other elections" to include more examples of the specific political activities that are prohibited:

Elections. Members share with their fellow citizens the right and responsibility to exercise their franchise and voice their opinion on public issues. However, in order not to impair their effectiveness on behalf of the local governments they serve, they should not participate in any political activities (including, but not limited to, fundraising, endorsing candidates, and financial contributions) for representatives to city, county, special district, school, state, or federal offices.

Tenet 7 reflects one of the most important principles for the profession: that managers must avoid those political activities that could harm their reputation for fairness and impartiality. They enhance their professionalism by treating all members of the governing body equally and impartially. Their responsibility to avoid political activities beyond their immediate jurisdiction is essential because those activities have the potential to harm the community or the profession.

Employment agreements and appointment commitment
Ethics, personal financial concerns, family considerations, and the relationship with the governing body are all intertwined when an offer of employment is extended to a prospective city or county manager. The mix creates many ethics complaints and numerous requests for advice.

Once the local government has concluded its interviews and is prepared to make an offer to a prospective manager, the candidate usually has taken the following steps:

- Evaluated the community, its values, and the political environment to determine if it is a place where the manager can succeed
- Engaged in serious conversations with family members about the community, making sure that it will be a good place for them and fully understanding their feelings about moving

- Determined which provisions are essential in an employment agreement with this local government
- Waited to accept the position until absolutely sure that another offer would not tempt the manager to renege on his or her commitment.

Sadly, a few managers have behaved in a cavalier way in this dance with a prospective employer. ICMA members have been censured for accepting a position as city manager and then abandoning that position hours after reporting for work. Still others have pleaded special circumstances for a change of mind: "My wife just didn't want to leave her extended family, and I didn't realize how strongly she felt until I told her I had accepted the job."

The trend to negotiate an employment agreement before accepting a position has eliminated some of the problems that used to occur when managers believed that they had certain understandings that later evaporated when they reported for work. It has also created some new problems for the profession, especially when the public perceives that a manager had negotiated a "golden parachute" that had not been clearly disclosed to the city or county council.

Employment agreements were unusual twenty years ago. In 1971, only fifty-three managers responding to an ICMA survey had such an agreement. But by 1980, 27 percent of managers had them, and today more than 40 percent have a written agreement. To the manager, one of the most important provisions is severance pay. While six months' severance pay is the most common amount of severance found in today's agreements, the range is broad. Elected officials usually support some severance pay because they understand that along with their need to be able to fire the manager for any reason, the manager needs basic financial security so that he or she can provide the elected officials with professional advice without fear of financial disaster if the recommendation proves unpopular.

The ethical imperative for the manager is to be sure that the city council or county board of supervisors has impartial and adequate advice when entering into an agreement with a manager. Disclosure of the financial implications of the agreement is important so that there are no misunderstandings. Professional managers understand that they begin building trust with their elected officials in those first discussions.

The ethics of the golden parachute has been hotly debated, particularly in California. An editorial published in *The Oakland Tribune,* 27 April 1995, shows how the general public views some of these severance clauses: "Wouldn't you like to have a contract with your boss that made it nearly impossible for him or her to fire you? A contract that included a severance package that was so expensive the boss would break his budget if he or she got rid of you? . . . If public servants are only motivated by the salaries, then maybe they should be working in the private rather than the public sector."[1]

Some of the golden parachutes came not from employment agreements but from a practice called "pension spiking." Several widely publicized cases described local officials, including city managers, who had converted benefits into salary for the last two years of work in order to receive a higher pension. This practice was discontinued after California passed legislation to bar it but not before the image of the profession was damaged.

As Robert Christofferson, former chairman of the Committee on Professional Conduct, wrote in the September 1992 issue of *Public Management,* the problem arises when "the manager . . . secures a level of compensation that far exceeds reasonable norms and whose compensation may appear to be obscene in the eyes of the less well-paid people who pay the bills."[2]

In discussions about employment agreements, members have stressed the need for such agreements to be good, fair, and enforceable. In some situations, newly elected officials do not want to honor the terms of an agreement negotiated by a prior city council. State laws vary on this point. Georgia law requires that an agreement be renewed any time there is a new council member. As a result, agreements are rare in Georgia. There is no groundswell to make any changes in the ethics advice ICMA provides on employment agreements or appointment commitment.

ICMA asked members about their views of a statement in the tenet 3 guideline on appointment commitment: "Oral acceptance of an employment offer is considered binding unless the employer makes fundamental changes in terms of employment." While one or two members expressed concern about their ability to stay in a community because of turnover on the council or other shifting political considerations, most could not fathom why ICMA would be asking the question. "Your word is your word," was the typical refrain. So in a world of carefully negotiated employment agreements, the profession still believes that integrity is reflected in a handshake or a simple, "Yes, I accept your offer."

Enforcement and education

ICMA typically reviews twenty to thirty ethics complaints each year, most of which are lodged by other members of the association. In 1996, ICMA issued four public censures, including one membership bar, and seven private censures, including one expulsion; it dismissed fifteen cases. In 1997, the ICMA Committee on Professional Conduct issued nine private censures and dismissed eleven cases. The public censures were issued for stealing from public funds to make credit card and car payments; making highly political contact with a faction of the council after leaving the jurisdiction and without notifying the current manager; misrepresenting work experience on a résumé by indicating service in a position where the member had never been employed; and failing to publicly disclose ownership interest in real estate within the member's jurisdiction.

The committee issued more private censures for inaccurate résumés than for any other ethical violation. Members claimed to have degrees they did not earn or used misleading position titles. The violations relating to political activity included running for a county elected office while serving as city manager and endorsing two candidates for federal office who would serve in the member's jurisdiction if elected. Two members were privately censured for accepting a position but failing to report for work. Use of the city credit card for personal purposes, a classic error that can easily lead to an ethics violation, resulted in two private censures. There was only one private censure related to investments that could create a conflict of interest with official duties; this may indicate that members are becoming more careful in this area.

While ICMA has received complaints from individuals over the years who describe themselves as whistle-blowers, no complaint resulted in an ethics violation until 1996. In that case, the city manager fired an individual who had raised complaints about the city's landfill operation. This was the first individual fired by that city manager in more than fifteen years, and the sequence of events was clear. The committee found that the manager had violated tenet 11, which requires the member to "handle all matters of personnel on the basis of merit so that fairness and impartiality govern a member's decisions pertaining to appointments, pay adjustments, promotions, and discipline."

Since ICMA started an ethics column in *Public Management* magazine to publicize the advice it provides to members, more individuals call ICMA with ethics questions. Most of the time, the questions deal with sophisticated issues; many of the questions have to do with political rather than ethical judgment. The public airing of the real problems that the profession struggles with every day has generated a healthy discussion of issues. Some readers have suggested that the scenarios are too "far-fetched" to be true. Those asking those far-fetched questions only wish they were not living that particular reality!

An unmarried county manager needed advice to deal with a delicate problem. He had finally met someone he would like to date, but she also worked for the county! He concluded that he needed to face this conflict of interest and wanted advice on how to minimize the difficulties he might encounter. His first instinct was a good one: to talk with the county board. This is consistent with the guideline for tenet 12 dealing with personal relationships: "Members should disclose any personal relationship to the governing body in any instance where there could be the appearance of a conflict of interest." He also decided to ask the assistant county manager to review any personnel actions that might involve the woman he wanted to date, in order to avoid a direct conflict with tenet 11. He recognized that it might be necessary at some point for one of the two to seek other employment. In this case, the manager was willing to take whatever steps were necessary to pursue his heart's desire.

Those outside of the profession might see some of ICMA's advice as overly cautious. What ICMA tells its members is that even if an action is legal, it may not be ethical. And even if it may not violate the ICMA code of ethics, members may be uncomfortable seeing their action described on the front page of the local newspaper.

First adopted in 1924, the ICMA code of ethics remains central to the local government management profession. Members proudly display it on their walls, share it with their elected officials so that they can learn about the values of the profession, and provide ample feedback to the ICMA Executive Board on ethical issues that concern them. The interpretation of what is inappropriate political activity or a conflict of interest may change over the years, but the sense of the ICMA member's responsibility to the community as a whole is as strong today as it was in 1924.

Notes

1. "The Gadzillion-Dollar Golden Parachute," *The Oakland Tribune,* 27 April 1995, p. A 14. Editorial.

2. Robert Christofferson, "How Much Is Too Much?" *Public Management* (September 1992):22.

Appendix A: ICMA Code of Ethics with guidelines

1. Be dedicated to the concepts of effective and democratic local government by responsible elected officials and believe that professional general management is essential to the achievement of this objective.

2. Affirm the dignity and worth of the services rendered by government and maintain a constructive, creative, and practical attitude toward local government affairs and a deep sense of social responsibility as a trusted public servant.

Guideline

Advice to officials of other local governments When members advise and respond to inquiries from elected or appointed officials of other municipalities, they should inform the administrators of those communities.

3. Be dedicated to the highest ideals of honor and integrity in all public and personal relationships in order that the member may merit the respect and confidence of the elected officials, of other officials and employees, and of the public.

Guidelines

Public confidence Members should conduct themselves so as to maintain public confidence in their profession, their local government, and in their performance of the public trust.

Impression of influence Members should conduct their official and personal affairs in such a manner as to give the clear impression that they cannot be improperly influenced in the performance of their official duties.

Appointment commitment Members who accept an appointment to a position should not fail to report for that position. This does not preclude the possibility of a member considering several offers or seeking several positions at the same time, but once a bona fide offer of a position has been accepted, that commitment should be honored. Oral acceptance of an employment offer is considered binding unless the employer makes fundamental changes in terms of employment.

Credentials An application for employment should be complete and accurate as to all pertinent details of education, experience, and personal history. Members should recognize that both omissions and inaccuracies must be avoided.

Professional respect Members seeking a management position should show professional respect for persons formerly holding the position or for others who might be applying for the same position. Professional respect does not preclude honest differences of opinion; it does preclude attacking a person's motives or integrity in order to be appointed to a position.

Confidentiality Members should not discuss or divulge information with anyone about pending or completed ethics cases, except as specifically authorized by the Rules of Procedure for Enforcement of the Code of Ethics.

Seeking employment Members should not seek employment for a position having an incumbent administrator who has not resigned or been officially informed that his or her services are to be terminated.

4. Recognize that the chief function of local government at all times is to serve the best interests of all the people.

Guideline
Length of service A minimum of two years generally is considered necessary in order to render a professional service to the local government. A short tenure should be the exception rather than a recurring experience. However, under special circumstances, it may be in the best interests of the local government and the member to separate in a shorter time. Examples of such circumstances would include refusal of the

appointing authority to honor commitments concerning conditions of employment, a vote of no confidence in the member, or severe personal problems. It is the responsibility of an applicant for a position to ascertain conditions of employment. Inadequately determining terms of employment prior to arrival does not justify premature termination.

5. Submit policy proposals to elected officials; provide them with facts and advice on matters of policy as a basis for making decisions and setting community goals; and uphold and implement municipal policies adopted by elected officials.

Guideline
Conflicting roles Members who serve multiple roles—working as both city attorney and city manager for the same community, for example—should avoid participating in matters that create the appearance of a conflict of interest. They should disclose the potential conflict to the governing body so that other opinions may be solicited.

6. Recognize that elected representatives of the people are entitled to the credit for the establishment of municipal policies; responsibility for policy execution rests with the members.

7. Refrain from all political activities which undermine public confidence in professional administrators. Refrain from participation in the election of the members of the employing legislative body.

Guidelines
Elections of the governing body. Members should maintain a repu-

tation for serving equally and impartially all members of the governing body of the local government they serve, regardless of party. To this end, they should not engage in active participation in the election campaign on behalf of or in opposition to candidates for the governing body.

Elections of elected executives Members should not engage in the election campaign of any candidate for mayor or elected county executive.

Elections Members share with their fellow citizens the right and responsibility to exercise their franchise and voice their opinion on public issues. However, in order not to impair their effectiveness on behalf of the local governments they serve, they should not participate in any political activities (including but not limited to fundraising, endorsing candidates, and financial contributions) for representatives to city, county, special district, school, state, or federal offices.

Elections on the council-manager plan Members may assist in preparing and presenting materials that explain the council-manager form of government to the public prior to an election on the use of the plan. If assistance is required by another community, members may respond. All activities regarding ballot issues should be conducted within local regulations and in a professional manner.

Presentation of issues Members may assist the governing body in presenting issues involved in referenda such as bond issues, annexations, and similar matters.

8. Make it a duty continually to improve the member's professional ability and to develop the competence of associates in the use of management techniques.

Guidelines

Self-assessment Each member should assess his or her professional skills and abilities on a periodic basis.

Professional development Each member should commit at least 40 hours per year to professional development activities that are based on the practices identified by the members of ICMA.

9. Keep the community informed on local government affairs; encourage communication between the citizens and all local government officers; emphasize friendly and courteous service to the public; and seek to improve the quality and image of public service.

10. Resist any encroachment on professional responsibilities, believing the member should be free to carry out official policies without interference, and handle each problem without discrimination on the basis of principle and justice.

Guideline

Information sharing The member should openly share information with the governing body while diligently carrying out the member's responsibilities as set forth in the charter or enabling legislation.

11. Handle all matters of personnel on the basis of merit so that fairness and impartiality govern a member's decisions

pertaining to appointments, pay adjustments, promotions, and discipline.

Guideline

Equal opportunity Members should develop a positive program that will ensure meaningful employment opportunities for all segments of the community. All programs, practices, and operations should: (1) provide equality of opportunity in employment for all persons; (2) prohibit discrimination because of race, color, religion, sex, national origin, political affiliation, physical handicaps, age, or marital status; and (3) promote continuing programs of affirmative action at every level within the organization.

It should be the member's personal and professional responsibility to actively recruit and hire minorities and women to serve on professional staffs throughout their organization.

12. Seek no favor; believe that personal aggrandizement or profit secured by confidential information or by misuse of public time is dishonest.

Guidelines

Gifts Members should not directly or indirectly solicit any gift or accept or receive any gift—whether it be money, services, loan, travel, entertainment, hospitality, promise, or any other form—under the following circumstances: (1) it could reasonably be inferred or expected that the gift was intended to influence them in the performance of their official duties; or (2) the gift was intended to serve as a reward for any official action on their part.

It is important that the prohibition of unsolicited gifts be limited to circumstances related to improper influence. In de minimus situations such as tobacco and meal checks, for example, some modest maximum dollar value should be determined by the member as a guideline. The guideline is not intended to isolate members from normal social practices where gifts among friends, associates, and relatives are appropriate for certain occasions.

Investments in conflict with official duties Members should not invest or hold any investment, directly or indirectly, in any financial business, commercial, or other private transaction that creates a conflict with their official duties.

In the case of real estate, the potential use of confidential information and knowledge to further a member's personal interest requires special consideration. This guideline recognizes that members' official actions and decisions can be influenced if there is a conflict with personal investments. Purchases and sales which might be interpreted as speculation for quick profit ought to be avoided (see guideline on "Confidential Information").

Because personal investments may prejudice or may appear to influence official actions and decisions, members may, in concert with their governing body, provide for disclosure of such investments prior to accepting their position as local government administrator or prior to any official action by the governing body that may affect such investments.

Personal relationships Members should disclose any personal relationship to the governing body in any instance where there could be the appearance of a conflict of interest. For example, if the manager's spouse works for a developer doing business with the local government, that fact should be disclosed.

Confidential information Members should not disclose to others, or use to further their personal interest, confidential information acquired by them in the course of their official duties.

Private employment Members should not engage in, solicit, negotiate for, or promise to accept private employment, nor should they render services for private interests or conduct a private business when such employment, service, or business creates a conflict with or impairs the proper discharge of their official duties.

Teaching, lecturing, writing, or consulting are typical activities that may not involve conflict of interest or impair the proper discharge of their official duties. Prior notification of the governing body is appropriate in all cases of outside employment.

Representation Members should not represent any outside interest before any agency, whether public or private, except with the authorization of or at the direction of the appointing authority they serve.

Endorsements Members should not endorse commercial products or services by agreeing to use their photograph, endorsement, or quotation in paid or other commercial advertisements, whether or not for compensation. Members may, however, agree to the following, provided they do not receive any compensation: (1) books or other publications; (2) professional development or educational services provided by non-profit membership organizations or recognized educational institutions; (3) products and/or services in which the local government has a direct economic interest.

Members' observations, opinions, and analyses of commercial products used or tested by their local governments are appropriate and useful to the profession when included as part of professional articles and reports.

The ICMA Code of Ethics was adopted by the membership in 1924 and most recently amended in May 1998. The guidelines were adopted by the ICMA Executive Board in 1972 and most recently revised in January 1998.

Appendix B:
For Further
Reading

Barrett, Edith J. "The Role of Public Opinion in Public Administration." *Annals of the American Academy of Political and Social Science* 537 (January 1995): 150–162.

Bennett, William J., ed. *The Book of Virtues: A Treasury of Great Moral Stories.* New York: Simon & Schuster, 1993.

Berman, Evan M. "Rebuilding the Bridges of Trust: Attitudes of Community Leaders toward Local Government." *Public Integrity Annual* 1 (1996):31–40.

Berman, Evan M., and Jonathan P. West. "Managing Ethics to Improve Performance and Build Trust." *Public Integrity Annual* 2 (1997):23–32.

Berman, Evan M., and Jonathan P. West. "Values Management in Local Government." *Review of Public Personnel Management* 14, no. 2 (1994):6–23.

Berman, Evan M., Jonathan P. West, and Anita Cava. "Ethics Management in Municipal Governments and Large Firms: Exploring Similarities and Differences." *Administration & Society* 26, no. 2 (1994):185–203.

Bonczek, Stephen B. "Ethical Decision-Making: A Practical Approach for Local Governments." *Public Personnel Management* 21, no. 1 (1992):75–88.

Bowman, James S., ed. *Ethical Frontiers in Public Management.* San Francisco: Jossey-Bass, 1991.

Bowman, James S. "Ethics and Quality: A 'Right-Good' Combination." In *Quality Management Today: What Local Governments Need to Know*, ed. J.P. West, 64–69. Washington, D.C.: International City/County Management Association, 1995.

Bowman, James S., and Frederick A. Elliston, eds. *Ethics, Government, and Public Policy: A Reference Guide.* New York: Greenwood Press, 1988.

Bowman, James S., and Donald Menzel, eds. *Teaching Ethics and Values.* New York: SUNY Press, 1998.

Brown, M. *Working Ethics: Strategies for Decision-Making and Organizational Responsibility.* San Francisco: Jossey-Bass, 1990.

Bruce, Willa. "Ethics Education in Municipal Government: It Does Make a Difference." In *Teaching Ethics and Values*, ed. J. Bowman and D. Menzel, 231–249. New York: SUNY Press, 1998.

Burke, F., and A. Black. "Improving Organizational Productivity: Add Ethics." *Public Productivity and Management Review* 14 (Winter):121–133.

Carter, S. *Integrity*. New York: Harper Perennial, 1996.

Cody, W.J.M., and R.R. Lynn: *Honest Government: An Ethical Guide for Public Service*. Westport, Conn.: Praeger, 1992.

Cohen, Steven, and William Eimicke. "Ethics and the Public Administrator." *Annals of the American Academy of Political and Social Sciences* 537 (January 1995):96–108.

Cohen, Steven, and William Eimicke. *The New Effective Public Manager*. San Francisco: Jossey-Bass, 1995.

Cooper, Terry, ed. *Administrative Ethics*. New York: Marcel Dekker, 1994.

Cooper, Terry L. *An Ethic of Citizenship for Public Administration*. Englewood Cliffs, N.J.: Prentice Hall, 1991.

Cooper, Terry L., and N. Dale Wright, eds. *Exemplary Public Administrators*. San Francisco: Jossey-Bass, 1992.

Daigneault, Michael G. "Why Ethics?" *Association Management* 49 (1997):28–33.

Denhardt, Kathryn G. "Unearthing the Moral Foundations of Public Administration: Honor, Benevolence, and Justice." In *Ethical Frontiers in Public Management*, ed. J.S. Bowman, 91–113. San Francisco: Jossey-Bass, 1991.

Etzioni, Amitai. *The New Golden Rule: Community and Morality in a Democratic Society*. New York: Basic Books, 1996.

Frederickson, H. George, ed. *Ethics and Public Administration*. Armonk, N.Y.: M.E. Sharpe, 1993.

Frederickson, H. George, and David G. Frederickson. "Public Perceptions of Ethics in Government." *Annals of the American Academy of Political and Social Sciences* 537 (January 1995):163–172.

Garment, Suzanne. *Scandal: The Culture of Mistrust in American Politics*. New York: Times Books, 1991.

Gutmann, Amy, and Dennis Thompson, eds. *Ethics and Politics*. 3rd ed. Chicago: Nelson-Hall, 1997.

Guy, M.E. *Ethical Decision Making in Everyday Work Situations*. New York: Quorum Books, 1990.

Hagan, Frank E., ed. *Political Crime: Ideology and Criminality*. Needham Heights, Mass.: Allyn & Bacon, 1997.

Hermann, Frederick M. "Bricks without Straw: The Plight of Government Ethics Agencies in the United States." *Public Integrity Annual* 2 (1997):13–22.

Hopkins, W. *Ethical Dimension of Diversity*. Thousand Oaks, Calif.: Sage, 1997.

Hosmer, L.T. *The Ethics of Management*. Homewood, Ill.: Irwin, 1991.

Kellar, Elizabeth, ed. *Ethical Insight, Ethical Action*. Washington, D.C.: International City Management Association, 1988.

Kidder, R., ed. *Shared Values for a Troubled World*. San Francisco: Jossey-Bass, 1994.

Kweit, Mary G., and R.W. Kweit. "Ethical Responsibility for Reinvented Bureaucrats; Working for Customer-Citizens." *Public Integrity Annual* 2 (1997):3–12.

Lewis, Carol W. *The Ethics Challenge in Public Service*. San Francisco: Jossey-Bass, 1991.

Madsen, Peter, and Jay M. Shafritz, eds. *Essentials of Government Ethics*. New York: Meridian, 1992.

Menzel, Donald C. "Ethics Complaint Making and Trustworthy Government." *Public Integrity Annual* 1 (1996):73–82.

Menzel, D. "Teaching Ethics and Values in Public Administration: Are We Making a Difference?" *Public Administration Review* 57 (May/June):224–230.

Menzel, Donald C. "Through the Ethical Looking Glass Darkly." *Administration & Society* 27 (November 1995):379–399.

Moore, Mark H. *Creating Public Value: Strategic Management in Government.* Cambridge, Mass.: Harvard University Press, 1995.

Moore, Mark H., and Malcolm K. Sparrow. *Ethics in Government: The Moral Challenge of Public Leadership.* Englewood Cliffs, N.J.: Prentice Hall, 1990.

Morgan, Peter W., and Glenn H. Reynolds. *The Appearance of Impropriety.* New York: Free Press, 1997.

Nash, L.L. *Good Intentions Aside: A Manager's Guide to Resolving Ethical Problems.* Boston: Harvard Business School Press, 1993.

Reynolds, Harry W. "Educating Public Administrators about Ethics." *Annals of the American Academy of Political and Social Science* 537 (January 1995):122–138.

Richardson, J., ed. *Business Ethics.* Guilford, Conn.: Dushkin, 1997.

Richardson, W., L. Nigro, and R. McNinch. "Ethics Workshop in State Government: Teaching Practitioners." In *Teaching Ethics and Values,* ed. J. Bowman and D. Menzel, 203–217. New York: SUNY Press, 1998.

Richter, W., F. Burke, and J. Doig. *Combatting Corruption / Encouraging Ethics.* Washington, D.C.: American Society for Public Administration, 1990.

Rohr, John A. *Ethics for Bureaucrats.* New York: Marcel Dekker, 1978.

Rohr, John A. "Public Administration Ethics and Professional Ethics." *Public Integrity Annual* 2 (1997):49–54.

Sanders, G., E. Berman, and J. West. "Municipal Government Financial Reporting: Administrative and Ethical Climate." *Public Budgeting & Finance* 14 (Summer 1994):65–78.

Selznick, Philip. *The Moral Commonwealth; Social Theory and the Promise of Compromise.* Berkeley, Calif.: University of California Press, 1992.

Shaw, R. *Trust in the Balance: Building Successful Organizations on Results, Integrity and Concern.* San Francisco: Jossey-Bass, 1997.

Steinberg, Sheldon S., and David T. Austern. *Government, Ethics and Managers.* New York: Praeger, 1990.

Terry, L. *Leadership of Public Bureaucracies.* Thousand Oaks, Calif.: Sage, 1995.

Terry, R. *Authentic Leadership: Courage in Action.* San Francisco: Jossey-Bass, 1993.

Trevino, L., and S. Youngblood. "Bad Apples in Bad Barrels: A Causal Analysis of Ethical Decision-Making Behavior." *Journal of Applied Psychology* 75 (1990):378–385.

Van Wart, Montgomery. "Trends in Types of Control of Public Organizations." *Public Integrity Annual* 1 (1996):83–98.

West, Jonathan P., Evan Berman, and Anita Cava. "Ethics in the Municipal Workplace." In *Municipal Year Book*, 3–16. Washington, D.C.. International City/ County Management Association, 1993.

Wilson, James Q. *The Moral Sense.* New York: The Free Press, 1993.

Zauderer, D. "Integrity: An Essential Executive Quality." In *Business Ethics,* ed. J. Richardson, 26–30. Guilford, Conn: Dushkin, 1997.

Practical Management Series

The Ethics Edge

Text type
New Century Schoolbook

Composition
Barton Matheson Willse & Worthington
Baltimore, Maryland

Printing and binding
Victor Graphics, Inc.
Baltimore, Maryland

Cover design
Becky Geanaros

6399